THE
THIEF-TAKER
HANGINGS

THE
THIEF-TAKER
HANGINGS

How Daniel Defoe, Jonathan Wild, and Jack Sheppard
Captivated London and Created the Celebrity Criminal

AARON SKIRBOLL

Guilford, Connecticut

For Hank

LYONS
PRESS

An imprint of The Rowman & Littlefield Publishing Group, Inc.
4501 Forbes Blvd., Ste. 200
Lanham, MD 20706
www.rowman.com

Distributed by NATIONAL BOOK NETWORK

Copyright © 2014 by Aaron Skirboll

Lyons Press paperback edition 2020

British Library Cataloguing in Publication Information available

Library of Congress Cataloging-in-Publication Data available

ISBN 978-1-4930-5000-0 (paperback)
ISBN 978-1-4930-1423-1 (e-book)

∞™ The paper used in this publication meets the minimum requirements of American
National Standard for Information Sciences—Permanence of Paper for Printed Library
Materials, ANSI/NISO Z39.48-1992.

The Annals of Criminal Jurisprudence . . . present tragedies of real life often heightened in their effect by the grossness of the injustice and the malignity of the prejudices which accompanied them. At the same time real culprits as original characters stand forward on the canvas of humanity as prominent objects for our special study.
—EDMUND BURKE, CELEBRATED TRIALS AND REMARKABLE CASES OF CRIMINAL JURISPRUDENCE

The introduction of detailed realism into English literature in the eighteenth century was like the introduction of electricity into machine technology.
—TOM WOLFE, THE NEW JOURNALISM

ENGLISH CURRENCY IN THE EIGHTEENTH CENTURY

4 farthings = 1 penny
12 pence (d.) = 1 shilling (s.)
5 shillings = 1 crown
6 shillings, 8 pence = 1 noble
13 shillings, 4 pence = 1 mark
20 shillings = 1 pound (£ or l.)
1 pound, 1 shilling = 1 guinea (gold coin)

Source: http://www.oldbaileyonline.org/static/Coinage.jsp

CONTENTS

DANIEL DEFOE

Engraving by Michael Vandergucht after a portrait by Jeremiah Taverner

INTRODUCTION

A BRAWLING BACK-ALLEY BUNCH

Perhaps the first true modern literary journalist: Daniel Defoe,
whose 1725 tract on the criminal Jonathan Wild offers a prototype
of the modern true-crime narrative.
—KEVIN KERRANE AND BEN YAGODA, *THE ART OF FACT*

Today criminal investigations rule the media. Once or twice each year, a trial transfixes the public, a new cause célèbre born seemingly each season. Spectators travel hours to courthouses; tickets to trials are distributed by lottery; and the term *media circus*, coined in the 1970s, comes into its own.

If it bleeds, it leads—so goes the old journalistic saw. Readers and viewers can't tear their eyes away from true crime stories, and the grislier the details, the better. But when did it all begin, this mixing of criminal and celebrity? Searching for the origin of the phenomenon took me back three centuries to the nascent years of the newspaper and across the Atlantic to London. In the middle of it all stood Daniel Defoe, a wily old newspaperman and the aging author of *Robinson Crusoe*, who battled for the scoop amid the muck and grime of the eighteenth century. His coverage of two men—Jonathan Wild, the chaser, and Jack Sheppard, the mark—enthralled a kingdom and birthed a genre.

An eighteenth-century Al Capone, Jonathan Wild was the first man to organize crime for profit and the first criminal whose name everyone in the city knew. A burglar and a prison breaker, Jack Sheppard had much in common with John Dillinger. In late 1724, a manhunt for him grabbed the city's attention like no other story and drove newspaper sales skyward. Sheppard the housebreaker ran, thief-taker Wild chased him, and reporter Defoe wrote about both.

With Sheppard on the loose, the story evolved in real time, but nothing about the case was clear-cut, nor was it easy to know for whom to root. The grandeur of the once-popular hunter was fading, and the criminal was incorrigible and eminently quotable. In the middle of it all, we have a man known today primarily as a novelist, his skills as a journalist mostly forgotten. His colorful tales about the pair teemed with details, but as with nearly everything he wrote, his name was nowhere to be found, and in Sheppard's case, Defoe wrote his account of the man's deeds as if it were the thief's autobiography, as he'd done with Robinson Crusoe and Moll Flanders.

In 1724 and 1725, more than thirty unsigned pamphlets were published on Wild and Sheppard. Five of these tracts have been attributed to Defoe, and the British Library has cataloged them under his name. In the story ahead, I privileged only the two pamphlets that have met with near universal agreement on the attribution to Defoe: *The True and Genuine Account of the Life and Actions of the Late Jonathan Wild* and *A Narrative of All the Robberies, Escapes, &c. of John Sheppard*. A third, *The History of the Remarkable Life of John Sheppard*, was probably part of a group effort in which Defoe had a hand, among others.

Entering the world of Defoe scholars with virgin eyes, I had no idea what awaited me. This is one brawling back-alley bunch of bibliophiles, many waging pissing matches to see who knows Daniel best. One camp of scholars charges another with corpus swelling, while the latter assails the former for deflating the number so as to remove works of lesser quality. In Defoe's day, it was more the exception than the rule to put your name to pamphlets, so attribution makes for a thorny issue, and with over five hundred works credited to him, there's no definitive universal agreement here. Nonetheless, the scholarly scrap proved entertaining. Among those who've studied the man, it's a no-holds-barred, back-and-forth assault complete with name calling. Academic insults fly to and fro: "simpletons or rascals," "lack of brains," "a disaster." Charges of canon forgery and "power moves" have been made, and as one set of authors answered a particular onslaught, they decided it would "look craven if we do not give him one or two back—though a 'Forum' may not really be the place for fist-fights."

To an outsider, for the most part, more of a consensus appears about the Wild and Sheppard pamphlets credited to Defoe than not. If only it weren't for the Law Firm. That's the collective nickname I have given to scholars P. N. Furbank and W. R. Owens, who seem to want something close to DNA evidence before ascribing anything to Defoe. In their book, *Defoe De-Attributions*, they've called into question some 252 of the works in Defoe's canon, including many of his criminal tracts. The vast majority of Defoe biographers and others who've studied the period have kept Defoe's criminal pamphlets and his work at *Applebee's Original Weekly Journal* under his name. As Maximillian Novak, who has studied Defoe for most of his life and penned the Defoe entry in the *New Cambridge Bibliography of English Literature*, noted of the author's work at *Applebee's* it "was an accepted fact by every Defoe scholar until 1997. In that year, P. N. Furbank and W. R. Owens published an essay with the title 'The Myth of Defoe As *Applebee's* Man.'"

The Law Firm muddied the waters with doubt, and others have followed suit.

However, even the Law Firm acknowledges that these pamphlets *could* be Defoe's. They just don't have the evidence to prove the 300-year-old pamphlets are his. Scholar Pat Rogers, who has studied and written on Defoe and many of his contemporaries, told me that these attribution questions dog Defoe far more than any other writer of the time. Not only did he write an incredibly large amount—signing practically none, or publishing under a pseudonym—but he did so on an equally dizzying array of topics.

I have sided with the majority regarding the tracts on Wild and Sheppard, as well as Defoe's tenure at *Applebee's*. Dozens of men and women who have made a careful study of the man's life and work have counted them his, which is good enough for me. Besides, instead of trying to prove that Defoe wrote these tracts on criminals, maybe it's more fitting to leave it with a glint of doubt, as with all of his writings. After all, he never signed *Robinson Crusoe* or *Moll Flanders* either, and *Roxana*'s authorship didn't fall to him until half a century after its publication. Three centuries have passed since the author's death, and he remains shrouded in mystery, each year his life growing more so. His major works of fiction were all written in the first person, as true stories, while his nonfiction works read like novels.

But then, that's part of the attraction: The definitive biographies of two infamous criminals were written by a novelist. Picture an aging

Defoe, near his life's end, running around London between the gallows and Newgate Prison, where he met the inspiration for *Moll Flanders*, a writer mixing it up with thieves, murderers, and rogues of all inclination amid dirt, despair, and deprivation. That image stirred the London of the past back to life for me. Left with the choice of leaving Defoe out of the story—hemming and hawing over attribution bitchery—or moving forward with the majority, I chose the latter. Defoe and Mr. Applebee made the cut. When telling the stories of Wild and Sheppard, you have to include the best and most accurate tracts written by their contemporaries, and the British Library lists those under Defoe's name.

It's also worth underscoring that this book isn't a biography of Defoe. My intentions are far less noble. My aim is merely to entertain. Defoe had a vast collection of interests—economics, politics, religion, and trade among them—and I've touched on little to none of it. Only his criminal writings and the aspects of his life that related to crime in general—and, specifically, the careers of Wild and Sheppard—concerned me. For a full treatment of the man, pick up the biographies by Paula Backscheider or Maximillian Novak.

I'm no scholar. Yet neither was Defoe. An unpolished outsider, he gained little respect from his peers. No one conferred on him the same prestige as the likes of Addison, Pope, or Steele. He warned of grammatical errors, and likewise, I can guarantee that, absent an editor's hand, you'd find the pages ahead marked with similar mistakes. I'm also thankful to Lyons Press for a point of the upmost importance to this work: a firm deadline. After years of research, there's always more. As Arthur Griffiths, a nineteenth-century prison inspector and author who wrote on Sheppard, remarked in the preface to *The Chronicles of Newgate*: "Now at the termination of my labours ... I found at length that I *must* be satisfied with what I had instead of seeking for more."

Defoe said it best in his final days, in *Augusta Triumphans*, his tract on civic improvements: "As I am quick to conceive, I am eager to have done, unwilling to overwork a subject; I had rather leave part to the conception of the readers, than to tire them or myself with protracting a theme, as if, like a chancery man or a hackney author, I wrote by the sheet for hire. So let us have done with this topic and proceed to another."

PROLOGUE

THE TRIPLE TREE

To close the scene of all his actions he
Was brought from Newgate to the fatal tree;
And there his life resigned, his race is run,
And Tyburn ends what wickedness begun.
—FROM "JACK SHEPPARD'S THREE FATAL STAGES," 1724

Flip through old books depicting the executions of eighteenth-century England, and chills will run down your spine. The Bell-Man, eerily dressed in black, lurks on the wall of St. Sepulchre's churchyard like a prophet rising. The long white faces of the crowd stand out against the dull gray sky. Animals rummage for scrapings from the corpses hanging above. You can almost smell the stench of death in the air and hear the words coming from the Bell-Man's lips: "All Good people pray heartily unto God for these poor sinners, who are now going to their death, for whom this great bell doth toll."

Today the location of the Tyburn gallows lies just off the Marble Arch at the southernmost point of the Marylebone district of London. The spot is marked not by a circular plaque or even an X, but by the spine of a triangle, symbol of the Tyburn Tree, otherwise known as the Triple Tree or the "Deadly Nevergreen." In the eighteenth century, the gallows occupied a space on Edgware Road, near the northeast corner of Hyde Park, some two and a half miles west of London. More than 50,000 people were executed there. At the Triple Tree, criminals met their maker. Shakespeare wrote of the place in *Love's Labour's Lost*—"The shape of

STEPHEN GARDINER DRESSED IN HIS DEATH SHROUD
MAKES HIS DYING SPEECH AT TYBURN.
from THE NEWGATE CALENDAR

love's Tyburn that hangs up simplicity"—while poet John Taylor later pondered the deadly tree some decades later:

> *I understand the root of it is dry,*
> *It bears no leaf, no bloom, or no bud,*
> *The rain that makes it fructify is blood.*

Legal executions had taken place around the village of Tyburn for centuries, spread out across the countryside, beginning in 1196 with William Fitz Osbert, also known as "Longbeard," a leader of an uprising by the poor. In 1571, the Tyburn Tree was constructed with its innovative triangular design: a wooden triangle laid horizontally atop three support legs. Its design efficiently allowed more hangings at one time, up to twenty-four simultaneously—eight from each beam of the triangle.

On June 1, 1571, Dr. John Story became the first person to hang from the newfangled and quickly infamous triangular gallows. "Blessed John," a Catholic condemned for high treason under Queen Elizabeth I, was sentenced to be hanged, drawn, and quartered—that is, hanged *almost* to death, then disemboweled, beheaded, and cut into fours. A fire burned nearby to incinerate his entrails and spare body parts, but Blessed John didn't go quietly. During the disembowelment, as "the executioner had cut him down and was 'rifling among his bowels,'" the doctor arose and dealt him a shrewd blow on the head." (In January 1661, King Charles II hanged the completely dead body of Oliver Cromwell there in a gruesome but effective act of revenge.)

Executions by burning were falling out of favor toward the end of the 1600s—though a stake stood conveniently opposite the Triple Tree, just in case. Beheadings also declined with the 1686 death of cutter and hangman Jack Ketch, notorious for mangling his wards and needing additional hacks to perform his duties. As such, England moved into an era of simple hangings—simple, perhaps, but still ample.

Nearly any infraction, including theft of as few as five shillings, could result in a trip to the gallows. Men died for stealing a single candlestick. For such petty larceny, men, women, and even children were dragged nearly three miles from Newgate Prison—the awful dungeon in London—up Holborn Hill, past St. Giles in the Fields, and out Oxford Street to the "fatal tree," which stood in the middle of the roadway, an ever-present warning. Countrymen near and far knew the name, and a trip to Tyburn became known simply as "Going west."

Executions occasioned a great deal of fanfare at the time. Some criminals dressed extravagantly for the "Tyburn Fair," while others were dragged practically naked, but either way great crowds always gathered to watch. A country gentleman wrote to his brother after his first viewing of a public execution: "The Sight has had an extraordinary Effect upon me, which is more owing to the unexpected Oddness of the Scene, than the affecting Concern which is unavoidable in a thinking Person, at a Spectacle so awful, and so interesting."

On the way from Newgate, conveyance was modernized to a wooden cart, with criminals—often sitting on their own coffins—accompanied by the hangman and the prison chaplain. After a brief stop at St. Sepulchre Church to greet the Bell-Man, the procession, which included the marshals, the constables, and the jailers (known as "Javelin Men") began the nearly three-hour trip to Tyburn. Depending on the popularity of the criminal, he or she was either pelted or cheered along the way. En route, the condemned could stop at taverns, where all—hangman, chaplain, and the soon-to-be-deceased—tipped one back together.

Upon arrival, the cart stopped under the gallows, and the criminal's neck was tied by rope to the hanging bar. Spectators jostled for better viewing on scaffolds and stadium-like seating. A final speech was expected and often delivered, with copies of the speeches transcribed and then sold to the crowd, making for instant bestsellers. Lastly, the criminal was hanged.

In previous years, by means of a gibbet (not isolated to Tyburn), the corpse remained strung up until it rotted away, poisoning the air with the stench of slowly decaying flesh. In the enlightened eighteenth century, surgeons hounded the Triple Tree for bodies to dissect . . . but not without battling the assembled mob, which wanted grisly souvenirs of the day's proceedings, or a superstitious touch of the corpse for its supposed healing properties.

The shocking number of deaths may supply the reason why these public executions failed to deter crime. Social reformer and author of

Tom Jones, Henry Fielding, wrote concisely of a nation desensitized: "Many cart loads of our fellow creatures are once in six weeks carried to slaughter." But every thief, every lawbreaker in the land knew the score. Get caught with your hand in another's purse, and you risked a trip to the Tyburn Tree.

Today the facts of the Tyburn hangings are as ghastly as they are hard to fathom. The courthouse publication *State Trials* records in great detail the 1570 executions of Christopher Norton and his uncle Thomas, both accused of high treason. Of Christopher it was written: "And being hanged a little while, and then cut down, the butcher opened him, and as he took out his bowels, he cried and said, 'Oh Lord, Lord, have mercy upon me!' and so yielded up the ghost." The account continues in horrific detail. He was quartered, his bowels burned, his remains carried in a basket to Newgate Prison, as was custom, where they were parboiled. His head was set on London Bridge and his cooked quarters tacked onto the gates of the city. Even by the eighteenth century, such a report was neither grisly nor uncommon. It was a matter of course.

THE
THIEF-TAKER
HANGINGS

DEFOE IN THE PILLORY FOR SEDITION IN 1703
Engraving by James Charles Armytage after Eyre Crowe

I

THE DISSENTER

*The poor Author was a great while, call'd hard Names on every side,
by one sort of People because they did understand him, and by another
because they did not understand him.*
—DANIEL DEFOE, THE *REVIEW*, DECEMBER 20, 1705

Defoe was a dead man. On January 3, 1703, Daniel Finch, Second Earl of Nottingham, had issued a warrant for his arrest. A week later, the *London Gazette* published a proclamation offering a £50 reward for information leading to his capture and giving a physical description of him: "a middle-sized spare man, about 40 years old, of a brown complexion, and dark-brown coloured hair, but wears a wig, a hooked nose, a sharp chin, grey eyes, and a large mole near his mouth."

The charge against Defoe? Seditious libel.

The news no doubt troubled him greatly. In under a week, he wrote to Finch, pleading for pardon. Until now, Defoe, age forty-two, had never shied away from taking a contradictory view. A Presbyterian, and therefore outside the Church of England, he had stood by his core beliefs despite his chosen religion keeping him from the advantages of an elite education or public office. He didn't waver in his faith and still managed to gain prominence. In years past, he'd even had the ear of King William III.

But King William died unexpectedly in 1702. Tories—no friends to Dissenters, as those beyond the state religion were known—took over the government, and Defoe lost what influence he'd had. In the first few years of her reign, Queen Anne tied church and state very much together. The situation wasn't likely to improve for the Dissenters.

Defoe didn't wait around to see what the government might do. He went into hiding.

Published anonymously a month prior, in December 1702, Defoe's pamphlet, "The Shortest Way with the Dissenters; A Satire against High Church Tyranny," sold well, to Defoe's surprise. It also prompted his arrest warrant. He had a few successes under his belt as a writer, but at this point he was still primarily a businessman, the recent owner of a rather profitable brick and tile factory in Tilbury.

Ironically, the sarcasm of advocating for the "rooting out" of Dissenters from the country gained legitimate support in some factions. He meant it to show the absurdity of the extremists' small-mindedness, but some High Church Anglicans—the side of the Church of England that more closely resembled Catholicism—missed the satire entirely and cheered for the nonconformists to be "hang'd," "banish'd," "destroy'd," or, better yet, for the "present Race of poison'd Spirits" to be "purg'd" from the Face of the land." On the other side of the aisle, many Dissenters took tone-deaf alarm at Defoe's essay. Not to be excluded, those in the middle—who really should have known better—somehow found it affronting as well. Most importantly, however, the Tory government took offense and considered it libelous that they might have had eyes on overpowering their opponents. Defoe's writing got under everyone's skin equally, it seemed.

Officials quickly discovered the author's identity and ordered all copies of the pamphlet destroyed by the common hangman—obviously not Defoe's aim. According to biographer Maximillian Novak, Defoe considered his words "no more outrageous than those he imitated." The initial reaction of praise and approval from many among the High Church substantiated this rationale. Only when they discovered that the author didn't belong to their number did they deem the pamphlet seditious. But Defoe had targeted not only the government but also the Queen, an ardent supporter of the Church. His words had consequences. As Novak observes, "Defoe was a gambler and could not resist the perverse pleasure of approaching the edge of abyss."

Queen Anne herself gave orders to the Earl of Nottingham "to make strict and diligent search for Daniel Defoe, and him having found, you are to apprehend and seize together with his papers for high crimes and misdemeanors, and to bring him before me to be examined concerning such matters." Backed into a corner and fighting for his freedom, Defoe begged for leniency, writing of a "mind impatient of confinement." He threw himself at Nottingham's feet: "I beseech your Lordship to assure her Majtie, that I am perfectly free from any seditious designs."

Defoe, the married father of six, had a seventh on the way and also took care of his father. He needed his freedom to support his family. In his letter to Nottingham, he wrote of how "prisons, pillories, and such like" were worse to him than death. In one last bid, he even offered to banish himself from the country to serve the British Army for a year in the Netherlands, where at least he could die in service to his country rather than uselessly in prison. Defoe later called himself a man deficient of "passive courage," and this letter proved it. Its suppliant tone made for a stark departure from someone who as a young man had been such a loud and ardent Dissenter.

Born Daniel Foe around 1660—later adding the aristocratic particle to his name—he had witnessed some of the most momentous events in the history of England. Born just as King Charles II ascended the throne and the Restoration began, Defoe had lived through the Great Plague and the Great Fire of 1666. In 1688, during the Glorious Revolution, he rode to join the army of Prince William of Orange, soon anointed King William III. A year later, he recollected what he had seen in the political pamphlet, "Reflections upon the Late Great Revolution."

Pamphleteering served as a major tool to form or often sway public opinion, and pamphlet wars were frequent. Rebuttals followed published attacks, then counter-rebuttals, and so on. The chosen venue for debating the day's controversies, anonymous pamphlets frequently sounded a single note and ranged from one sheet to many hundred. Anyone who had the money for the printing costs could author one—and a great many did. Many resembled present-day blog posts. Some looked more like modern-day letters to the editor, insult-driven and horribly written. But Defoe's well-conceived and executed pamphlets stood out from the pack.

As a youth, Defoe studied to enter the ministry, but instead he chose a life in trade. In his business career, he sold many products, notably hosiery, wine, tobacco, and, most recently, brick and pantile. At the turn of the century, when he reached middle age, Defoe found his pulpit and a place in life as a writer. He wrote what he knew and saw. He wrote about business while also turning his focus to the Church and the country's political unrest.

As a pamphleteer, he was working in a genre that relied on directness. Until the release of "The Shortest Way," nothing illustrates Defoe's moral code and fearlessness more than his strongly worded Legion's Memorial. Defoe hand-delivered the pamphlet to the House of Commons after the imprisonment of a group of Kentish petitioners. Writing on behalf of "Two hundred thousand Englishmen," Defoe demanded the release of the wrongly imprisoned men, asserting that citizens had the right to petition, and that elected representatives should serve the people rather than the other way around. If not outright threatening, the pamphlet certainly challenged Parliament. It was signed dramatically, "Our name is Legion, and we are Many."

Defoe keenly supported King William, but many disliked the foreign-born king. In "The True-Born Englishman," a satiric poem, and one of his most successful works ever, Defoe decried the irrational way that his countrymen looked down on foreigners despite their own "mixtures of Blood." Tens of thousands of copies of the poem were sold, and it led to an introduction to the King in 1701. Regrettably, their friendship had a short shelf life. The King died a year later, in March 1702.

While Defoe certainly enjoyed writing poetry, the businessman in him saw the public demand for a voice in the religious debate. At the end of 1702, after Parliament passed a bill barring Dissenters from government, Defoe published a twenty-nine-page pamphlet, "The Shortest Way with the Dissenters," in an attempt to slap the country awake. As biographer Paula Backscheider notes, he wanted the publication to act as "the dramatic gesture that would hold a mirror up to men and bring them to a right perspective on their actions and the Dissenter's character."

It accomplished neither end. In a perverse testament to his skills as a writer, nearly everyone believed that a High Church Anglican had written it. This wouldn't be the last time that he artfully took on a character to conceal his authorship. His first novel wouldn't appear for another seventeen years, but here we have an early demonstration of his power—even if he did pass it off as nonfiction. He gained more than a few critics for using a fictitious narrator to discuss religious matters, one contemporary counterattack complaining that such a maneuver invaded "the Conscience."

His instincts led him to seek appeasement. But he did so less than humbly when he issued an apology in the form of a second pamphlet, "A Brief Explanation of a Late Pamphlet, Entituled, The Shortest Way with the Dissenters." In it, he heaped the onus of misinterpretation on his readers. He never believed himself guilty for shining a light on others' iniquity.

Many tongues wagged about the affair. Word had it that if he were caught, his punishment would be severe. Defoe stayed out of sight, on the lam, for nearly half a year, eluding search party after search party. Displaying a knack for fugitive life, he moved at night, often in disguise, and bounced around. He may even have ventured to Holland—and with good cause. The £50 bounty on his head was enough for someone to live on for a whole year, and it was for mere information, not even the capture itself.

One account from the period tells of a dashing, swaggering Defoe locked in a showdown with a man while walking in Hackney Fields. Unsure if he'd been recognized, Defoe took precautions. He drew his sword, drove the stranger to his knees, and forced him to "Swear that if he ever met him again, he should shut his eyes till he was half a mile off him." Another account described Defoe in a series of similar close calls, at least one of them sending the writer barreling out a window at the last moment.

The more time passed, the more the government smeared his name and transmogrified his satire into a full-fledged subversive manifesto. Before long, he was no longer merely seditious, but as it read in his indictment, he was of "a disordered mind, and a person of bad name, reputation and conversation."

On May 21, 1703, Defoe ran out of luck. The *Post Man and the Historical Account* broadcast that: "On Thursday Daniel de Foe, Author of the Pamphlet, entitul'd, The Shortest Way with the Dissenters, was taken, and after having been examined, he was committed on Saturday to Newgate." The arrest had gone down in Spitalfields after someone spotted him at the home of a French weaver named Nathaniel Sammen. There a pair of Nottingham's "messengers" seized him, according to the *London Post*. The nameless informer claimed the £50 reward.

The Earl of Nottingham had his man. In order to get him, he had brought in the printer of the pamphlet, George Croome, and the man who delivered it, Edward Bellamy. After questioning and probably a great deal of intimidation, both men agreed to testify against Defoe to save themselves. Nottingham cut an imposing figure, so severe in appearance and manner that he had earned the nickname "Dismal." The earl already had examined many of Defoe's personal papers and books seized during the manhunt. Nottingham was hoping for bigger fish, and seemed ready to trade Defoe's freedom for information on accomplices, or possibly Whig leaders with whom the writer was suspected of collaborating. Defoe spurned the requests. He described his unenviable position to William Penn, founder of the Pennsylvania colony, a fellow Dissenter, and a fan of "The True-Born Englishman."

> *Sir in Some Letters which I have Sent his Lordship I have Answer'd him with the Same Assurance. . . . That if my Life were Concern'd in it I would Not Save it at the Price of Impeaching Innocent men, No More would I Accuse my Friends for the Freedome of Private Conversation. . . . I have no Accomplices, No Sett of Men, (as my Lord Call'd Them) with whom I used to Concert Matters, of this Nature.*

Nottingham's offer fell on deaf ears.

On June 5, Defoe made bail. Court records show that it took the assistance of four others for Defoe to raise the necessary £1,500 bond. He agreed to appear at the Justice Hall in the Old Bailey on July 7 at nine a.m. to answer his charges.

The "True & Perfect Kallendar of the Names of All the Prisoners in Newgate for Fellony & Tresspasses the 7th Day of July 1703" shows him a man of his word. "Daniel DeFoe"—alias De Foo—appears fourth on the list, between Hannah Ford—accused of stealing a pair of shoes, a smock, and a petticoat—and Elizabeth Williams, suspected of stealing a silver cup. Defoe pled guilty on the advice of his counsel and stood trial that day. It surely didn't warm his heart to find the courtroom full of judges about whom he'd written in less than glowing tones. This was going to get personal.

Biographer John Robert Moore describes the lineup he faced. "Of the Lord Mayor, the sheriffs, and the aldermen who were most likely to be in charge of his trial, several had been lashed by Defoe in print by name for their public and private morals, their physical and mental infirmities, in a manner which no one of the men would be likely to forget or easily forgive." But it gets worse. "They had been attacked as individuals, as officials, or as members of a party. . . . Probably every one of them had some personal grudge to pay off against Defoe." Now, thanks to "The Shortest Way," in walked the writer who'd smeared them. Revenge on a silver platter.

Chief among the men was the hanging judge Sir Salathiel Lovell, city recorder and a member of the Society for the Reformation of Manners, a group that formed in 1691 to eradicate the city's immoral tendencies. This band of self-proclaimed do-gooders concentrated heavily on prostitution and sodomy, and it just so happened that Defoe had written a scathing treatise against the Society in 1702, entitled "Reformation of Manners." In it, Defoe pointed out "That no Man is qualified to reprove other Mens Crimes, who allows himself in the Practice of the same." He elided Lovell's name, but there was no hiding the target.

L——l, the Pandor of thy Judgment-Seat,
Has neither Manners, Honesty, nor Wit;
Instead of which, he's plenteously supply'd
With Nonsense, Noise, Impertinence, and Pride.

Defoe further exposed the recorder as amenable to the highest bidder.

He trades in Justice, and the Souls of Men,
And prostitutes them equally to Gain:
He has the Publick Book of Rates to show,
Where every Rogue the Price of Life may know:
And this one Maxim always goes before,
He never hangs the Rich, nor saves the Poor.

No, this wasn't going to go well at all. Needless to say, the court found Defoe guilty. Lovell sentenced him to pay a fine of two hundred marks (roughly £133), to stand in the pillory three times, and to languish in prison at the Queen's pleasure—that is, indefinitely. Defoe escaped the gallows, but in early eighteenth-century England, the pillory presented hazards all its own. There was no guarantee that he would survive the punishment; some had perished at the hands of unruly crowds eager to mete out their own justice.

On Thursday, July 29, 1703, Defoe faced the mob at the Royal Exchange in Cornhill, the financial center of London, where he once had lived and owned a hosier business. It lay near where he grew up, so he was no stranger to the crowd. In the distance stood St. Michael's, where his daughter, Mary, had been buried as an infant. Everywhere he looked, familiar scenes and faces greeted him. At noon, as rain drizzled down, Defoe took his first stand in the pillory.

Normally located in a public square, a pillory consisted of a pair of wooden boards erected on a pole and comprised of three holes: one for the head, two for the arms. The structure stood on an elevated platform for better public viewing with a sign above the stocks detailing the crime committed. The criminal generally had to stand for an hour, sometimes more, bent over with head and hands placed through holes in the stocks. The device usually punished crimes of dishonesty or treachery. Spectator participation added to the proceedings. Onlookers roused into a frenzy targeted the prisoner with fruits and vegetables (usually rotten), eggs, rocks, animals (usually dead, sometimes live), or anything else on hand. Even school-aged children shelled whatever they could find at the convict. A hangman officiated and occasionally wiped debris from the criminal's mouth or nose.

Prisoners often exited the pillory bludgeoned and bloodied, and as Samuel Johnson once noted of those who had endured the punishment, "He could not mouth and strut as he used to, and after having been there, people are not very willing to ask a man to their tables who has stood in the pillory." Anyone sentenced to the pillory also lost the right to vote.

Defoe had transgressed against abstract authority, not a neighbor. It was a crime the masses could stand. But inside the pillory area, seditious libel didn't hold such perquisites. Sedition often carried the additional punishment of floggings, branding of the face or tongue, or other mutilation, such as slitting the nose. *Fog's Weekly Journal* captured the use of these punishments to great effect a few years later in their coverage of forger Japhet Cook, alias Sir Peter Springer, and his pillory experience.

The time being near expired, he was sat on a chair in the pillory, when the hangman, dressed like a butcher, came to him, and with a knife like a gardener's pruning-knife cut off his ears, and with a pair of scissors slit off both his nostrils, all which Cook bore with great patience; but at the searing with a red-hot iron of his right nostril the pain was so violent that he got up from his chair . . . he went from the pillory bleeding.

No wonder Defoe pleaded feverishly with Nottingham and others for a pardon. He knew what physical harm a stint in the pillory could have, and he knew the damage it could cause to his reputation as a businessman and a writer. His letters to Nottingham showed him shaken, but as he entered the pillory near the Royal Exchange, he steadied.

The crowd buoyed him, the people on his side. Lines from his poem "Hymn to the Pillory," which he had dashed off and published while imprisoned, floated among the visitors drinking to his health. It was an unprecedented show. To his own great surprise, they regaled him as a hero and greeted him with applause. In yet another moment of irony, the pamphlet that had landed Defoe in shackles, "The Shortest Way," was being hawked among the crowd in great numbers.

For the next two days, in Cheapside then by Temple Bar, it was more of the same. He took his stand. Crowds gathered to show their support. In return, Defoe put on a brave face. He had risked his own life for what he believed and for the sake of others. Some dispute whether admirers tossed flowers at him instead of garbage, but his time in the pillory became an occasion of triumph. "No man in England but Defoe ever stood in the pillory and later rose to eminence among his fellow men," writes Moore.

Defoe returned to Newgate Prison none the worse for wear. Built in 1188, the ancient jail burned down in the Great Fire before being rebuilt in 1672. The new version remained a dirty, stinking, violent dungeon, however. Defoe paid at least twenty guineas to secure a place in the Press Yard, one of the better wards in the prison. There he took refuge in his writing, passing the time by taking down first-person accounts from Newgate's cast of thieves, highwaymen, and pirates. With their adventurous tales ringing in his ear, he wrote new pamphlets and oversaw a collection of his already published works.

He spent five months in jail, an ordeal that never left him. He recognized how firsthand experience altered perception and influenced narrative perspective. Interviewing subjects made the piece. That was the missing ingredient needed to paint a verbal picture. In *Aspects of the Novel*, E. M. Forster ponders Defoe's time as a prisoner: "The author had some great experience himself while in Newgate. We do not know what it was, probably he himself did not know afterwards. . . . But something occurred to him in prison, and out of its vague, powerful emotion Moll and Roxana are born."

Defoe was released from prison in November 1703. In the meantime, other writers had taken potshots at him and left his reputation in tatters. In his absence, his factory had gone belly-up. The business had been earning Defoe the handsome dividend of around £700 yearly. It marked the second time that he'd gone bankrupt. (The first had landed him in debtors' prison.)

While in prison, he had received a brief and cryptic communication. "Pray, ask that gentleman what I can do for him," came the message from Robert Harley, speaker of the House of Commons. Harley, the man who had initiated the hunt for Defoe in the first place, had interceded with the Queen and helped arrange for Defoe's liberation. He had eyes on higher office and understood, more than other politicians at the time, the benefits of having friends and allies in the press. Over time, Harley had observed Defoe's journalistic abilities and saw an opening of potential, for himself and the government. Perhaps Defoe nudged him into action when as a fugitive he'd written to Nottingham in conciliation and offered to serve the Queen "with my hand, my Pen, or my head."

Harley wrote the Earl of Godolphin to discuss his plan: "He is a very capable man, and if his fine be satisfied . . . he may do service, and this may perhaps engage him better than any other rewards, and keep him under the power of an obligation."

In a brilliant move, Harley not only rescued Defoe from prison but also restored much of his ruined finances. He also had taken care of Defoe's wife and family during his imprisonment. Surely Defoe owed him a debt of gratitude for such efforts. In a May 12, 1704, letter, Defoe displayed his appreciation.

> *I am your most humble petitioner, that you will please to abate me all those extasies and extravagancyes a necessary acknowledgement of your generous concern for me would lead me to. I can no more express myself, than I can forgett the obligation. . . . I humbly recognize as the first mover of your thoughts in my favor, will yet put an occasion into my hands, by faithfull, and usefull, application, to satisfye you, that I am the gratefullest wretch alive.*

Defoe never forgot the man who had secured his freedom from Newgate, nor did he disappoint his new benefactor, whether by producing pamphlets on behalf of Harley and the administration, or even working as a spy.

In February 1704, with Harley's backing, Defoe established one of the first newspapers in England. He named it the *Review*, and at the ripe old age of forty-three, Daniel Defoe became a reporter.

"THE COFFEEHOUSE MOB"
Frontispiece to Edward Ward's VULGUS BRITTANICUS

II

The Streets of London

The houses of old London are incrusted as thick with anecdotes, legends, and traditions as an old ship is with barnacles. Strange stories about strange men grow like moss in every crevice of the bricks.
—Walter Thornbury and Edward Walford,
Old and New London

The Great Plague raged and festered from 1665 to 1666. The Great Fire ravaged London in 1666. The Great Storm hit in 1703. The city endured, the slums remained. Some neighborhoods rebuilt themselves, rich beside poor, stacked in, crowded. Because of government planning laws, it was more cost-efficient to build onto existing dwellings, extending a structure out, up, or even beneath the earth. Passageways snaked between edifices, and poor neighborhoods became warrens.

London of the eighteenth century was nothing like the urban mecca it became. Outside the old city walls, in a matter of blocks, stacked tenements gave way to green fields dotted with cows. Despite those walls, little buffer existed between rural and urban. Cattle drives took place in the city. Animals and vermin scurried about. Smithfield had a massive sheep den, and the whole place reeked of barnyard. Fleet Ditch, which weaved through the city, offered a dumping spot for everything from offal to human excrement. The streets were just as filthy, full of sewage and garbage, both sometimes tossed from the upper windows of houses.

The Thames overflowed with vessels that bumped into one another, a massive parking lot of ships. More than three hundred church spires, towering above the rest of the city, dotted the skyline, St. Paul's Cathedral the tallest of all. Taverns, alehouses, and dram shops lined the streets. Among them, men, women, and children worked the streets, peddling fish, fruit, and vegetables. Beggars asked for alms, and street singers hawked their ballads.

The population of London at the beginning of the century—including Westminster and nearby villages like Stepney and Chelsea—hovered above 600,000, but population growth was stagnant to slow. Many people came from villages in the country, where they worked in agricultural jobs, to find work in the city. Women pursued jobs as domestics, while men targeted apprenticeships for skilled labor. Despite the influx, the population remained more or less stable because of the high infant mortality rate and, in general, a greater rate of deaths than births. When the city's rural immigrants died, more took their place.

Conditions proved "good for a few and bad for most," as Patrick Pringle writes in *Hue and Cry*.

> *While worshippers were thronging the churches, mothers were putting their babies out in the streets to die. For every beau in the coffee-house there were scores of people rotting in the gin-shops; for every lady in a toy-shop there were dozens of whores hiring out their undernourished bodies for the price of a loaf of bread. . . . For every pleasure thousands of pains, for every laugh a flood of tears.*

Newcomers packed into the low side of town and pushed the slums to their bursting points. "The city was seen as sucking in the healthy and devouring them," wrote author Fergus Linnane. "London was pestilential." When the new arrivals did find work, the low pay failed to keep them afloat, no matter how many hours a day they worked. They remained poor—and when the poor got desperate, they took to crime.

William Johnson—a butcher from Northamptonshire, some seventy miles north of London—opened a shop in Newport Market, but business didn't boom. He tried his hand as a corn chandler in Long Acre, then as a victualler running a public house. After some time at sea, he returned to London and became a thief. He robbed, was caught but pardoned, killed a prison turnkey, and then was executed. From butcher to thief to killer and dead—all in short order.

Estimates put the number of criminals during this period in London at around 115,000. For those with coins in their pocket, the street was a treacherous place. They took their lives in their hands merely by going for a stroll, day or night. On a single trip, a pedestrian could get mugged twice, coming and going. Many who could afford a dinner out, did so armed. Ladies of stature carried blunderbusses, an early kind of shotgun.

Few lights illuminated the streets, except along the chief roads or in the squares. The moon lit the rest, and without it darkness prevailed. Roads closer to the city fared better than elsewhere in England, but all were a mess, packed deep with snow and mud in winter and loose with thick swirling dust in summer. When it rained, ponds formed in the middle of the thoroughfares, stalling any semblance of easy passage. All of these conditions made for a pilferer's delight. But in England's age of capital punishment, a thief could pay with his or her life.

From 1660 to 1750, the number of offenses punishable by death increased from 50 to 160, then to over 200 by century's end. The Bloody Code, as the country's system of law enforcement later came to be known, largely aimed to protect private property. Parliamentary legislation in 1706 ended the practice of invoking the benefit of clergy—by which first-time offenders could obtain leniency for minor crimes—and all but condemned anyone arrested for even the slightest infraction. Stealing a single teaspoon or even uprooting a sapling could result in a trip to the gallows.

Despite this increase in felonies punishable by death, the number of hangings actually decreased from the preceding century. In many cases pardons prevented them. British law aimed at forestalling crime with the threat of death, leaving the final punishment to the discretion of court or king. Gibbets dotted the landscape around London to serve as warnings. But the sight of those structures, from which hung the rotting corpses of criminals, failed to inspire the desired effect. London had a strong stomach; death made little impression. Travelers passed these gruesome displays without a second thought. Beyond these visual deterrents, the city had little in place in the way of law enforcement. No police force existed, nor public prosecutors. If a person was robbed, it was up to him or her to prosecute. The laws were draconian and violence ever present.

When "people of quality," as they were known, ventured from their flawless estates and spotless manors, two worlds collided. On the way to church or the theater—through grimy streets and garbage-strewn environs—they mixed with the poor and the desperate. On many occasions the first to meet them as they traversed the London roads was the highwayman.

The call of *Stop, thief!* rang out far and wide during this period, and often announced the handiwork of a thief with a black mask over his face and pistol in hand. It was the highwayman, the so-called gentleman of the road, who told his prey to "stand and deliver." Only a small fraction of thieves lived in any kind of splendor, but at least highwaymen attempted to rob with style. Most hailed from respectable homes and had a higher social and educational standing than other thieving groups. Many highwaymen had fallen into bankruptcy or came to steal because of gaming debts. Henry Fielding called gambling "the school in which most highwaymen of great eminence have been bred."

Highway robbers worked in groups on horseback. One of the gangsters would stop a coach with pistol in one hand and hat in the other and politely inquire, "Your purse or your life?" The standard performance brimmed with apology and politeness, and the highwayman seldom lacked a handy excuse for why distress had driven him to rob. If met by a hard case, he fired a flintlock—a kind of pistol, the weapon of choice—into the air, which generally turned the situation around.

English highwaymen tended not to point their pistols directly, nor did they fleece their victims dry. They left a mark with enough money to complete his journey, and they often returned sentimental possessions to their victims. In 1708, Jack Ovet took politeness too far when he fell in love with the young woman he had robbed aboard the Worcester stagecoach.

"Madam, your charms have softened my temper," Ovet said to her. "Cast not your eyes down, nor cover your face with those modest blushes; and believe me, what I have taken from necessity is only borrowed, and shall be honourably restored, if you will let me know where you may be found."

His temper may have softened, but it didn't end well for Ovet. The thirty-two-year-old swung for his crimes later that year.

The highwaymen of France, Spain, and Germany had a reputation for being coarse and cold-blooded. But even the English gentleman thief lost his temper if his demands went unmet. In *Highwaymen*, Christopher Hibbert shares some of the surprisingly vile lines spouted by spurned road robbers: "God damn you, you double-refined son of whores!" and "You sodomitical sons of bitches." Those insults flew at men, but a bristling highwayman hardly eased up for the ladies, as evidenced by unpleasant remarks such as "You strumpetting whore's abortion."

Most highway robberies took place in or around London due to the ample opportunities for shelter within the city's passageways. Escape often lay just through the next street. As Fielding noted, "The whole appears as a vast wood or forest, in which a thief may harbour with as great security, as wilds beasts do in the deserts of Africa or Arabia."

The wretched roads only aided the highwayman's cause. Coaches often got stuck, broke down, or lost a horse, leaving many immobilized on the roadway with highwaymen circling like vultures. It was hopeless for a stagecoach to try to outrun a man on horseback, either to escape or apprehend him. But sometimes a highwayman made the transaction simpler. If a thief spotted someone packing bags in the city, he might leave a note offering safe passage for a price: a few guineas, perchance a watch. A bribe perhaps, or, if you like, a financial passport or turnpike fee. A traveler was advised to have money in hand or be "knocked on the head for his poverty," as one letter writer put it at the time.

Once their ventures were complete, highwaymen could kick back at an assortment of taverns or similar businesses in and around London that acted as safe houses. There they mingled with their own or were met with indifference. The Blue Lion, the Bull and Pen, and the Dog and Duck all served as thieves' dens. But highwaymen hardly monopolized the crime scene. The city abounded with footpads, pickpockets, housebreakers, prostitutes, and Mohocks.

Footpads elicited more fear than any of the others. They didn't ask or show politeness of any kind like their counterparts on horseback. They took what they wanted through force. Because they toiled on foot and a quick getaway wasn't always possible, they were quick to kill potential witnesses. An outcry could put a damper on their plans. If they had to murder or maim an onlooker, so be it. Footpads often joined forces to work in pairs or gangs. They plied their trade within the city, on the lookout for well-dressed denizens in dark or isolated pockets of town. One threatened the mark with a pistol to the throat while his partner relieved the victim of his valuables.

Pickpockets roamed the streets aplenty. They worked every nook of the city, and unlike footpads they preferred a good crowd, outside the theater or courthouse or at fairs, races, or public hangings. It took great skill to become proficient in the field. Children excelled in this domain, as did women, who were some of the most adept at it.

Many prostitutes also picked pockets. After all, it made good business sense. If a man was already under her spell, it wasn't hard for a woman to find a way into his unguarded pockets. Some girls fell into prostitution as young as the age of twelve, selling their bodies for as little as sixpence. Prostitution opened doors for further jobs, like the bully or pimp. Just as gambling halls brought forth gamesters and sharpers, underground London had a steady stream of short-term jobs. Affidavit men, informers, and confidence tricksters all plied their trades. Housebreakers burgled, and of course, run-of-the-mill murderers did their deeds as well.

The poor were by no means the only ones to turn to crime, as was the case with a gang of violent young aristocrats called the Mohocks. Taking their name from the Native American tribe, these heavies weren't in it for the money; they terrorized the city for kicks. English antiquarian John Timbs called them a "nocturnal fraternity." They might sleep till noon or later, but once awake, they drank themselves into a stupor before venturing out to poke old ladies with swords or toss a prostitute into a barrel headfirst down Snow Hill and into the river. The Mohocks bullied with swords, and while historians argue whether they actually flattened noses, bored out eyes, or cut off ears, their reputation preceded them, and sufficiently terrified pedestrians.

The Mohocks engaged in child's play compared to another group, the Bold Bucks, who, after avowing atheism and performing a set of rituals to prove their godlessness, then dedicated their club life to rape. If a woman couldn't be found out of doors, the Bucks had no problem breaking into a home to find one. Regrettably, they did so with near impunity.

Convictions were hard to come by for rape, and often the crime went unreported.

Making matters worse, officials were just as morally corrupt as criminals. London did, however, have watchmen to guard the streets. These men, often of advanced years, manned posts throughout the city, but were hardly up to the task of tackling the requirements of their employment. Besides, they were armed only with poles, so they didn't exactly meet the challenge of facing pistol-bearing thieves.

"There is no humour in my countrymen which I am more inclined to wonder at, than their general thirst after news," wrote Joseph Addison in the *Spectator* on August 8, 1712.

Whatever the people of London thought of crime, they all shared an unquenchable longing for news in general, and specifically for stories about the lives of criminals. Amid all the madness, they discussed the stories of the day at coffeehouses, more than five hundred of them in the city at the time. Within the confines of a coffeehouse lay a veritable library of books, newspapers, and pamphlets lying around or changing hands. Some people patronized the establishments with such frequency that they gave a coffeehouse's address for acquaintances to find them rather than their own lodgings.

In these places, patrons consumed more than just the electrifying brew from the New World. Tobacco smoke hung in the air. Theologians, economists, and experts on foreign trade—all self-proclaimed, of course—mixed with politicians. Friends sat by the fire and exchanged opinions on the events of the day. Details on affairs from all corners of the globe passed from the ships on the Thames and poured through the doors of the coffeehouse. Banking, trade, and shipping secrets mingled with affairs of state and gossip in an atmosphere warmed by burning logs and tinged with the steam of coffee and stench of tobacco. A touring Frenchman named Misson recorded his observations of the eighteenth-century coffeehouse: "These Houses, which are very numerous in

London, are extreamly convenient. You have all Manner of News there: You have a good Fire, which you may sit by as long as you please: You have a dish of Coffee; you meet your Friends for the Transaction of Business, and all for a Penny, if you don't care to spend more."

Those who couldn't afford a newspaper of their own pooled their money to share a copy. Londoners perused items on marriages, deaths, and the comings and goings of the distinguished and the royal. They read military and adventure stories and comic pieces, and they took in chronicles of crime and criminals. The rest of the paper consisted of advertisements, some of them odd by today's standards. One husband warned the public not to lend or sell his wife anything on credit. Elsewhere, charlatans promised to cure any ailment. London newspapers peddled an incredible array of antidotes. The "Liquor of Azam" offered to cure the "Stone." Also on sale was "Tinctura Amara Stomatica; or Dr. Andrew's famous bitter Stomach Tincture. Which is a most grateful, bitter, and pleasant Flavours and is found by long Experience to exceed all the Stomach Elixirs and Tinctures in the whole World."

The *Daily Journal* advertised an unnamed miracle tonic as "A Medicine of Inestimable Worth" to cure both the "Barrenness in Women, and Imbecility in Men, and that by promoting the chearful Curricle of the Blood and Juices, raising all the Fluids from their languid depressed State to one more florid and sparkling, opening all Obstructions, fortifying the Nerves, encreasing the Animal Spirits." Fertile women and smart men with increased libidos—what wasn't to like? Authors, publishers, and printers also hawked their wares, including this entrancing offering: *An Enquiry into the Question, where the Swallow, the Nightingale, the Woodcock . . . and other Birds of Passage, Go and Reside during their Absence from us.*

But those of a criminal nature took a far greater interest in the listings made by those who had been robbed and were promising rewards for the recovery of their goods.

III

Jonathan Wild Comes to the City

In those days, when English law was severe to a fault, it was not worth
while turning robber without possessing a genius for the business, nor
without a ready tact for taking advantage of any means invented by
the ingenuity of others for eluding the public prosecutor.
—Godfrey Holden Pike, *The Romance of the Streets*

He wasn't a shoddy buckle-maker. He could have been a decent one even, but in 1704, Jonathan Wild wasn't all that great at his work. It was less a matter of skill than desire. Contemporary accounts paint a picture of a ne'er-do-well not yet out of his teens with his head in the clouds. Defoe later wrote that Wild's thoughts were "above his trade." The job just didn't hold his interest. In a different line of work, Wild proved himself dedicated and hardworking, the very best in his business. It just wasn't a very honest one.

Records give Wild's baptism as taking place on May 6, 1683, at St. Peter's in Wolverhampton, 130 miles northwest of London. His father, John Wyld—names and other words often had multiple spellings at the time—worked as a joiner, or carpenter, and his mother sold fruits, flowers, and other items at local country markets. They were poor, but for the most part, they ate. The eldest of five siblings, Jonathan learned to read and write at the Free School in St. John's Lane, though he never really shone in grammar or spelling. His two sisters grew up and married respectable tradesmen in Wolverhampton. But the Wild boys lived up to their name. His brother John set out to live life on the straight and narrow, becoming a public officer and then the crier of Wolverhampton,

JONATHAN WILD IN AN EIGHTEENTH-CENTURY ENGRAVING

but in the end, Jonathan, John, and Andrew all saw the inside of a prison cell.

At age fifteen, Jonathan apprenticed to a Birmingham buckle-maker, and his father died shortly thereafter. He worked and lived in the country, and in all likelihood, odds were that he was going to die in the country, like his father. His mind wandered. He sought out eccentric characters, which led him to the local alehouses, where he met not only interesting folk but also those who didn't particularly obey the law. The troupes of actors who wandered past Wolverhampton enthralled him.

Not long after serving out his seven-year apprenticeship and beginning his career, Wild met a young girl, Amy, whom he married and with whom he had a son. But family life did nothing to ease his drifting mind. His interests lay elsewhere. Body soon followed mind, and in less than two years, he borrowed a horse and left for a life in the city.

In London, he hired on with an attorney from Staffordshire, surname Daniel, but for reasons undocumented, Counselor Daniel fired him, and Wild took employment as a "setter," working for some bailiffs from Clifford's Inn, Fleet Street. A setter, or bailiff's follower, chased debtors. The job was fraught with danger, and it didn't pay much. Wild returned to Wolverhampton in 1704, a failure.

Back in Wolverhampton, he worked joylessly again at making buckles. We have few details of the next four years of Wild's life. Some published accounts from the era share two great stories from this period, but then, some don't. The first involves the horse that Wild "borrowed" when he set out for London.

On his hangdog return home, Wild had to cough up for the horse, which he had sold when low on funds in London. The money was long gone, squandered on city living. The owner allowed him to set up a payment plan to stay out of prison, with Wild paying a shilling each month until the debt was settled. To ensure regular payments, the owner added to the arrangement that Wild had to work his trade so as to have an income. Wild made good on two payments. When pushed for the third, he told the owner that he was finished—no more payments would follow.

In a 1725 pamphlet titled "The Life of Jonathan Wild, from his Birth to Death," Wild showcased an early instance of his talent for double-talking that would benefit him so well in the future. He answered that the creditor had it right: Wild had run off with his horse, sold it, then pocketed the money. But the agreement into which they had entered had settled the affair. The head-spinning conversation continued:

"Very well," said the horse's owner, "why don't you pay me according to that contract, then?"

"No," said Wild, "that contract is obsolete and of none effect."

"How so?" asked the owner.

"Why, you'll allow that Articles of Agreement, or Contracts, not fulfill'd, are broken, and Articles once broken, cannot subsist afterwards: Now our Articles are broken, for I have made but two Payments, when there are three due long ago. Therefore I owe you nothing."

To summarize: Because they had agreed to a contract together, their business had to be settled according to said contract, which once broken no longer applied, and therefore, Wild had fulfilled his obligations. The quick-tongued declamation amazingly succeeded. Wild made no further payments for a debt he obviously owed. He also learned a valuable lesson: There had to be a better way to make money than by making buckles. So, according to the author of the pamphlet, "He easily perceiv'd he had Occasion for more Money than his Hands could procure him in that narrow Way of Business; therefore he spurn'd at the Trade and resolv'd, some how or other, to transfer the Labour from his Hands to his Head, as being the most likely Means of getting a Livelihood fit for a Gentleman."

Accordingly he gave London another shot. He set out—on foot this time—with nine pence to his name. From this latter voyage comes the second of the contemporary sketches of Wild in his early years.

Outside Wolverhampton, he came across a well-heeled woman traveling on horseback. She agreed that he could walk alongside her for a few miles, during which time the two learned about each other. A traveling doctress, she was visiting different parts of the countryside as a healer, at this point on her way to Warwick, on the other side of Birmingham. When Wild learned of her medical background, he figured he'd get her opinion on his trick hip, which he was able to pop out of its socket. By doing so, he could turn his leg around nearly 180 degrees. The result was a sickly mangled sight, his foot turned in the opposite direction, dragging along.

Distressed, the doctress dismounted her horse to give Wild a consultation, but he promptly popped his hip back into place. She was relieved—and intrigued.

Wild had been doing the trick for years, but never with more frequency than when he spotted soldiers or press gangs on the lookout for new recruits for the campaign against France. Wild disliked the thought of military service even more than manual labor. He had used his hip trick, when growing up, to conjure compassion instead of recruitment. Once past the soldiers in view, he realigned his hip and went on his way.

As the story goes, after learning of Wild's deceptive ways, the doctress revealed her own treachery: She knew as much about medicine as he did. The doc was a quack. But Wild's pain-free malady had inspired her. She concocted a scheme and asked him to participate. He agreed—but who wouldn't have? The bulk of his duties in her plan had him lying in bed, eating and drinking as much as his heart desired. Not a bad gig.

Off they went to Warwick, with Wild disguised as a beggar and limping behind.

The scheme was to have him examined by the town's doctor, who no doubt would find Wild's condition incurable. Then the quack doctress would come along and do the miraculous. Of course, her healing wouldn't come until after she'd placed a wager with the local physician that she could heal this unknown beggar. Prior to the cure, Wild would lie in bed for ten days, acting the part. Apparently he lost his voice from all the theatrical screaming as she worked on him.

The recovered con spared no flourish. He waxed lyrical about his lack of pain, describing a beautiful dream, complete with angels, flowers, gold, and ivory. He observed the kind doctress in this sleeping state, and then the sound of thunder jarred him awake. At that point, according to his telling, the pain dispersed and he was no longer lame. With her healing touch, Wild's bone had settled back into place. He was whole again—and the doctress fifty guineas the richer. Following Wild's testamentary recovery, the doctress then went to work on the poor sick folk in the town, cooking up all manner of placebos to heal their ailments, graciously charging only what the medicine cost her. Wild provided the muscle behind the operation, crushing bricks and using the dust for their medicine. All told, the pair pocketed around £100.

These two tales of a young Jonathan Wild, true or not, exemplify traits that later informed his reputation. First is an overwhelming belief in himself. He had an uncanny ability to make others believe he was right and then put their trust behind him, usually by means of the second trait: his acting chops.

Following their Warwick interlude, the quack and her muse packed up and departed for London, after which the partnership dissolved. Wild presumably wasted no time in spending his part of the bounty, because he once again went broke and was thrown into the Wood Street Compter for debt.

With his entrance into prison, the documented history of Jonathan Wild begins. He discussed his time in the Compter in the 1718 pamphlet, "An Answer to a Late Insolent Libel," which bears his name on the title page but was written by a stronger hand that recorded the events by dictation. Wild says he spent four years in the Compter, and records show he was released in 1712, so we can put him in debtors' prison from 1708 through 1712. Within the walls of the Wood Street Compter, Wild found himself both penniless and friendless. It was here that his true education commenced. As he stated in the pamphlet, it was impossible to spend such a prolonged time imprisoned without being "in some measure let into the secrets of the criminals under confinement."

A thief's first stop in the London justice system, the Wood Street Compter was founded in 1555 and rebuilt in 1670 following the Great Fire. Located between Cheapside and the London Wall, it also served as a way station for criminals who stayed for a couple of nights before being sent to Newgate or elsewhere. According to Patrick Pringle, prisons at the time weren't designed for "punishment, correction, or reformation." Relatively few crimes had sentences that included imprisonment. More often, punishment involved an action: paying a fine, standing in the pillory, receiving a whipping, transportation to the colonies, or hanging. Debtors waited at the Compter until they paid their debt, but again, according to Pringle, "Everyone who went into prison was required to pay an entrance fee, and also a fine, called 'garnish,' to his fellow prisoners; failing that, he had to surrender his clothes. 'Pay or strip' was the usual greeting." An inmate had to pay at practically every step and one last time upon release. If an inmate had the money, a private room could be had, and it wasn't beyond the norm for the well-off to throw parties and invite people from outside. Conversely, those at the bottom of the heap found themselves in the notorious "Hole," an overpopulated cesspool high on filth and low on food. Hundreds of souls struggled in dirty chaos, murderers mixing with children as young as five years old.

The Compter, like other prisons, consisted of a hierarchy of classes, known as "Sides," with a prisoner's station depending on the size of his wallet. At the top was the Master's Side. From there, in descending order, was the Knights' Ward, Two-Penny Ward, and the Common Ward, wherein lay the Hole. Unfortunately, Wild—after hearing the words "Sir, we arrest you in the King's Majesty's name, and we charge you to obey us"—found himself in the Common side and quickly became acquainted with the Hole. The less-than-spacious Common side lay in the cellar, the ceiling no more than nine feet high. Prisoners slept three or four to a bed, the beds stacked up the side of the walls like shelves. The only light or fresh air came through an eighteen-inch hole in the ceiling described as a "funnel." Biographer Gerald Howson described the scene:

> Here about seventy people lived, women and children, dependent entirely on such charity as the gaolers allowed to filter down for their food, crowded together in more filth than would be permitted in any pigsty, in freezing cold and damp, and in total darkness, month after month, year after year. Only an intermittent, faint, grey glow down the funnel proclaimed the march of successive days.

Starvation or "gaol-fever"—the common name for typhus—took the lives of Compter inmates weekly. Exact death rates from this period remain unknown because no inspections took place, and even parliamentary committees couldn't gain entrance to London prisons. But in Marshalsea Prison, in 1719, some 300 inmates, out of a total of 1,500, died in a single three-month stretch. Gaol-fever made the rounds via lice and fleas, which were legion, as were bedbugs. The popping of bugs underfoot had the unexpected benefit of alerting the prisoners that someone was approaching.

Making money and friends meant survival. Those who didn't get along met with "Making the Black Dog Walk," a severe hazing for new detainees. One alternative to the dire situation was to volunteer yourself into slavery on one of the American plantations. Another method for survival was sex. According to Pringle, "Women and children of both sexes commonly sold their bodies to the warders and to more affluent prisoners for bread, so prisons were also brothels." Some women gave themselves voluntarily, hoping to get pregnant, which would allow them to "plead their bellies" and avoid the hangman.

Wild suffered along with the rest. He'd never seen such conditions, and his fellow inmates were anything but accommodating. The atmosphere was cutthroat, the competition menacing. He worked to make his situation better. He took any job the Compter had to offer, no matter how awful, debasing, or downright disgusting. He worked for the turnkeys and the higher-class prisoners on the Master's Side. He listened. He learned. Most importantly, he made friends.

In time, he rose through the system. By 1711, he had gained some freedoms and greater responsibilities from the keepers. One such privilege was the "Liberty of the Gate." At night, whenever pickpockets, prostitutes, or other "rats" (new prisoners) came in, Wild guarded them till morning, occasionally chaperoning the prisoners to their next stop, whether it be the courthouse, magistrate's quarters, or elsewhere.

The term *rats*, for "new prisoners," derives from the thieves' argot, or secret language, known as cant. All walks of life and sociological standing can speak slang, which shifts with the times, but cant is private and unchanging. An old system, it was developed for secrecy, a way for a thief to talk to a thief without revealing his meaning to outsiders within earshot. Many who spoke cant were illiterate, so the words have simplicity in mind: A horse was a *prance*. A ladder was a *Jacob*. *Stampers* were shoes. A *push* was a crowd of people. A *cackling fart* was an egg. From single words to entire phrases, cant covered practically all of a thief's activities, thus allowing him to speak freely amid a crowd. *Bite the bill from the cull* was to steal a sword from a man's side. *Taking lobs from behind rattlers* meant nabbing luggage from a moving coach. *Nim the nab* was to steal a hat off a man's head.

At the Compter, Wild spent much time with thieves of all sorts. But one rat particularly caught his eye. A regular at the Gate, the hub where all of the characters of the night congregated, she was a true professional.

In *The Tyburn Chronicle*, Mary Milliner is described as "a common street-walker" who had "run the whole circle of vice, knew all the ways of the town, and most of its felonious inhabitants." But Milliner was more than a whore. She knew how to earn money from an array of shady activities. Both well versed and well connected, she usually didn't stay locked up for long. She was too smart for that. Milliner was the wife of a Thames waterman, but the underworld knew her as a "buttock and file" as well—a prostitute and a pickpocket. Skilled at her work, she often pursued both functions simultaneously, robbing some poor sot while she had sex with him.

Before meeting Milliner, Wild had been stockpiling knowledge of the underworld. Now he realized how little he knew. She revealed a whole new world to the young debtor. Milliner's domain consisted predominantly of thieves and whores. She introduced her new beau around, and soon he was learning myriad new techniques for making money.

Under Milliner's tutelage, Wild made numerous friends and associates. His aptitude concerning thievery had grown to the point where other inmates often called on him for advice, telling him the particulars of their plans. Wild's counsel often proved beneficial to the thieves, and like an ace handicapper, he became the man to see. One contemporary account referred to him in his new Compter role as "a kind of Oracle amongst the Thieves."

Two notable men among these new acquaintances were Obadiah Lemon, who ran his own gang, and William Field, a notorious informer who testified regularly and easily against others to improve his own lot. Field had come to the Compter on a pickpocketing charge in September 1712, but he went free after testifying at the Guildhall the next month against Under City Marshal Charles Hitchen. Wild and Hitchen soon met, and it's entirely possible that Wild entered the relationship with a bevy of inside information on the under marshal, thanks to Field.

In 1712, Wild finally paid off his debt, which wasn't excessive. Records include "A Schedule of what monies I owe," written out in Wild's handwriting, listing twelve creditors with amounts ranging from £1 19s to £12, as well as several other persons "I owe small debts to, but forgett their Names." His total debt ran to £61 6s. On a separate sheet, Wild listed four people who owed him a total of £33 pounds, and then in an addendum "Severall others which I cant remember being Small."

Wild's pardon was announced in the *London Gazette* on November 4, 1712. Come December, he was a free man again. He and Milliner moved in together, shacking up in Lewkenor's Lane, Covent Garden. Both were already married, but the two lived together as a married couple, Milliner the second of six Mrs. Wilds. The new lovers opened a brothel, and Wild officially began his life as a career criminal.

IV

The Review

*I grasp at any kind of opportunity. . . . I take the first subject that
chance offers. They are all equally good to me. And I never purpose to
treat them exhaustively.*
—Montaigne, *Of Democritus and Heraclitus*

Defoe was born in 1661 in the parish of St. Giles, Cripplegate, outside
the city walls but still very much a part of London. He lived the city life.
These streets were his home. These were his people. "Cities in general
fascinated Defoe," notes author Cynthia Wall, "but he wrote most particularly of London, its boundaries and buildings, streets and occupa-
tions, trade and crime, strengths and vulnerabilities, ancient patterns and
constant permutations."

London may have changed in the centuries since, but clouds of people still swarmed at each rung of society's ladder even then. Different
characters occupied every hall, bawdy house, shop, mansion, or political
office. City and people intertwined. On Grub Street, the synonymous
home of the hack, writers toed the line of literary respect, scribbling
away, willing to write anything for a penny. London hummed then as
now. Defoe gave witness to it all. "I remember in the time of the Popish
plot," Defoe wrote, "when murthering men in the dark was pretty much
in fashion, and every honest man walked the streets in danger of his life."

Defoe's father had been a tradesman, a butcher, a candle-maker, and
a merchant. Coming from a family of nonconformists, Defoe couldn't
attend Oxford or Cambridge—where he would have had to swear the
oaths of supremacy and allegiance (to the monarch and Church of

A
REVIEW
OF THE
Affairs of FRANCE:

Purg'd from the Errors and Partiality of News-Writers and
Petty-Statesmen, of all Sides.

Tuesday, November 7. 1704.

I Am oblig'd so often to Digress, by those
Gentlemen that pretend to blame me for
Digression, that I think they ought indeed to be call'd the Authors of it.

The Grand Cavil, of what's all this to the Affairs of France, has been so often thrown in my way, that I think my self under an Obligation to say something to it.

If the Gentlemen Objectors expected, That in Treating of the Affairs of France, I should have confin'd my self to the Limits of their Country, and only wrote a History of the Kingdom, my Title ought to have been A REVIEW OF THE AFFAIRS in FRANCE, not OF it: He that will write only of the Actions of the French, within their own Country, will have his Memoirs, full of little else but Edicts for Taxes, Regulations, Creations and Dispositions of Old and New Offices; Orders for Te Deums for Victories; Promotion of Generals; Introduction of Ambassadors; Coining Vainglorious Medals, to the Honour of Immortal, Invincible Lewis XIV. These things interlac'd with Matters of Love, Intrigue, fine Balls, Entertainments, now and then a great Marriage, and not a little Whoring, must have been the Subject of my Worthy Undertaking.

Alas! How little of the active Part of the Affairs of France have been within their own Kingdom? The Glorious Duke of Marlborough has had the fairest for bringing France to be the Scene of Action, of any Man in the World; and could his Grace, that has Conquer'd like Joshua, done one thing more that Joshua did, viz. Cause the Sun to have stood still; could he have Commanded the Season to have gone back, and added three Months more to the Summer, that the French might not have had a Winter to Recruit their Cavalry, Regulate and Refresh their Old Troops, and raise New, I dare not mention how far he might have push'd, this most advantageous Campaign.

In short, He that will hear of the Affairs of France, so great has been her Influence in all the Courts and Countries of Europe, he must be content to ravel almost into universal History; at least he must Concern the active part of Europe in it, or the Story will be Nonsence, Imperfect, Inconsistent with it self, and unworthy both the Author, and any Reader that he ought to Value.

If I do not shew the hand of France in the Affairs of Hungary; then indeed I have launch'd too far; but I demand the Justice of Time to end it, and wonder any Man should be tyred with the Particulars.

Nor let any Man be uneasy for the Protestants in Hungary; as to this Story, if it does not do them right, as far as can be expected in Reason; I am mistaken; and as for those who expect more Right than Reason demands, I have no regard to their Demands, and shall never answer their Expectation.

Cccc　　　　　　I have

England)—so as a teen he was sent to Dissenting School in Newington Green, northeast of the City, destined for a life in the clergy. But when the time came, Defoe chose a secular life. He went into business, and he married a businessman's daughter.

In 1704, when Defoe first published the *Review*, newspapers were still in their infancy. England's first newspaper, the *Oxford Gazette* (later the *London Gazette*) first appeared in 1665, and the nation's first daily paper, the *Daily Courant*, appeared in March 1702. Across the Atlantic, America's first newspaper, the *Boston News-Letter*, appeared weekly, starting in 1704, as well. Journalism was exploding into the eighteenth century.

Prior to these developments, all written news had appeared in pamphlet form. According to J. B. Williams, author of *A History of English Journalism*, "A pamphlet in the seventeenth century was a book of one or more sheets of paper folded into quarto pages and—if stitched together— unbound. Hence these pamphlets of news were invariable called 'books,' 'books of news,' and finally 'news-books.'" News books eventually became newspapers, with the first recorded use of the term as we know it found in a 1670 letter to Charles Perrot, the *London Gazette*'s second editor; the correspondent wrote, "I wanted your newes paper Monday last past."

In 1681, the two-paged, single-sheet political newspaper *The Observator: In Question and Answer*, edited by Roger L'Estrange, came out irregularly, usually at least three times a week. *The Observator*'s format remained true to title, but the Q&A resulted in clunky dialogue, which Defoe thankfully avoided in his own venture. Taking heed of his predecessors, he aimed for a cleaner page. In John Dunton's 1691 *Athenian Mercury*, Defoe found elements to include in the *Review*, such as inspiration for its "Scandal Club" section. Dunton also published *The Ladies' Mercury*, a targeted publication, and although it lasted only four weeks in February and March of 1693, the new demographic focus was ingenious.

The *Review* was a solitary achievement for Defoe, but hardly his only work at the time. He continued as a pamphleteer and contributed articles to other newspapers. He was gaining a reputation as a man with an ink-stained hand, and in 1704 he published in excess of 400,000 words, including his first book, *The Storm*, about the events and aftermath of the

Great Storm, which struck just as Defoe was emerging from prison in November 1703.

The storm hit on Friday, November 26, and continued for a week straight. Rain, flooding, and high winds pummeled the country and the sea. Over eight thousand people died, a great many on the water. The storm wiped out one-fifth of the Royal Navy. Just one of the ships, the *Newcastle*, lost 197 of its crew of 233. Houses blew away and entire forests were uprooted. No one had ever seen anything like it, and it remains the worst natural disaster in England's history. It had affected everybody, and held everyone's interest. Defoe saw an opening.

Defoe took to the country to gather intelligence on the disaster, visiting devastated areas and witnessing the effects of what he called "the greatest and the longest storm that ever the world saw." He also gathered reports from others, soliciting accounts through advertisements. In the end, the book consisted of approximately 75,000 words and upwards of sixty different perspectives. *The Storm* stands out as a pioneering achievement. Even three centuries later, it still warrants appreciation and has been called "the first substantial work of modern journalism," and "one of the earliest extended journalistic narratives in English." John J. Miller of the *Wall Street Journal* says of *The Storm* that "Defoe's eyewitness account is valuable, but his real innovation was to collect the observations of others. Journalism was then in its infancy, and there was nothing like systematic and objective reporting on contemporary events."

The *Review* first appeared on February 19, 1704. Defoe's paper, yet another early example of modern journalism, ran with little interruption for nearly a decade, until June 1713, publishing essays on politics, trade, economics, and religion on Tuesdays, Thursdays, and Saturdays. The publication's original title—*A Weekly Review of the Affairs of France: Purg'd from the Errors and Partiality of News-Writers and Petty-Statesmen, of all Sides*—made it clear that the paper intended to criticize others. After a month, its circulation had risen to four hundred, although between five to ten people probably read each copy. More who couldn't read congregated around someone who could to hear the paper read aloud.

England was fighting France, among other nations, in the War of the Spanish Succession, so matters dealing with the enemy held high interest. In the introduction to the first issue, Defoe stated the paper's goal as "setting the Affairs of Europe in a Clearer Light, and to prevent the various uncertain Accounts, and the Partial Reflections of our Street-Scribblers, who Daily and Monthly Amuse Mankind with Stories of Great Victories when we are Beaten," and likewise distortions, which had "this Effect, That People are possest with wrong Notions of Things, and Nations Wheedled to believe Nonsense and Contradiction." As such, Defoe reported facts in a straightforward fashion, listing the occurrences without inclination to beautify. Years prior, in the preface to "The True-Born Englishman," he drew attention to his "mean Stile" and called his verse "rough." His directness appealed to the coffeehouse and alehouse sensibilities of the average middle-class Englishman.

His episode with "The Shortest Way" lay behind him, but it now offered unexpected benefits, including a certain amount of credibility as a fearless writer, a muckraker ready to take on church, state, and fellow man. He set aside a special section in the *Review* just for this type of mudslinging, which he meant to lighten the mood: "After our Serious Matters are over, we shall at the end of every Paper, Present you with a little Diversion, as any thing occurs to make the World Merry; and whether Friend of Foe, one Party or another, if any thing happens so scandalous, as to require an open Reproof, the World may meet with it there."

He initially called this section "Mercure Scandale: or Advice from the Scandalous Club: Being a Weekly History of Nonsense, Impertinence, Vice and Debauchery." Like the paper's title, it ran through a few iterations before settling on "Advice from the Scandal Club, To the Curious Enquirers; in Answer to Letters sent them for that Purpose." Here he offered conversation on everyday interests and devoted space for answering readers' questions on courtship, marriage, vice, etiquette, friendship, and civic duties—anything and everything. He even covered the supernatural. One reader asked, "Whether there is, or ever were any such Apparitions, Ghosts, Phantomes, or by whatsoever Name you may call them?"

Defoe had no reservations about dealing in scandal. A few months into the paper's run, he imagined an array of possible targets, such as "a drunken Justice fallen into the Mill-pond, or an eminent Citizen taken with a Twelve-penny Whore," or "a Magistrate stabbing a Man into the Back in the Dark, or a Man of Letters corresponding with our Enemies abroad. If these things are true and can be made out; if these Men have Names and are to be found out by their Characters," then all was fair in printing the sordid details.

So the "Scandal Club" provided entertainment, which counterbalanced the "Solemn and Tedious Affair." He was right on target. The paper was in every sense a huge hit, and as Maximillian Novak observes, "Advice from the Scandal Club was an important journalistic innovation."

The only problem was that his so-called "Club" was a party of one. Defoe eagerly pointed out the "lyes" in other periodicals, but if he spun parables into letters or gossip, this absence of fact didn't bother him. The device allowed him to reach as many readers as possible; if not for easy reading, they might not have read anything at all. In other words, leisurely edification was better than no edification. After all, "All men are not Historians," Defoe wrote—but they could still buy papers. "If it had been always serious, and had proceeded too fast, had been too Voluminous, too Tedious, either for their Leisure or Inclination; and thus we weedle them in, if it may be allow'd that Expression, to the Knowledge of the World, who rather than take more Pains, would be content with their Ignorance and search into nothing."

The *Review* had found a new market and brilliantly capitalized on it. Readers at coffeehouses, inns, and alehouses read it, but women also discussed the paper's bright tales at the tea table. As Christopher Flynn notes, "Defoe's *Review* was actually intended to be read and discussed according to a rhythm dictated by its periodical circulation and coffee shop consumption. It was meant to move in time and space." This was something new.

Robert Harley had saved Defoe from wasting away in Newgate Prison. Harley, like Defoe, was a man of the city, a Whig, and a nonconformist, but Harley was speeding through the offices of British politics, first as secretary of state, and then first lord of the treasury and de facto prime minister. To do so, he used the media to his advantage. Harley saw the value of having someone else write about what a great job he was doing as a politician. In came the *Review*, which, as one of its foremost functions, gave Harley's team good marks.

Defoe wrote about whatever he liked, but Harley put him on the government's payroll, thereby financing the paper and prompting essays that touted a certain agenda. Defoe liked to speak of irony—an unexpected twist—and here he was, publishing a periodical in support of the very government, the exact people, who had hunted and imprisoned him.

The first years of the *Review* covered the war with France. When Harley began pushing in 1706 for political union between England and Scotland, thereby creating Great Britain, Defoe filled the *Review* with words encouraging the cause. He even pulled on his boots and went into action as a secret agent. He traveled to Scotland, and in Edinburgh he feigned the part of an interested businessman (or other times even an expert gardener) to push for an accord between the nations among the people. A reporter and spy, he conveyed the information that he gathered on the mood of the Scots back to Harley.

With the War of the Spanish Succession playing out on the continent, the Act of Union provided a great journalistic opportunity domestically. Defoe published stories in the *Review* based on his firsthand reporting. He even printed an Edinburgh edition of the *Review* for a time. His propaganda efforts succeeded. In 1707, England and Scotland united. He had performed a great duty on behalf of his government, but in his own city, he couldn't catch a break. He won little respect. He wasn't the only writer Harley had employed to do his bidding. Jonathan Swift, future author of *Gulliver's Travels*, was also on the payroll. But since Swift hadn't done time in the pillory, Harley touted him openly as a friend, welcoming him through the front door. In an earlier letter to Harley, Defoe had branded himself "a Man in the Dark"—a prophetic description. Instead of receiving public gratitude, his service remained under wraps.

"The Shortest Way" earned Defoe a stalwart reputation, and the *Review* sold nicely, but his peers remained less than impressed. They didn't invite him to literary gatherings or their clubs, such as the exclusive Scriblerus Club, which counted Jonathan Swift, Alexander Pope, and John Gay as members and convened in Dr. Arbuthnot's austere quarters at St. James's Palace. "Satire upon the abuse of human learning was their leading object," wrote John Timbs in *Club Life of London*.

The Scriblerus was also a Tory club—"so self-conceited as to believe that nothing was good outside their narrow precincts," according to biographer Thomas Wright—but beyond politics the haughty group never really cared for Defoe. Swift, a well-respected intellectual, hated Defoe, and Pope remained critical of Defoe for decades, while to other writers, like Joseph Addison and Richard Steele, he was disregarded as an outsider.

Though Defoe certainly didn't hold himself above the fray. In the very first issue of the *Review*, he essentially threw down the gauntlet. "As to our Brethren of the Worshipful Company of News—writers, Fellows of Scriblers College, Students in Politicks, and Professors in Contradiction; we prepare them this Hint as a fair Warning. Let them please to be careful, not to Impose Absurdities and Contradiction in their Weekly-Papers, and they shall meet with no Ill Treatment from this Paper." Defoe brashly announced that "we will forgive them small Errata's, and slips of the Pen; nor will we always quarrel with them for Errors in Geography; but if they tell us a Lye, that a Man may feel with his Foot, and not only Proclaim their own Folly, but their Knavery too, and tell the World they think their Readers are Fools too, *that is intolerable.*"

To move papers, Defoe strove to present his periodical as the final word on matters, and it was hard to argue with the success that the paper enjoyed. In time he began signing some of his other works as "by the Author of the *Review*," having done the same with "by the Author of 'The Hymn to the Pillory'" and "by the Author of 'The True-Born Englishman.'"

By 1710, it was Swift's turn to take jabs at Defoe. In his paper, the *Examiner*, Swift grouped Defoe and John Tutchin, publisher of *The Observator*, together, calling them "two stupid illiterate Scribblers." Easily offended by such criticism, Defoe didn't remain silent, and alluded to settling the matter via fisticuffs: "I am perfectly illiterate in the polite style of the street, and am not fit to converse with the porters and carmen of quality, who grace their diction with the beauties of calling names, and cursing their neighbor with bonne grace. I have had the honour to fight a rascal, but never could master the eloquence of calling a man so."

Years later, this line of snobbery still enraged Defoe. In *The Compleat English Gentleman*, he posed the question anew: "Will nothing make a man a schollar but Latin and Greek?" As put by John Robert Moore: "If we think of his contemporaries in velvet coats, smoking church-warden pipes at ease, we must picture Defoe in a rough weatherproof coat, on horseback or on foot." He had dirt under his nails. Others looked down on him.

They had further reason in 1713 when Defoe was arrested again, this time for debt. After nine years, the *Review*'s run was coming to a close. At its end, Defoe found himself back where he was when it started: imprisoned in Newgate. The last issue appeared on June 11, 1713.

Harley came to his aid once more and arranged for his release. But Defoe found himself amid a slump of legal predicaments. Another brush with the law came after he had composed a trio of controversial pamphlets: "Reason against the Hanover Succession," "What if the Queen Should Die?," and "What if the Pretender Should Come?" Each of the documents contained treasonous passages, it was charged—anonymous, yes, but credited to Defoe with little question.

Defoe claimed the mantle of irony once again. Harley saved him again, arranging for a pardon from the Queen. But his release came with an admonition from Judge Powys on the Queen's Bench that his pamphlets could have him "hang'd, drawn, and quarter'd" if he wasn't careful.

Defoe saw how prisons made thieves. Men and women went to jail for being poor and came out criminals, like Jonathan Wild and countless others who learned their crafts behind bars. Defoe did as he always had and observed, but he also had timing on his side. Since the late seventeenth century, the demand for criminal literature had grown. So many citizens lived lives of desperate poverty, and to escape the drudgery of their day-to-day life, they looked for inspiration in the rebel—anyone who dared to take his life into his own hands and fight against a society stacked against him.

In addition to the steady influx of naive country folk looking for work in the city, the war with France and Spain was ending. Military men returning from the continent would be unable to find work, and many would drift into lawlessness. Defoe might not have recognized his unique position to accommodate his readers, but he knew penitentiary life, and he wrote what sold.

Defoe had scored a success with the *Review*, but as the paper's operations were shuttered, proper credibility still eluded him. As John Gay observed in a letter to a friend, "The poor *Review* is quite exhausted, and grown so very contemptible that, though he has provoked all his brothers of the quill, none will enter into a controversy with him." So Defoe moved on to other literary pursuits. As Paula Backscheider writes, "Still convinced that novelty drew the most readers, Defoe found it in three intriguing groups of criminals: pirates, gangs, and women."

Pope and Swift put the writer-for-hire beneath them. Swift couldn't even tax himself to mutter Defoe's name. "One of these authors (the fellow that was pilloried, I have forgot his name) is indeed so grave, sententious, dogmatical a rogue, that there is no enduring him." Defoe had been pilloried. No matter what he wrote or how much he published, he could never dig himself out of that singular hole. It defined him. There was no getting around it: Defoe was a hack.

V

THE MARSHAL AND
THE BUCKLE-MAKER

*These are some of the remarkable adventures of the Marshal and
his man the buckle-maker after the Marshal's suspension, and many
others might be enumerated.*
—JONATHAN WILD, "AN ANSWER TO A LATE INSOLENT LIBEL"

When Charles Hitchen's father-in-law died in 1711, Hitchen used his
wife's inheritance to purchase the vacant post of under city-marshal in the
City of London at auction for £700 on January 8, 1712. Many purchased
their jobs at the time, and decades would pass before the City unveiled its
first police force. In the meantime, the province of law enforcement fell
to the patchwork efforts of the marshal's office, magistrates, constables
(and their assistants, the beadles), and watchmen.

The men filling these positions often did more to pad their own
pockets than they did to deter crime. Not all of these positions came
with a salary, so the gentlemen in these roles more often than not made
their money through a combination of bribery and the levying of arbi-
trary fines. Constables often paid others to perform their duties, since the
job wasn't voluntary but more akin to being drafted. A constable's service
time was for one year before another recruit took his place. A reward
system at the time supplied an exemption from this post, among others,
to anyone brave enough to have captured a bandit.

When he took the marshal's job, Charles Hitchen became virtually
omnipresent in London. Then again, it was hard to miss the tall broad

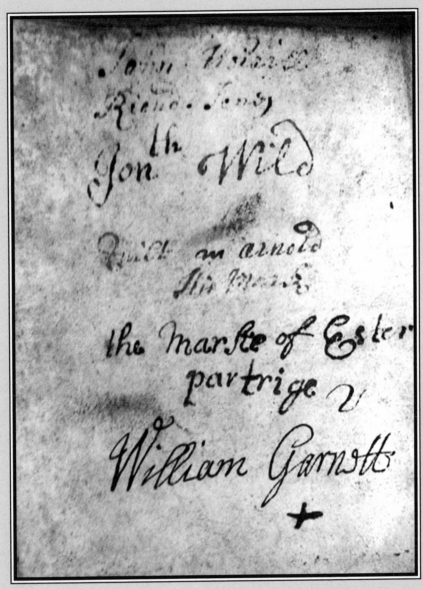

ONE OF THE MANY BLOOD MONEY CERTIFICATES BEARING WILD'S
SIGNATURE, FOR APPREHENDING THIEVES

man in the periwig and tricorn hat who carried a sword and never failed to throw his title in the air when making an entrance. Not only did Hitchen like to hang out at all the taverns and brothels around Temple Bar and Aldgate, but he often surrounded himself with clusters of pickpockets and other ill-mannered young toughs, whom he called his "mathematicians." He based his operations in coffeehouses like Masey's in Old Change, or Mear's near his home, which he used in lieu of an office. There he read the *Daily Courant* for news of lost property and wrote circular letters drumming up business, such as the following—under a fictional, initialed alias—advertising the services of the marshal to London shop owners victimized by robbery:

To Mr. A— Merchant,
Sir,

I am inform'd that you have lately had the Misfortune to be Depriv'd of your Pocket-Book. It is not long since I labour'd under the same calamity, and perhaps to a greater Degree than you, I having Notes for very considerable Sums enclos'd in the same; but upon applying my self to Mr. C—s H—n, in St Paul's Church-Yard, whom I was inform'd was the greatest Proficient in the Business of Thief-Taking in England, he took care to serve me effectually. There is no doubt but he will serve you likewise to the Extent of his Abilities, and I can assure you he has universal Acquaintance with, and Influence over all Persons in the Town Employ'd in Thefts of this Nature. But I must give you this Caution, that you go to him with your Pockets well lin'd, or He'll have nothing to say to you.

I am, tho' unknown,
Your Friend &c.
A.B.

The £700 price tag of his post didn't serve as a financial token of the marshal's devotion to service. Hitchen planned to recoup his costs as a blackmailer and a receiver, also known as a fence—a person who deals in stolen goods. He also dabbled in prostitution by selling protection to whores and the owners of brothels. Hitchen had a three-pronged approach when it came to those who could earn him a penny: intimidation, confession, and possession. Whenever he learned of a theft committed by a pickpocket or whore, Hitchen threatened the offender into a confession and then took possession of the stolen goods.

By and large, he was heavy-handed and shortsighted when dealing with thieves. When fencing stolen goods, his high prices benefited only his own wallet, and his demeanor angered most everybody with whom he dealt. In addition to bribing and hassling pickpockets and whores, he also began to extort from honest shop owners and tradesmen.

By September 1712, complaints against Hitchen—after less than a year on the job—had reached such a pitch that news of his transgressions had reached the Court of Aldermen, elected officials overseen by the lord mayor of London, who sat among their number. The court formed a committee to investigate evidence from ten cases against the marshal, the direst involving one of the solicitation letters he liked to pen that directed victims of robbery to call on him for assistance. During subsequent discussions concerning £200 worth of missing Bills of Exchange, Hitchen stuck his foot in his mouth when he bragged that he knew of "2,000 persons who lived by Thieving within the Bills of Mortality"—a roundabout reference to London and parts of Middlesex and Surrey— and on whom he could call to find the missing loot.

Another complaint against Hitchen came from the constable of Shoreditch. Constable Wise conveyed that the marshal frequented two Moorfields taverns, the Three Tuns and the Black Horse, with such regularity that it was hard to differentiate Hitchen from the cast of bandits and gamblers who also patronized the establishments. Wise indicated that the marshal held recurrent meetings with pickpockets from the Clerkenwell Workhouse, among them Jonathan Wild's associate from the Wood Street Compter, William Field.

Hitchen answered his accusers on December 16, when he appeared before the committee and presented an "Answer of Charles Hitchen to the Severall Informations . . ." Wild biographer Gerald Howson kindly calls the document "nine pages of foolscap without a comma or a stop," written in "a semi-literate attempt at 'legalese.'" But Howson allows that the document contains many intriguing particulars about London street life at the time. In his defense to the aldermen's committee, Hitchen tried to shift attention away from himself and establish his accusers as less than credible, and some as thieves themselves. This appearance by Hitchen in front of the committee on December 16, 1712, also marks the exact date that Wild gained his release from the Compter.

Wild and Milliner set up "shop" in Lewkenor's Lane—Macklin Street today—between Holborn and St. Giles in Covent Garden. Whorehouses and boozing dens dotted the short, dark, slim street of packed dirt. The neighborhood dripped with sex and crime—sometimes simultaneously, thanks to Milliner.

Peter Cunningham, in his 1850 *Handbook of London: Past and Present*, describes Lewkenor's Lane as "a rendezvous and nursery for loose women," making it the perfect setting for the pair to open a brothel. In the years to come, other prostitutes followed. But not long before, Covent Garden had accommodated the upper crust. The neighborhood's atmosphere radically shifted following the Great Fire of 1666. Soon public houses surrounded the piazza, and with them came colonies of harlots and hustlers. By day, Covent Garden hosted the city's largest outdoor market, but with the cover of night, the neighborhood transformed into the sex capital of London.

Soldiers visited the area looking for a good time. Covent Garden catered to all proclivities, with no inclination deemed over the edge. Consequently, not all people of quality deserted the area. The all-look-and-no-touch posture molls stripped nightly, sometimes presented on oversize platters, the women cinched into the shape of a "trussed chicken." They dealt floggings to many a well-heeled gentleman who paid handsomely for the pleasure. In the 1766 tract, *The Midnight Spy: Or, A View of the Transactions of London and Westminster From the Hours of Ten in the Evening, till Five in the Morning, Exhibiting a great Variety of Scenes in High and Low Life, With the Characters of some Well known Nocturnal Adventurers of both Sexes*, the dance between the posture moll and her masochistic clients, known as "flogging cullies," played out: "During the time of discipline, they beg for mercy like a soldier on the parade, and beseech forbearance; but the more importune they seem for lenity, the severer vapulation the woman is to exercise."

Not far from Wild and Milliner's Lewkenor's Lane abode, next to the Drury Lane Theatre, stood the anchor of the neighborhood, the rowdy Rose Tavern. Among other nightly activities, the Rose featured gambling, women's wrestling, and gambling on women wrestling. Straight, gay, and those in between all mingled. Private rooms were available upstairs here and at other nearby taverns for anyone with the money to spare. But the Rose was a particularly violent locale, where the occasional murder took place.

Milliner and Wild used the setting to their benefit, growing proficient at a scheme known as the "buttock and twang." Wild played the part of the *twang*, cant for "bully," offering protection to Milliner, the prostitute, or *buttock*. Defoe later defined the twang as "One of the Cant Words for those who attend upon the Night-walking Ladies in their Progress, and who keep at a distance, that if the Lady they are employ'd by, happens to fall into a Broil, they may come in timely to her Assistance, and making a Noise and a Quarrel, if possible fall a-fighting to give her an Opportunity to walk off." So Wild lurked in the shadows, ready to attack should Milliner run into any problems while robbing her client. They worked this trick both in-house and elsewhere, since Milliner could accomplish her acts—both of them—standing up or against a building.

Physically, Wild had grown into the part of the heavy. Contemporary renderings depict him with a strong face and a heavy, piercing glare. (Then again, all of the artists' representations come from a decade later, when he certainly presented a more burdened appearance.) Performing his duties with merit, Wild continued to expand his circle of acquaintances, again, thanks to Milliner, who knew most everyone trying to make a penny on the streets. Wild met criminals of all sorts—mill kens, files, bridle culls, and buzzes—and a few gangs invited him to join their ranks, but he always declined. He wanted to know *all* the gangs without pigeonholing himself to a single group, or even a single avenue of crime. He learned where they did their business, how they performed their acts, and what they did with the goods after they stole them.

In short time, Wild made himself useful to many different bands of thieves, and he did so ingeniously, without ever partaking in the thievery himself. He became a manager of sorts, and as he'd promised himself, he learned to make a profit with his head and not his hands. He used the information presented to him and advised and directed individual gang members into paths of profit. Various gangs depended on him to plan their schemes.

Two parliamentary acts aimed at the receiving trade—one in 1691, and a second in 1706, with the latter making the receiver of goods known to be stolen guilty of a felony—put the days of easy thieving on the verge of extinction. Before, thieves could find a buyer for their goods or a warehouse or liquidator to take their booty for a fair price—often close to full value—practically anywhere. But this pair of acts made it nearly as dangerous to peddle stolen goods as it was to steal them in the first place.

After a few of the top receivers were hanged for their troubles, the number of people taking the risk to fence stolen goods dropped precipitously. The rare souls who continued to dabble in this trade drastically lowered the amounts they paid for stolen items. Defoe nicely summarized a thief's dilemma: "when the poor Adventurer had, at the hazard of his Neck, gotten any Purchase, he must run all that Hazard over again to turn it into money."

A third piece of legislation, the Highwayman Act of 1692, further changed the thievery landscape. A £40 reward now went to anyone for the apprehension and conviction of a highwayman (in excess of £3,000 or $5,000 today). The brave person receiving the reward also won a free pardon, as well as the highwayman's horse and holdings, such as weapons or money, unless they were obtained in the specific crime. Ratting within the ranks rose dramatically.

Marshal Hitchen and other officials, such as constables, jumped in to fill the void. Left with a dearth of solutions for how to unload a score, many thieves took up with Hitchen and other crooked lawmen. Wild and Milliner sought a better approach, though. They conjured up ways around this legislation. One trick they developed was the "Trap," defined in canting dictionaries from the period as: "He that after a Buttock and file, has bit a Cull of his Pocket-Book, makes it his Business to find out where the Man lives, and extort Money from him to prevent his being exposed."

The scam worked best when a person was in a legally suspicious location, such as a brothel. If Wild and Milliner came to possess a gentleman's wallet, and if the gentleman desired to salvage his respectability, or simply didn't want his wife to find out, the trick worked. The Trap also redefined the value of stolen goods. No longer was it necessary to seek out diamonds, watches, or snuffboxes made of gold or silver. Blackmail dramatically increased the relative worth of diaries, letters, or even mere scraps of paper with writing on them.

Wild and Milliner fared increasingly well in their undertakings, and in 1713, they moved from Lewkenor's Lane to the nearby rookery of Cock Alley, Cripplegate, the same neighborhood where Defoe was born, and a place suitably constructed for a thief or receiver to hide for a spell. There, throwing up a cloak of respectability, Wild opened a brandy shop in their residence across the street from the Cripplegate church.

Wild had placed himself in a unique position: Technically he wasn't a thief, nor was he a receiver. But he did want to make thieving profitable again. He aided other thieves in returning stolen pocketbooks and papers to their rightful owners. Unlike Hitchen, who was busying himself in the same con, Wild monetized both sides of the equation to mutual benefit. Wild had what Hitchen lacked: subtlety.

As marshal, Hitchen wasn't shy about overseeing groups of pickpockets or soliciting victims of theft to purchase their goods back. On June 24, 1713, after all of the public conniving—the multitude of infractions and threatening solicitation letters—Hitchen was finally suspended. He did manage to keep his title, however, and he wanted to keep affairs running smoothly until he returned to full service. He immediately sought out an up-and-comer to assist him during his suspension.

Wild described his meeting with Hitchen near Cripplegate, at which the marshal said:

> *I am very sensible that you are let into the Knowledge of the Intrigues of the Compter, particularly with relation to the Securing of Pocket Books. But your experience is Inferior to mine. I can put you in a far better Method than you are Acquainted with, and which may be Facilitated with safety. For tho' I am Suspended, I still retain the Power of Acting as a Constable; and notwithstanding I can't be heard before my Lord Mayor as formerly, I have Interest among the Al———n [Aldermen]. But I must first tell you that you'll spoil the trade of Thief-Taking in Advancing greater Rewards than are necessary. I give but a Half-a-Crown a Book; and when the Thieves and Pick Pockets see you and I Confederate, they'll submit to our Terms and likewise continue their Thefts for fear of coming to the Gallows by our means. Concluding, you shall take a Turn with me as my Servant or Assistant, and we'll Commence our Rambles this Night.*

The tightfisted marshal predictably disliked Wild's practice of paying thieves near full value on the goods they pilfered. Nevertheless, Wild acquiesced to Hitchen's request. He joined the marshal, who wasted little time teaching him the ins and outs of his trade. They sought out thieves to shake down, whores to blackmail, and even bullied innocent onlookers. Hitchen was despicably vicious, and Wild found it mesmerizing. As at the Compter and with Milliner, he was learning advanced techniques and fresh methods of criminal enterprise.

In "An Answer to a Late Insolent Libel," Wild documented his time under Hitchen's wing, extensively describing their "rambles" into the night together. The marshal did his round of the city. Near Temple Bar, he stopped at "several Brandy-Shops and Ale-Houses" where the marshal had for his welcome all the drinks he desired: brandy, punch, and ale. The marshal took nothing else, but he made it clear that he wanted to know if any items had gone missing. He wouldn't accept not being part of a score.

When addressing the women of the night, according to Wild's account, Hitchen plainly stated the motive for his investment in becoming under marshal, warning the prostitutes that if all stolen pocketbooks weren't delivered to him, there would be trouble. "What do you think I bought my Place for but to make the most of it." Then he presented his new assistant to the women. "You are to understand this is my Man (pointing to the Buckle-Maker) to assist me, and if you at any Time for the future Refuse to yield up the Watches, Books, &c. as you take or come to your Hands, either to me or my Servant, you may be assur'd of being all sent to Bridewell"—a London Prison—"and not One of you shall be permitted to walk the Streets." For good measure, the marshal added: "I have still a Power of Punishing, and you shall dearly pay for the least Disobedience to what I have commanded."

With that, Hitchen strutted off down the street to hassle a group of his "mathematicians," warning them that the marshal and the buckle-maker were always watching. If the young pickpockets didn't heed this notice, they would surely "Swing for it." To which, the boys quickly bowed to "their master" and pledged their faithfulness.

Witnessing Hitchen's wicked tactics firsthand wasn't without benefit for Wild and his criminal career. He learned foremost always to know the particulars of a robbery: who robbed what from whom, and where. Wild had caught a break. Not only was he gaining an education, but running around with a government agent, however corrupt, also gave Wild an air of legitimacy.

As Wild's knowledge of the London underworld grew, his reliance on Mary Milliner's instruction correspondingly decreased. Milliner wasn't exactly waiting expectantly at home for her man to return. The two were going their separate ways. After laboring under Hitchen for about a year, Wild wasn't faring any better with his new boss than he was with Milliner. The work remained lowbrow at best. The two men searched houses of ill repute to see what they could scare from its inhabitants. They worked the city day and night. They cleared the streets of the drunk and unruly. It was no way to get ahead.

In fact, they were quarrelling with greater frequency. Hitchen bullied innocent clergymen, and he once flew off the handle, unprovoked, at a respectable bailiff's wife, calling her a whore for no apparent reason. Then he forced her to buy him a meal at the Nag's Head Tavern, which he ate at a table alone, telling her that "he did not commonly permit such Vermin to sit in his Presence"—this as the innocent women shivered at a nearby table, hungry and cold. Hitchen, according to Wild, fell to his supper "Lustily." Wild couldn't help but be annoyed.

Beneath the coarseness, however, Hitchen masked an utter lack of courage. On occasion after occasion, Hitchen's base cowardice let Wild down. If a score turned ugly, Hitchen fled at a moment's notice, regardless of whether Wild was under attack. Hitchen once left him on his own to wage battle against a crowd armed with a "poker, fire-fork," and "fire-brands," which left Wild's face "mangled."

On another evening, in pursuit of a group of young thieves who failed to keep the marshal privy to their plunderings—Hitchen shouting, "We'll catch the Whores Birds!"—he and Wild ultimately wound up at a house on Beech Lane in the Barbican, where a crowd of ten or eleven immediately fell into "a great rage" upon them. The marshal faced the hostility by scampering away. Once more, Wild had to fend for himself. This time, Hitchen returned for his assistant, but he'd enlisted nearly ten watchmen and a constable before returning to the home. At the door, the constable and Hitchen halted to discuss who should enter first, "both so long in their Compliments that the man [Wild] thought neither of them would venture in." Ultimately, Hitchen prevailed in the battle of ingratiating spinelessness, and the constable went first, "with his long Staff extended."

Hitchen followed behind, shouting, "Where are the Rebels? Villains! Why don't you secure them?"

At the end of this ordeal, it turned out that neither of the two savage brutes whom they apprehended had yet reached the age of twelve.

Other rambles with Hitchen just plain flummoxed Wild.

One evening Hitchen invited him to a molly house (gay brothel) after dark, saying that he wanted to introduce him to a crowd of "he-whores." Unsure what Hitchen meant, Wild asked his boss if they were hermaphrodites.

"No, ye fool," answered Hitchen, "they are sodomites, such as deal with their own sex instead of females."

Inside the house, a host of men in female dress greeted the pair, and a great number hugged, tickled, and kissed among themselves, speaking a unique language. Wild overheard the breezy threat of a spanking as punishment for a prolonged absence from the house. The attendees spoke with familiarity to Hitchen, who seemed gleeful. They greeted him as "Madam" and "Your Ladyship."

Wild remembered, "The Marshal was very merry in this assembly and dallied with the young sparks with a great deal of pleasure."

However, when Hitchen was surprised by a group of outsiders in attendance, his demeanor swung. He became severely agitated.

VI

Thief-Catcher General of Great Britain and Ireland

He was now master of his Trade, Poor and Rich flock'd to him: If any Thing was Lost, whether by Negligence in the Owner, or by Vigilance and Dexterity in the Thief, away we went to Jonathan Wild.
—Daniel Defoe, *The True and Genuine Account of the Life and Actions of the Late Jonathan Wild*

In 1714, Queen Anne, the last Stuart monarch, died, giving way to Protestant King George I and the Hanoverian dynasty that ruled Great Britain for the next two centuries. That year the War of Spanish Succession also ended, prompting the demobilization of thousands of British soldiers. Scores of young men had enlisted for battle from small country towns, such as Wolverhampton, where Wild had played lame for the Red Coats. These young soldiers and sailors, the taste of war still fresh in their mouths, saw no reason to return to the country. Instead, they came to the bustling metropolis for the first time. A crime wave ensued, which Hitchen used to his advantage, promising the aldermen a plan to tackle increased street crime.

The ploy worked. They reinstated Hitchen to active duty in April 1714. Shortly thereafter Hitchen and Wild concluded their business together, no doubt a mutual parting. Wild had tired of Hitchen's ways, and the marshal, officially back in the game, had his own staff of men under him. He didn't need Wild anymore, nor did he have room for a subordinate with an inflated sense of self-worth.

WILD IN A 1725 PAMPHLET

By the end of 1714, Wild's relationship with Milliner had also run its course. The pair split just before the New Year. Some accounts say little to nothing before moving on to Wild's next wife; other accounts speak of a violent parting, such as the 1768 *The Tyburn Chronicle: Or, The Villainy Display'd in All Its Branches*, which says of Milliner: "She had some time so provoked him to wrath, that he swore he would mark her for a bitch, and thereupon drawing his sword, he cut off one of her ears—This occasioned a divorce." The author then stated that Wild gave Milliner a weekly pension after their parting, "in a grateful consideration of the service she had done him, by bringing him into so large an acquaintance."

Hitchen and Wild, meanwhile, became rivals.

Wild's house on Cock Alley had been attracting thieves from all across London, all eager to obtain his assistance. He had successfully expanded the inner workings of the Trap, realizing that with receivers and fences in short supply, and taking too large a percentage, it didn't make sense to complicate matters further. Why not start at the top? Who would want a particular item more than the person who had owned it in the first place?

Wild went after honest businessmen who might have been robbed of important pocketbooks, receipts, account books—known as waste books or day books—or other items integral to their business, and worth the hassle of buying back. Unlike Hitchen, who tried to gouge his customers, Wild learned that making his clients feel as if they'd made a good deal was well worth taking a little less in an exchange. If a woman had her watch stolen, she was probably going to replace it, so why not see if she'd like her old one back first—at a lesser price than a new one, of course.

When the time was right, Wild called a meeting with a group of the city's top prigs (thieves) to discuss existing options. Eager to hear about the possibility of improved profits, a band of miscreants met and offered him their attention. Wild shared what he had in mind:

You know, my Bloods, that as Trade goes at present, you stand but a queer Chance; for, when you have made any Thing, if you carry it to the Fencing Culls and Flash Pawn-Brokers, these unconscionable Dealers in contraband Goods will hardly tip ye a quarter of what it is worth; and, if ye offer it to a Stranger, its ten to one but you are habbled [arrested]. So that there's no such Thing as a Man's living by his Labour; for, if he don't like to be half-starved, he must run the Hazard of being scragg'd, which, let me tell ye, is a damn'd hard Case. Now, if you'll take my Advice, I'll put ye in a Way to remedy all this. When you have upon any Lay [enterprise], and spoke to some Purpose [made a good score], let me know the Particulars; and I'll engage to pay-back the Goods to The Cull that owns them, and raise ye more Cole upon that Account, than you can expect from the rascally Fencers. And at the same time take care that you shall be all Bowmen [safe].

So it was agreed. With his crew on board, Wild began keeping track of all the illicit action going on in the city. In essence, he was sharpening a tactic he had learned while roaming the streets with Hitchen, who always made sure to query his mathematicians as to where they'd been so as to know the corners where each set of rogues normally worked. Wild took this technique further, religiously recording every detail in a logbook: name, inventory, location, etc. By observing Hitchen, Wild also learned about the art of patience when negotiating. He saw that Hitchen lacked that skill, and when the marshal couldn't agree to terms with a client, he looked to unload the goods some other way. Wild, on the other hand, stayed the course when looking to strike a deal. In fact, he often compelled the client to wait under the pretense that he was running himself ragged over the ordeal, thus driving up the price.

Wild's techniques weren't groundbreaking. Some elements of his method came from Hitchen, while other aspects dated a century or so back to the days of Mary Frith, also known as Moll Cutpurse, who ran a shop on Fleet Street and kept tabs on the underworld. Even further back were thief-takers, known as *coney-catchers*, as described in the 1597 book *The Discovery of a London Monster Called the Black Dog of Newgate* by Luke Hutton. Still, Wild had a few points in his favor that neither Hitchen nor

Cutpurse had. With regard to Hitchen, it was tact, and with Cutpurse, it was the weekly and daily newspapers.

Londoners used the *Daily Courant*, for example, to place advertisements for items lost or stolen. Wild perused these ads daily, and after ascertaining the particulars of a crime, he reviewed his account books. When he had identified the location of the stolen goods, he called on the victim.

I happen'd to hear that you have lately been robb'd, and a Friend of mine, an honest Broker, having stopp'd a Parcel of Goods upon Suspicion, I thought I could do no less than give you Notice of it, as not knowing but some of them might be yours, and, if it should prove so (as I wish it may), you may have them again, provided that no Body is brought into Trouble, and the Broker has something in Consideration of his Care.

Other times, he acted solely on a thief's word, with or without a newspaper account of the goods stolen. But Wild himself never possessed the stolen goods; he just made it his business to know their location. In fact, Wild didn't even handle the merchandise when the exchange took place. Instead, either he had the thief and the victim do so on their own, or in many cases, he arranged for a proxy to go between the parties.

The scheme succeeded. Thieves were making money again, and the people of London were getting their purloined items back. Wild was merely an "honest broker." Even when he couldn't negotiate a deal for a stolen item, he kept his word and didn't leave a thief with nothing to show for his work, stowing the object for another time. He was said to be "jealous" of his reputation as an honest man, and he defended his reputation stridently. In the beginning, he didn't even accept rewards from his clients when offered. He was doing a public service out of the goodness of his heart. Or so he'd have you believe.

Wild wasn't exactly going hungry. He made his money initially by sharing in the thief's loot, which the general public didn't know. Hitchen later gave a fairly accurate assessment of how Wild (speaking in the depiction) divvied up the money for a heisted item worth £20: "Let us see how the Bear Skin is divided. You will have ten pounds, and I shall have six, and the Cull, alias the fool [the rightful owner], will save four pounds."

The thief gained only an extra pound from Wild versus the normal fence, but the real value in this transaction stemmed from working for Wild and the prospect of return business, as the client would be encouraged "to come to my felonious ware-house, as often as he has occasion: and this will likewise be an Encouragement for you to Robb as often as you can, and if this is not doing Business, the Devil's in the Dice," according to Hitchen.

Another key ingredient to the success of Wild's recovery system was the selfishness of the age. By and large, robbery victims had short-sighted interests: They wanted their things back, nothing more. As Frank McLynn explains in *Crime and Punishment in Eighteenth-Century England*, the people as a whole lacked any "conception of public good" or "civic duty." McLynn suggests that this lack of moral obligation also explains the rabid fear of fire during this period. If flames broke out, there was little chance of getting everyone to pitch in to put them out. And when a crime was committed, people cared only about getting their property back, not about the apprehension of the thief. Thus, Wild's business thrived.

On the rare occasion when a robbery victim asked too many questions, Wild said that he was merely in the right place at the right time. He elaborated on how fortunate he felt to have learned of this information and to offer his assistance. He had equipped himself with a stock speech for just the occasion:

> *Sir, I only come to serve you, and, if you think otherwise, I must let you know that you are mistaken; I have told you that some Goods being offered to pawn by a suspected Person, the Broker had the Honesty to stop them; and therefore, Sir, if you question me about Thieves, I have nothing to say to you; but that I can give a good Account of myself, my Name is Wild, and I live in Cock-Alley by Cripplegate, where you may find me any Day in the Week; and so, Sir, your humble Servant.*

After Wild's elocution, he came to terms with the cull more often than not. He had broken no law. Everybody was happy.

But soon he developed a severe ruthlessness, a trait that would serve him well. To be successful as a crime lord, he had to be feared. Wild masterfully played criminals against one another to exploit the Highwayman Act and the £40 reward for the apprehension of a bandit. Other crimes soon joined this reward system at various monetary values, footpads, for instance, fetching the same £40. These rewards meant that more people were on the lookout to secure bandits. Notable among the seekers was the thief-taker.

Technically, a thief-taker was a private citizen with no official standing who was compensated ad hoc for each capture he made. As with Hitchen, sometimes officials got in on the action. Common criminals also got involved, particularly attracted to the complimentary pardon. When Wild expanded his operation and became a thief-taker, he gained further control over the trafficking of stolen goods, and he tolerated no confusion on this matter. If a thief didn't deal with him, he handed the criminal over for the reward. Wild cashed in either way.

The thief-taking system understandably perpetuated violence. A cornered bandit didn't give another thought to fighting a thief-taker to the death. As a result, the most violent criminals, or those in the larger gangs, were left alone. It was just too messy. Also, should a criminal subsequently be acquitted, the thief-taker not only didn't get the reward, but he'd also earned an enemy in the process.

Because Wild saved the thieving trade by making it profitable again, he rarely faced the same pushback that other thief-takers had to endure. Criminals never bothered to point the finger at Wild; this is because not only had he won their respect, but more importantly, he had also made himself indispensable to them. When he wasn't arresting them, he was still helping bandits find money for their stolen goods. He wasn't just a thief-taker; he was also a thief-maker.

Like Hitchen before him, Wild read the newspaper and in time contributed to it to promote his business. On May 26, 1714, this ad appeared in the *Daily Courant.*

Lost on Friday Evening 19th March last, out of a Compting House in Derham Court in Great Trinity Lane, near Bread Street, a Wast Book and a Day Book; they are of no use to any one but the Owner, being posted into a Ledger to the Day they were lost. Whoever will bring them to Mr. Jonathan Wild over against Cripplegate-Church, shall have a Guinea Reward and no Questions asked.

In the years to come, hundreds of announcements advancing Wild's name and services appeared in London papers. Wild ostensibly placed the ads on behalf of his clients to aid in locating their goods. The ads showed that Wild was pulling out all the stops to recover their belongings. In reality, on most occasions the thief was already known, as were the whereabouts of the goods. The ad merely masked the ruse. Of course, it didn't hurt Wild's business to have his name regularly in the press as the person to see in case of a robbery. It also demonstrated—to the government, among others—that Wild himself didn't have the stolen property.

The ads ran differently when Wild and the thief wanted old-fashioned blackmail money. For instance, if an ad sought a pocketbook with "notes of Hand" lost near a well-known brothel, it was sending a message to the owner of the pocketbook that Wild already knew his name, and that it would be wise for the man to pay Wild a visit. The *Post Man and the Historical Account* ran this notice: "Whereas there some time since several Goods lost between London and Weedon, and some of the said Goods were taken upon a Person coming out of an Inn in Drury Lane." If the gentleman or family man who had been robbed while leaving a Drury Lane inn—a place well known for sex and gambling—didn't want Wild to pay him a visit at his home or business, he had to go to Wild and pay for the return of his property, regardless of whether he wanted the items back.

Wild also encouraged his clients to place ads on their own, listing what had been lost or stolen. The nascent nature of the newspaper contributed to this practice; perhaps seeing your name in print was its own reward. Defoe, for one, struggled to see what his countrymen hoped to accomplish with this public airing of details concerning missing items, calling it a "weak foolish Practice . . . namely, that after this, when any

Person was robb'd they always publish'd the Particulars of their lost Goods, with the Promise of a Reward to those who should discover them." It may have been ineffectual for the citizens who did so, as Defoe described it, but not for Wild.

The money rolled in. In the winter of 1714–15, Wild had earned at least £200—approximately $25,000 in today's money—through seven arrests and the conviction of five people. In December 1714, an ad directed the public to see "Mr. Jonathan Wild at the Blue-Boar in the Old Bailey," revealing that Wild had moved once again, this time to a tavern owned by a Mrs. Seagoe.

In time, Wild began dabbling in the goods that most fences feared or avoided, such as furniture, clothes, and apparel. Breeches, coats, handkerchiefs, hats, shirts, stockings, and suits were all worth stealing. Even wigs, customary for men during this era, could fetch a nice return, particularly when made of real hair. Linens and fabrics of all sorts could be sold: calamanco, damask, drugget, fustian, shagreen, silk, and velvet. Even the leather portmanteaus that contained them counted toward the price. An ad in the *Post Man and the Historical Account* reported this list of items looted from a church: "a Velvet Pulpit Cloth and Cushion, with Gold Fringe and Tossels; a Velvet Cloth and two Cushions, belonging to the Communion Table; a Damask Table Cloth and two Napkins; a large Velvet Pall trimmed with Scarlet; a Doctor's Starlet Hood, and 3 fine Holland Surplices."

Jonathan Wild was known as a man of his word, for better and worse. To the thieves working under him, this honesty presented a double-edged sword. As his sway over the criminal element in London spread, the relationship between Wild and the city's thieves grew trickier. If you did as Wild said, he would be a loyal friend, but if you opposed him, you'd find yourself behind bars or swinging from the gallows. Wild had three fundamental rules when it came to dealing with thieves and their spoils: First, if he knew about a robbery—more and more a certainty—then the thief had to leave it to Wild to deal with the goods; second, the thief had to agree to a "reasonable" and fair price when an offer was made by the object's owner. Third, no trashing fellow thieves or, as Defoe termed it, making "threatening Speeches against their Comrades."

Although Wild's stock continued to rise, it was time to take out the competition—the city's other thief-takers, as well as any receivers who may have been poaching his business. There had to be a sense of fear. His rivals needed to be nervous. Because of his reputation for honesty, whenever Wild sent for a prig with a guarantee that he could safely come and go, the thief trusted this assurance. But Wild didn't tolerate independence. If crossed, he didn't rest until he had settled the matter.

The first person sent to the gallows on his account was Elizabeth Shirley. In January 1715, she was convicted of housebreaking. She and a pair of associates had stolen a silver candlestick off the communion table at a banqueting house in Whitehall. Wild named her in an inventory he penned, aptly titled: "A List of the persons discover'd, apprehended, and convicted of several Robberies on the Highway; and also for Burglaries and House-breakings; and also the several Persons here-under named, for returning from Transportation, by Jonathan Wild."

One way or another, he systematically cleared the city of competition as well as the uncooperative from within his own ranks. In the fall of 1714, three men—Parrot, Parker, and Chance—robbed the Whitehall house of the bishop of Norwich and made off with valuable jewelry. They sold the spoils to a fence in Holborn named William White. Wild arrested Chance, who sold out his coconspirators and gave information on White. (Presumably, Wild also had a fifth person ready to falsify information against Chance if necessary.) Chance's trial testimony reveals how easy it was for Wild to knock out his competition.

> *The Prisoner [Parrot] came to me, and said, there was a large Parcel of rich Goods brought from Norwich to the Bishop's House, and that he knew it, because he help'd to unload 'em, and that he would shew me how to get into the House. We agreed upon the Matter, and he, and I, and Will. Parker, who is not yet taken, broke open the House and stole the Goods, which we sold to one White, in Holborn.*

In one swoop, he had shut down three members of the Whitehall gang and a rival receiver. For turning on his comrades, Chance was allowed to walk, though he didn't remain free for long, later making an appearance on Wild's "List" for housebreaking.

Those who played by his rules had Wild's protection. Even other thief-takers couldn't hurt a loyal bandit. When his men were nabbed, Wild often took care of the situation with bribery, or he fixed the evidence of a case so someone else took the fall. On occasion, if he couldn't free a thief at the outset and the case went to trial, Wild would sway witnesses on behalf of his friends—or make them disappear.

The mutual trust and loyalty of Abraham Mendez and Quilt Arnold had earned them upper-tier positions in Wild's ever-evolving business. Mendez had the longer tenure and served as a reliable confidant to Wild. Diligent, committed, and the brains of the operation, Mendez kept a keen eye on the books, earning the title of clerk of the western roads. A Portuguese Jew—his religion always mentioned prominently along with his name—Mendez lived on Berry Street in the parish of St. Katherine Cree-church. Quilt Arnold was christened in the parish of St. Dunstan, Stepney, on January 15, 1687, making him four years Wild's junior. As Wild's second assistant and the brawn of the group, he had the position of clerk of the northern roads. Other records listed him as Wild's "Secretary, and Groom of the Chambers."

Today, in a nondescript box at the National Archives in Kew, England, amid maddening cursive and parchment paper, survives a mountain of "blood money" certificates—the receipts for apprehension and payout of the rewards under the Highwayman Act. Wild's and his underlings' names appear prominently throughout, year after year, collecting rewards.

On Saturday, March 31, 1716, in Jockey-Fields, just north of Holborn, the widow Mrs. Mary Knap was shot to death while walking home from Sadler's Wells with her son. A band of five footpads remained on the loose following the attack. The night prior, one Thomas Middlethwaite was also murdered, presumably by the same gang of men. On April 3, the

London Gazette gave a description of the crimes, while noting a startlingly high reward for apprehension of the shooter. (As mentioned, spelling of names was inconsistent during the era.)

> *Whereas on Friday the 30th of March last, about Eight a Clock in the Evening, eight or nine Foot-Pads assaulted and fired upon Thomas Micklethwaite, Esq; in the Road betwixt St. Pancras-Church and the End of Gray's-Inn-Lane; And whereas the Evening following, about Ten a Clock, Mrs. Mary Knapp, Widow, was shot through the Head under the Wall of Gray's-Inn-Garden, facing Bedford-Row; His Majesty is pleased for the better Discovery of the said Offenders, to promise his most gracious Pardon, and the Reward of One Hundred Pounds to any one of the Persons concerned in either of the Said Facts, who shall discover any of his Accomplices, so as they or any of them may be Apprehended and Convicted.*

The *Weekly Packet* further reported that Middlethwaite, on horseback during the assault, didn't go down without a fight, firing on his assailants and wounding at least a couple of them.

The murder of Widow Knap seized the attention of London, and a manhunt ensued. In addition to the King's £100 reward, the standard £40 for capture of a highwayman or footpad still applied. That made for one hell of a score. The average income for poor or working families then ranged between £15 and £50 annually. Whoever captured the Knap shooter was in for a windfall.

Wild needed little urging. He and Mendez went to work right away, gathering intelligence, and they had a list of suspects inside of a week. Isaac Rag, Timothy Dun, Will White (the same receiver for the Whitehall Gang), John Chapman (alias Edward Darvel, alias Ned Darvel), and Tom Thurland were chief among the targets. Wild and Mendez swiftly rounded them up. First they nabbed White at Jack Wetherly's Café in Newtoner's Lane. Later the same evening, they found Thurland near the Bell Inn in Smithfield, armed with multiple pistols, but they secured him before he could shoot. The next evening, they took Chapman in Drury Lane, and shortly thereafter captured Rag. Only Timothy Dun remained at large.

Wild persuaded Rag—already a wanted man for two additional crimes—to give evidence against the others. Before Rag had finished talking, he gave information on a total of twenty-two accomplices for an assortment of crimes.

In May 1716, White, Thurland, and Chapman were charged for the murder of Widow Knap and levied with additional indictments for other crimes. But White and Thurland refused to deliver a plea—both men refusing to speak at all, or to recognize the authority of the Court—thereby delaying the proceedings. The trial notes for the case describe the Court's persistent attempt to get the two men to cooperate: "The two Prisoners, however, continued mute. The Court directed their Thumbs to be tied together with Whipcord: This was done by two Officers, who drew the Cord tight with their whole Force, and so held it for above a Quarter of an Hour. This working no effect, the Court passed sentence upon them to be pressed to Death."

White and Thurland remained steadfastly silent all the way to Newgate Prison. There, fitted for the press and meeting the executioner busily readying his tools, they had a change of heart. They returned to the Old Bailey where they both finally pleaded not guilty.

Widow Knap's son, John, took the stand first as a witness. He detailed his mother's final moments, which took place just forty yards from occupied homes in the area. "In an instant, some fellows coming up, my Link [torch] was blown out, my Hat and Wig were taken off, and I was knock'd down, upon which my Mother scream'd out, and thereupon one of them fired a Pistol close by me, and immediately I heard my Mother cry, *Lord help me! Help me*, and then the Rogues fled."

Isaac Rag gave testimony against his conspirators on the charge of murder. The bandits began the night at the Broken Trooper Tavern. There, according to the *Weekly Journal or British Gazetteer*, they made plans to hit the road and "rob any they should meet." Rag gave the court a description of the slaying from the malefactors' nonchalant perspective:

I and the Prisoners were concerned in this Fact; but White was the Man that killed the Gentlewoman, for each of us had a Pistol with a Brace of Bullets, and, after the Fact, we went to drink together, and we all pulled out our Pistol to see who had fired, and we found that White had discharged his; we asked him, why he did so? And he said, he did it to frighten the Woman, and make her hold her Tongue.

William White, thirty-four, was a ten-year veteran of the British Navy. Thomas Thurland, thirty, was a miller, who at one time kept a shop at Colchester in Essex. John Chapman, thirty-two, was a gardener by trade. The three men were found guilty of murder and additional indictments. They were hanged at Tyburn on June 8, 1716. A repeat offender, Isaac Rag hailed from the Parish of St. Botolph, Bishopsgate, and had been arrested twice the previous year, one of the occasions resulting in a three-day pillory sentence. His situation, regarding his role in the Knap murder, remained in flux.

In the meantime, there was the unresolved matter of Timothy Dun. Reports snaked their way through the London newspapers in mid-May that Dun had surrendered himself to the turnkey at Newgate Prison, but in actuality he was still in hiding. Which didn't please Wild.

The Irish-born Dun, age twenty-seven, had at one time belonged to the Regiment of Foot Guards. A hard case, he had been in and out of trouble for years, and had been sentenced to hang on April 7, 1714, when caught stealing a silver watch. But he landed a reprieve after he promised to transport himself out of the country. Wild knew that someone with Dun's pedigree couldn't stay in hiding for long, that "he must follow the old Business, or starve," as he was reported to say. So confident was Wild that he threw down a ten-guinea wager that he'd have Dun in custody before court was back in session.

As if on cue, Dun's wife paid Wild a visit at the Blue Boar shortly thereafter. According to *Select Trials at the Sessions-House in Old Bailey*, Dun had indeed "grown weary of his confinement," and had sent his wife to gauge Wild's interest in continuing his search. The details of the conversation between Wild and Mrs. Dun remain unknown, but after their meeting Wild had one of his men follow her, setting off a game of cat and mouse for the rest of the afternoon, through Blackfriars, Whitefriars, Westminster, Lambeth, and finally back to her quarters in Maid-Lane, in Southwark. Wild's man marked her door with chalk and reported the location back to his boss.

Early the next morning, Wild and Mendez took a few men to pay Timothy Dun a visit. One of these men, William Riddlesden, an erstwhile attorney, had been in and out of trouble himself, checking in to Newgate Prison repeatedly. In fact, he had been caught along with Elizabeth Shirley as part of the banqueting house robbery in Whitehall the previous year. Shirley was hanged at Tyburn, but Riddlesden received a sentence of transportation (essentially deportation), only to return and end up a servant to Wild, protected under his supervision and working as an associate thief-taker. One person hanged, and one set free. In the Knap case, it was through Riddlesden's information and familiarity with William White and the Whitehall Gang that Wild had been able to build his initial inventory of suspects so quickly.

Wild's posse scaled two sets of stairs to reach Timothy Dun's door. The fugitive, hearing the commotion, jumped from a rear window in hopes of making a quick escape. But Mendez smartly scrambled to the backyard, where he found Dun descending to a lower roof. Mendez fired his pistol and struck Dun in the shoulder, dropping him eight feet to the earth below. Riddlesden met Dun in the yard and finished the job, shooting him directly in the face. Amazingly, Dun survived both gunshots. He was hanged at Tyburn on July 23, 1716, neither confirming nor denying his involvement in the Knap murder.

Wild won his wager and the reward. In the *Calendar of Treasury Books* listed under "Treasury Warrants," an entry verifies payment.

Money order for 100£ to Jonathan Wild for the reward published in the Gazette 3 April 1716 for discovery of the footpads who assaulted and fired upon Mr. Thomas Micklethwaite, Esq., and the evening following murdered Mrs. Mary Knap: the Recorder of London having certified that the said Wild did apprehend and take most of the offenders who were convicted and executed for the same.

The total haul for the Knap case came to the considerable sum of £270.

Isaac Rag, for all his help in securing the arrests, received no great favors for his troubles. His stint as a turncoat had earned him the chance to live, but not his freedom. Documents show that he remained in prison for years. In November 1716, at the New Prison in Clerkenwell, Rag petitioned the justices for release on account of the plentiful information he had offered, which aided in numerous arrests and convictions. We know they denied his petition because newspaper accounts show that the following December, he and two other New Prison inmates attempted escape but failed. For their efforts, they were transferred to the more-secure Newgate Prison, and Rag was finally transported in 1720.

An ad in the *Post Man and the Historical Account* on May 24, 1716, demonstrates that Wild continued to conduct business as usual throughout the Knap affair. Despite his growing status, he didn't rest on his laurels. The ad urged the return of goods lost by a person exiting a Drury Lane Inn: "If the same Person who hath the Remainder of the said Goods in his Hands, will return them to Jonathan Wild at the Duke of Grafton's Head in the Old Baily, in two or three Days time after this Advertisement, he may be assured that there shall be no Prosecution; if not, he may expect to be brought to Justice." But the thief-taker no longer asked. He warned.

Every good business needs a name. At his Blue Boar workplace, Wild finally branded his creation. He called it the Office for the Recovery of Lost and Stolen Property. A clerk manned the desk to handle bookkeeping, and on the face of it, the Lost Property Office, as it became known, had all the trimmings of a genuine business. Anyone searching for lost items needed to set aside time for a series of visits. On most occasions, the production played out in three acts.

First visit: Prospective clients paid a one-crown application fee for the thief-taker to consider the case. Wild greeted customers in his calamanco (a glossy woolen fabric) nightgown, slippers on his feet, and turban on his head, all typical attire for indoor business at the time. He asked a series of questions purely for the customer's benefit; Wild already knew the details. Nevertheless, he stuck to the script and had every detail recorded in his books. As Defoe later noted, "Perhaps the very Thing you came to enquire after, was in the very Room where you were, or not far off: After all this Grimace was at an end, you were desire'd to call again." Then Wild let the client know whether he would take the case.

Second visit: Negotiations commenced. Having located the goods, Wild communicated the thief's demands, usually at a higher rate than Wild originally quoted the customer. To justify the increase, he typically threw in an anecdote or two to strengthen his position: The thief was being brazen and difficult, or was contemplating a higher offer for the item elsewhere. But not to worry; Wild would do his best to bring the price down. Please come again.

Third visit: Wild quoted the bandit's final asking price. If agreed, the client had to give his or her word that, following a satisfactory exchange, nothing further would be said of the matter. At this point, Wild gave the time and place for the swap, and his work in the matter came to an end. A porter could handle the delivery of the stolen item if desired, so the client and thief didn't have to meet, and Wild recommended tipping the porter as well. By now Wild had eased his policy against accepting gratuities, so if the client was satisfied with Wild's service, he happily accepted whatever the client gave. After all, at this point in the ruse, he hadn't received anything beyond the single crown at the outset.

At the end of the song and dance, another satisfied customer had his or her property returned, and on the face of it, Wild had broken no laws. No one needed to know whether Wild took a cut of the thief's pay or a piece of the porter's share, or that Wild would babble if a thief didn't handle matters precisely as ordered, or if Wild had sent the thieves to steal an item in the first place. The traveling actors who roamed the countryside near Wolverhampton in Wild's childhood would have delighted at the impression they'd made. His performance at the Lost Property Office was top-shelf. He conveyed uncertainty—*Nothing was for sure; it could take time*—and his range was spectacular, from shock to disappointment. The man had undeniable talent. He was a great showman.

The publicity surrounding the Knap murder attracted a wave of new clients. After all, who better to turn to than Wild if something was stolen? No doubt, there was substance behind the show. He was real; he shot it out and took part in knife fights. He chased, he hunted. His grit and courage put him in the thick of it. With the increase in business, he rented a more expansive property across the street from Mrs. Seagoe's Blue Boar. His new, more ornate, more spacious office at 68 Ship Court was known as the King's Head because of the signboard in front depicting King Charles I. It adjoined the Cooper's Arms public house, and lay next door to the birthplace of painter William Hogarth.

From the King's Head, Wild divided the London underworld into districts, assigning captains to oversee the action therein. He pushed his operatives to specialize in their strengths. By having thieves focus on a specific area—churches, racetracks, county fairs—he could further detect the culprits of unauthorized crimes or the unshared booty from said crimes. If a client had been the victim of the Rattling Lay in Aldgate, Wild knew both by style and geography the identity of the perpetrator. He had only to check his logbooks.

And just to be sure, every time a robbery went down, Wild jotted down the thief's name and placed beside it a cross denoting that the person had committed a felony. If a thief rebelled against him or if Wild needed to send someone to the gallows in order to save the neck of a better earner—or, for a quick £40—Wild simply thumbed through his ledger, found a thief with a single cross, and beside the first he struck a second cross. And though the term wasn't yet used, for the thief the meaning was unmistakable—he'd been double-crossed.

Wild played both rogue and regulator. One technique he used lives on today within law enforcement agencies, as well as organized crime syndicates. He separated individual members of the same gang when conducting his questioning. As has become common, he told each person that a conspirator had already betrayed him. It was time to do the smart thing—give up your buddies and save yourself.

Thieves generally supported his plan of having them work in one domain since it was easier for them to stick to what they knew. Wild knew not to force a square peg into a round hole. If a man lacked the tenacity for highway robbery, the thief-master found a use for the bandit elsewhere, perhaps pickpocketing, or the more refined art of the Spruce

Prig. For the latter role, Wild equipped his men with the fine attire necessary to attend theaters or balls, where they could rob people of quality for high-end scores. Wild even paid for some of his staff to learn to dance under the tutelage of dancing master Mr. Lun.

Wild's scope was vast. He had artists on the payroll to alter stolen jewelry and valuables, rendering items not slated for return unidentifiable to their former owners. He kept counterfeiters and coiners. He regularly paid musicians to rouse crowds at country dances so his thieves could better help themselves to the guests' swords and canes. Some of Wild's more personable workers obtained jobs as footmen, or posed as such to seduce maids at mansions, sleeping their way to intelligence on a grand home's swag. In time, Wild's company even took on Parliament and pickpocketed a lord at the House of Commons.

Always on the lookout for extra hands, Wild often scanned Whitefriars, St. Giles, and other slums for new recruits. Children had a place in the Wild enterprise, too. Once, after a boy successfully lifted a pair of silver buckles from a man's shoes in a crowd, Wild greeted the youngster and his mother with the fostering pledge, "My Life on't, he'll prove a great man." The acclaim imbued the new bandit's mother with pride—even if the words missed the mark in the long run. The boy didn't make it past the age of fifteen before being hanged. Defoe later observed:

> *Many a poor Boy he has pick'd up in the Street pretending Charity, and a willingness to do them good, which, when it has come to the Issue, has been no more or less than to breed them up to Thieving, and ripen them for the Devil . . . Horrid Wickedness! . . . several of these his own foster Children, he has himself caused afterwards to be apprehended and Hang'd for the very Crimes which he first taught them how to Commit.*

"So, Mr. Son of a Bitch! I have caught you at last?" Wild said.

Wild had spent the better part of a morning searching for Jack Butler around Bishopsgate Street. At an alehouse, Butler had evaded Wild and his pistol by way of a window. The chase reconvened in the basement of a dyer's shop, and after combing the area unsuccessfully, Wild finally found Butler hiding under an overturned wash tub.

"What have ye done with the Gold Watch, the Lace, and the other Moveables that ye stole out of your Lodgings, ye runnagate Rascal?" Wild asked. "Ye shall certainly swing for it; I'll take care of you, if there's never another Rogue in England."

Wild had learned of Butler through the Lost Property Office's account books. He'd ascertained that the gold watch and a parcel of fine lace remained unaccounted for, and from his intelligence network, he discovered the name of the rascal who had kept the prize to himself. Butler knew the price of his disloyalty and had disappeared for more than two months. It wasn't long enough, though. Wild never forgot a transgression.

The details of this encounter come from the popular eighteenth-century collection of trial accounts, *Select Trials at the Sessions-House in the Old Bailey*. Trial reporting was also in its infancy at this time. According to professors Robert Shoemaker, Clive Emsley, and Tim Hitchcock—who extensively studied the archival court documents for the websites The Old Bailey Proceedings and London Lives—the first surviving publication of proceedings from the Old Bailey came in 1674, as *News from Newgate: or An Exact and true Accompt of the most Remarkable Tryals of Several Notorious Malefactors*. At first, these trial accounts were sensationalistic and selective, an account running only four to ten pages long. But in time these publications, known either as the "Sessions Papers" or the "Proceedings," grew more objective. By 1712, their coverage of some of the city's more celebrated or interesting trials included verbatim testimony. According to Shoemaker, Emsley, and Hitchcock, "This became common practice in the 1720s, facilitated by the use of shorthand note takers."

The Proceedings present an important record. Although not a complete rendering of every part of the court process or a stenographical documentation of the trial, these transcripts offer a lively depiction of the action on the streets of London at the time. They offer a glimpse at Wild's style and manner of speech, and they note how Butler replied: "If you'll step to my Room again, and look behind the Bed's head, you may find something that will make you amends for your Trouble." Butler was allowed to live, though transported following his arrest, through Wild's influence.

As Shoemaker, Emsley, and Hitchcock note:

Although initially aimed at a popular rather than a legal audience, the material reported was neither invented nor significantly distorted. The Old Bailey Courthouse was a public place, with numerous spectators, and the reputation of the Proceedings would have quickly suffered if the accounts had been unreliable. Their authenticity was one of their strongest selling points, and a comparison of the text of the Proceedings with other manuscript and published accounts of the same trials confirms that what they did report was for the most part reported accurately.

The focus of popular writing was shifting toward ordinary people. Newspapers ran their own reports of crimes and trials, including testimony transcribed from the court. The public actively sought criminal and legal information, a whole new realm of news. Readers wanted unspoiled realism in what they read. Soft-core reenactments no longer sufficed. Along with *Select Trials*, they read dying speeches, ordinary accounts, magazine articles, criminal biographies, and, later in the century, the mix of truth and fiction of *The Newgate Calendar*. The true crime genre had begun.

Wild's name pops up repeatedly throughout it all. He became an expert witness, routinely turning up at the Old Bailey, where he was introduced with grandeur, as evidenced in the case of Samuel Kempton from St. Brides, indicted for "privately stealing." The Proceedings from the September 6, 1716, trial document that the aggrieved party applied to "Jonathan Wild with a Description, he was known to be particularly famous for Facts of that sort." Kempton was found guilty.

His steady courtroom presence represented only a piece of Wild's self-promotion. He was paying newspapers to flaunt his illustriousness. He was visiting the condemned in Newgate Prison, where he offered money and other comforts to prisoners in exchange for acknowledgment of his thief-taking skills or prowess in their dying speeches at the Triple Tree. Wild practically had his own publicity team.

By 1718, he had brought down some fifty thieves. Wild arrested his old pal Obadiah Lemon and his gang, and, besides the high-profile Knap murderers, he nabbed the dangerous highwayman James Goodman. Goodman had escaped from the Bail Dock at the Sessions House while awaiting sentencing. An ad in the Proceedings in the wake of his escape surely frightened Londoners, and had them eager for Goodman's recapture.

> *He is about 37 Years of Age, 5 Foot 10 Inches high [tall for the time], much Pock-fretten, has many Freckles in his Face and Hands, a wide Mouth, down Look, speaks very broad, a reddish beard, but did wear a brown Wig. . . . He was shot in the Nape of the Neck about a month since, when he was taken, which Wound is not yet well, and several small Pieces of his Scull taken out of the Wound.*

Goodman was spotted at Mackerel's Quaker Coffee House in Holborn, and word immediately went out to Wild, who secured the fugitive with the aid of Newgate turnkeys following a fierce struggle.

On January 19, 1717, Wild's name appeared in the *Weekly Journal or British Gazetteer* with the grandest of titles: "Head Theif-Catcher [*sic*] in England." The following year, his title was refined to "Thief-Catcher General," and, finally, "Thief-Taker General of Great Britain and Ireland."

After studying Wild, Defoe came away impressed. He wrote of a man with "inimitable Boldness" and "a kind of brutal Courage." He called Wild's handling of the vast pieces of machinery in his system "wonderful." But Defoe wasn't blind to Wild's treachery. He didn't let his countrymen wholly off the hook, pointing instead to the naiveté of the people for Wild's success:

> *Nay, Advertisements were Publish'd, directing the Finder of almost every Thing to bring it to Jonathan Wild, who was eminently impower'd to take it, and give the Reward. How infatuate were the People of this*

Nation all this while? Did they consider that at the very time that they treated this Person with such a Confidence, as if he had been appointed to the Trade? He had perhaps the very Goods in his keeping, waiting the advertisement for the reward; and that perhaps, they had been Stolen with that very intention.

Perhaps some knew, but if so, no one was willing to go against him. If they did, Wild didn't allow it.

London was a tough town. For Wild to have gained influence over the majority of the crime gangs was no small task—to say nothing of the control he enjoyed over law enforcement. Outliers remained, but for the most part, everything was going according to plan. But for how long? Defoe described him as having "a pushing, enterprizing Nature, he could content himself with nothing but every thing he could get, nor could he act moderately in any part of his conduct." More and more, but to what end?

An 1870 engraving of Wych Street, where Sheppard
apprenticed
Courtesy of the Theatrelands London Metropolitan Archive

VII

JACK SHEPPARD, APPRENTICE

*Sheppard was the very embodiment of the wild spirit
of the eighteenth century.*
—FERGUS LINNANE, *LONDON'S UNDERWORLD*

In 1702 when Jonathan Wild was shuffling between Wolverhampton and London, carpenter Thomas Sheppard and his wife, Mary, were delivered of a sickly baby in the parish of Spitalfields in London's East End. They named John Sheppard after his two-year-old brother, who had died just five months earlier. New baby John was so undersized and weak that his parents didn't hold out much hope for him to outlive his brother.

John Sheppard did live—later growing into a thorn in the side of Jonathan Wild—but for now, death continued to plague the Sheppards. Paterfamilias Thomas died at his workbench in 1706, and a baby sister followed in 1708. The Widow Sheppard now had to care for six-year-old John, known as "Jack," and eleven-year-old brother Thomas. Mary Sheppard, an earnest and resourceful woman, soon found work as a servant in the home of William Kneebone, a woolen draper. Jack went to Mr. Garrett's Workhouse School on Bishopgate Street, but Thomas's history remains a bit less clear. Some believe he became a footboy in the home of a noble family, but others suggest that headstrong Thomas, a troublesome child to rear, went directly to the streets and embarked on a life of crime.

At the workhouse school, Jack learned rudimentary reading, writing, and arithmetic, but for the most part, Jack and the other children spent the twelve-hour day sewing, knitting, and mending. Garrett and others managing workhouses kept expenditures down by moving children out the door and into apprenticeships as quickly as possible. Children as young as four years old began apprenticeships as chimney sweeps, where their slender frames came in handy. Conditions at workhouse schools weren't unlike prisons: overcrowded, infested, and providing meager nourishment. Jack "studied" at the workhouse for at least a year and a half, and shone as a pupil.

In 1710, Mary Sheppard rescued her younger son by getting him work as a shop boy with Kneebone, her employer. Kneebone behaved kindly toward the boy, going above and beyond his duties as employer, encouraging Jack to continue his education. He quizzed Jack with reading and writing work after the shop closed in the evening. Kneebone was a fine man, and Jack and his mother lived a tranquil life with him.

In Spitalfields, the working-class manufacturing center of London, weavers produced world-famous silks. But Jack's father, grandfather, and great-grandfather had all worked as carpenters, helping to build the neighborhood. So it came as no great surprise that when the time came to seek out a vocation of his own, Jack chose carpentry. Kneebone helped the hard worker land an apprenticeship with Owen Wood, a joiner and carpenter in Drury Lane. Kneebone had struck a deal with Wood, avoiding the customary apprenticeship fee, by offering Wood a contract to build his Hampstead country home.

With Sir William Fazakerley, the chamberlain of London, looking on, Sheppard was bound to Wood for a term of seven years on April 2, 1717, moving into the third floor garret of Wood and his wife's Wych street home. Sheppard became a skilled carpenter as well as a locksmith of great acuity and finesse. He was a clear-headed, temperate young man and a fine apprentice.

The labor involved in carpentry sculpted Jack's scrawny frame, packing his five-foot-four-inch body with a shield of muscle. His hands were large, his joints strong, and though he was small, as author Horace Bleackley wrote, he was "a complete pocket Hercules." As a newborn, he had had to fight for his life, and this same tenaciousness for living made him a carpenter of impressive power.

Bleackley remarked that his facial features "bore no little resemblance to those of a pug-dog," although portraits of the era depict an almost angelic face. *Parker's London News* described Sheppard as "having a perfect Boy's Countenance and Stature," and the *Daily Post* made note of a minor stutter: "an Impediment, or Hesitation in his Speech." He had a cheerful demeanor for the most part, but like most young men, he didn't lack a temper.

Sheppard had been fortunate. From Kneebone to Wood, he twice had met with kindness uncharacteristic of the age. Masters often ruled with an iron fist, or worse. But Sheppard possessed a valuable opportunity, as had Wild back in Birmingham when he'd learned buckle-making. In seven years' time, at the age of twenty-two, Sheppard would be well placed to begin his career and support himself.

There was only one problem: He had a young man's patience. First Jack Sheppard found a girl, and then a bar.

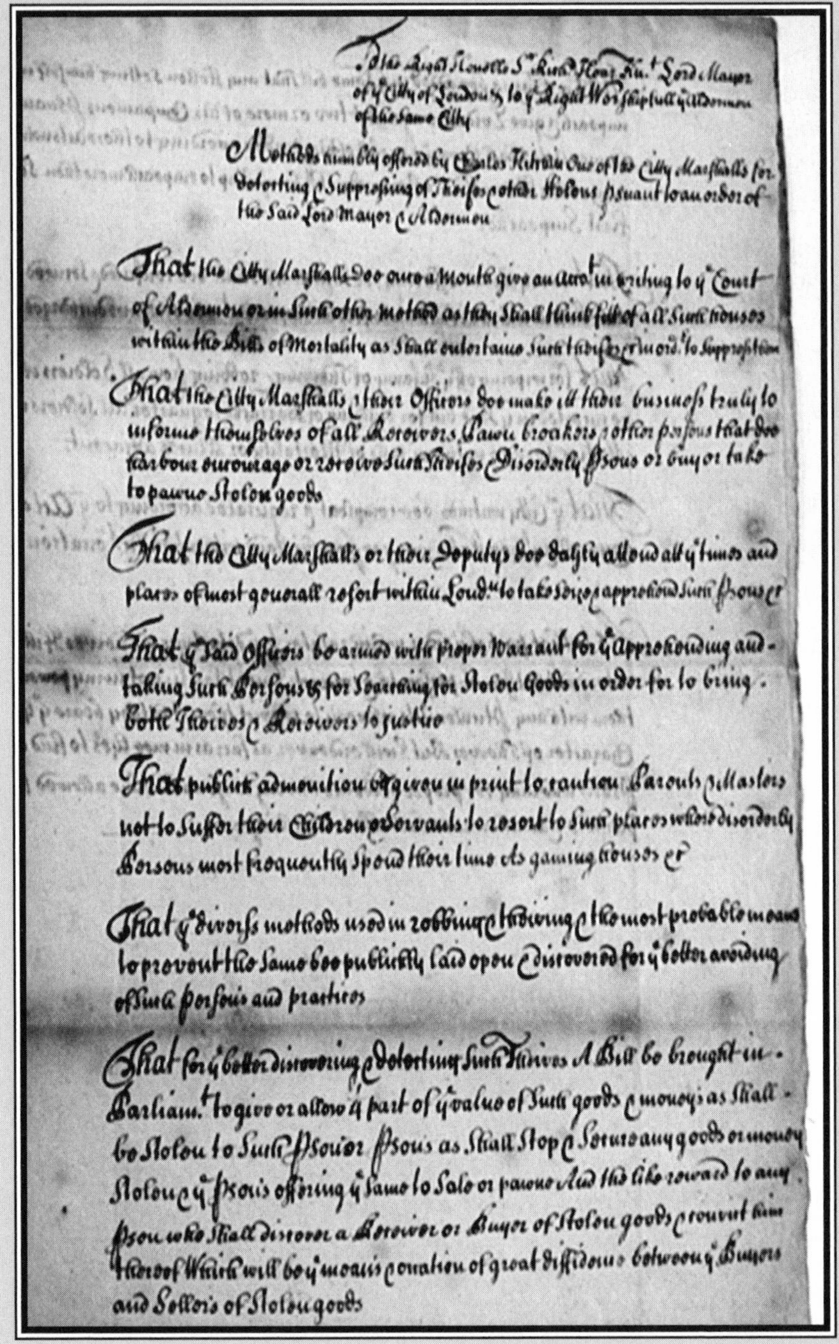

To the Right Honble Sr. Richd Hoar Knt Lord Mayor of ye Citty of London, to ye Right Worshipfull ye Aldermen of the same Citty

Methods humbly offered by Charles Hitchin One of the Citty Marshalls for detecting & Suppressing of Theives & other Felons pursuant to an order of the Said Lord Mayor & Aldermen

That the Citty Marshalls doe once a Month give an Accot in writing to ye Court of Aldermen or in such other method as they shall think fitt of all such houses within the Bills of Mortality as shall entertaine such theives & in ord. to suppress them

That the Citty Marshalls & their Officers doe make it their business truly to informe themselves of all Receivers, Pawn brokers & other persons that doe harbour encourage or receive such Theives & Disorderly persons or buy or take to pawne Stolen goods

That the Citty Marshalls or their deputys doe dayly attend all ye times and places of most generall resort within Londn to take dirrect & apprehend such persons &c

That ye said officers be armed with proper Warrant for ye Apprehending and taking such persons & for searching for Stolen goods in order for to bring both Theives & Receivers to justice

That publick admonition be given in print to caution Parents & Masters not to suffer their Children & Servants to resort to such places where disorderly persons most frequently spend their time as gaming houses &c

That ye divers methods used in robbing & thieving & the most probable means to prevent the same bee publickly laid open & discovered for ye better avoiding of such persons and practices

That for ye better discovering & detecting such Thieves A Bill be brought in Parliamt to give or allow a part of ye value of such goods & moneys as shall be Stolen to such person or persons as shall Stop & Secure any goods or money Stolen & ye persons offering ye same to Sale or pawne And the like reward to any person who shall discover a Receiver or Buyer of Stolen goods & convict him thereof Which will be ye means & occation of great diffidence between ye Buyers and Sellers of Stolen goods

Hitchen's methods for preventing crime

VIII

THE REGULATOR

Set Forth in Several Entertaining Stories, Comical Intrigues, merry Adventures, particularly of the M—L and his man the Buckle-maker. With a Diverting Scene of a Sodomitish Academy.
—JONATHAN WILD, *"AN ANSWER TO A LATE INSOLENT LIBEL"*

Charles Hitchen hadn't been happy when he'd parted ways with Wild, and he certainly wasn't happy about Wild's success and rise in power. It must have driven Marshal Hitchen crazy that he had paid £700 for the right to round up criminals only to have Wild, the man he had taught, gain such notoriety, influence, and profit from doing exactly that. Wild had used the very methods that Hitchen had taught him—bullying, bribery, and corruption—to usurp him. More than three years had passed since the pair had last worked together, but the span did nothing to lessen the marshal's ire, nor did it dampen his desire to destroy the newly crowned thief-taker general. Revenge weighed on Hitchen's mind. In 1718, the time was right.

Wild had blood on his hands. By his own calculations—and he shortly made them public—he had brought approximately sixty criminals to justice by hanging. But the government was looking to put a stop to Wild's business. In 1717, Parliament introduced the Piracy Act, which eventually became law in 1718, known as the Transportation Act. This act, among other legislation, made it a felony to take money for returning stolen items to a robbery victim without also apprehending and prosecuting the thief. The "Act for the Further Preventing Robbery, Burglary, and Other Felonies, and for the More Effectual Transportations of Felons" (etc.) stated that "there are several persons who have secret acquaintance with felons, and who make it their business to help persons to their stolen goods and by that means gain money from them, which is divided between them and the felons, whereby they greatly encourage such offenders." Then the kicker for Wild: "Unless such person doth apprehend, or cause to be apprehended, such felon who stole the same, cause such felon to be brought to his trial for the same, and give evidence against him, [he or she] shall be guilty of felony, and suffer the pains and penalties of felony."

Everyone knew where the Transportation Act was pointing; in fact, it became known colloquially as Jonathan Wild's Act. "This Act was so directly aimed at Jonathan's general practice, that he could not be ignorant enough to see it," wrote Defoe.

> *But good advice to Jonathan Wild was like talking Gospel to a kettle Drum, bidding a Dragoon not to Plunder . . . he that was hardened above the Baseness of all cautionary Fear, scorn'd the Advice, and went on in his wicked Trade; not warily and wisely as he had formerly done, but in short, with more Impudence and shameless Boldness than ever, as if he despised laws and the governors.*

The government was itching to gain control over the thief-taker, and with more and more of his underlings swinging at Tyburn, a healthy disdain was growing within Wild's own ranks. The tide had begun to move against him.

But he was no fool. From the *Weekly Journal or Saturday's Post*: "A Fellow, who by his Conduct, 'tis believ'd, had but newly commenc'd a Thief, brought a large Silver Tankard, which he had Stol'n from an Ale-House in Fetter-Lane, to Jonathan Wild, the famous Thief-Taker, to sell, but Jonathan became rather a Prosecutor than a Purchaser, for he presently secured the Fellow and got him committed to Newgate."

Hitchen also knew that Wild had amended his approach in order to minimize his exposure to the new law. If he could only nudge matters along, Hitchen might be able to bring down the thief-taker. The moment had come for the disgruntled city marshal to take his shot.

The marshal took his knowledge to the press, intent on exposing Wild's true nature. In early 1718, Hitchen released a pamphlet titled "A True Discovery of the Conduct of Receivers and Thief-Takers, In and About the City of London: To the Multiplication and Encouragement of Thieves, Housebreakers, and other loose and disorderly Persons." He shortly followed it with another, titled "The Regulator," which rehashed the first, added a canting dictionary, named names, but dropped notice of Hitchen's authorship.

Hitchen gave his pamphlet away for free. It indicted Wild with numerous charges—everything from counterfeiting to being the "King of Gipsies." The tract even ventured all the way back to Wild's days as a twang to Milliner's buttock. Hitchen's attempt was valiant in its way, but in the end, it was panned. Some of the more glowing reviews called it "an ignorant and impudent insult to the reader," "far too stupid to be effective," "a clumsy performance," "illiterate," and "excruciating." Its only redeemable quality was "the unintended humour, for which the Marshal had an unusual gift." Despite the terrible reviews, it accurately detailed how Wild conducted business. It also set off a pamphlet war between the former allies.

Hitchen composed a numbered list of the methods he would take to fight crime, but his list reads like a litany of complaints:

1. The city's watchmen were "defective" if not "corrupted."
2. Peace officers were "discouraged," and would not confront criminals for fear of retribution.
3. Wild made matters worse by jailing people who then met and learned from thieves. Wild couldn't win for losing.
4. City gates were useless.
5. "The Thief-taker is a Thief-Maker." Whores wouldn't steal if Wild wasn't paying them for the goods.
6. Everything was going to hell: "There is not any one Method yet put in Practice, to put a stop, much less to reform and suppress the Torrent of Debaucheries, which at this time, like a Flood-Gate, is pouring in upon you."

The marshal did have a plan, though. He wanted to throw all thief-takers into prison—thereby mitigating Wild's power, his only real concern. Hitchen urged Londoners to put a stop to Wild's practices. "The Thief, the Gaol, the Justice, and the King's Evidence, all of them seem to be influenced and managed by him, and at this rate none will be brought to the Gallows, but such as he thinks fit." He also urged the Society for the Reformation of Manners to shut down Wild's business. Hitchen's plan perhaps expectedly included an increase in the power of the city marshal. He also wanted a bodyguard and higher pay.

Much of the pamphlet consists of a question-and-answer session between the owner of The Goat tavern—located in Long Lane, and actually owned by "Country" Tom Edwards—and a dolt who asks stupid questions about the thief-taker and the bar's patrons, a cast of various criminals. The Q&A wanders for many pages before coming to a faux advertisement mocking the classified ads that Wild employed. "By His Skittish and Baboonish Majesty: A Proclamation" satirized Wild's directive that the city's thieves dismiss their former "Locks, Fences, and flash Pawn-Brokers" to distribute solely through him henceforth. The proclamation noted that disloyalty or competition wouldn't be tolerated—a fair description of Wild's takeover of the city's receiving trade.

> *Be it known to All and every one of them by these PRESENTS that my BABOONISH Will and Pleasure is that on sight here of, they immediately repair to their duty and allegiance; And for the future to bring all such Goods to me at my office, where they as well as others of my beloved subjects, shall have the greatest Encouragement and Protection, by skreening them at all times, and uppon all Felonious Occasions from Justice: And that they shall also find, that I will give more money to pay back to the right owner, than they can Lock, Pawn or sell them for to any of those Rebellious Receivers &c.*

The naysayers were right: Hitchen's pamphlet was "most stupid," as the *Tyburn Chronicle* called it. The premise is ridiculous, the writing childlike. But the dirt was in the details, and there's no denying that the pamphlet brims with insider knowledge and minute detail of the London underworld. Along with Wild's counter pamphlet, Hitchen's volleys have immense value. Gerald Howson calls the tracts "the only 'exposés' of this underworld written by insiders." Hitchen's use of cant offers a glimpse at how this faction of London spoke. He even provides a list of "The names of the Flash Words now in Vogue amongst Thieves," so that a passage like "Those three young Lads, altho' they are young, yet they are *Bowman-Prigs*, and are such as go on the Lay call'd the Dub," can be understood to mean that the three young men are dexterous and bold thieves who steal by picking locks. Thieves looked for "a *suit*, alias gold watch-cases" or "*wedges*, alias gold or silver snuff boxes." Others went on the "*sneake*: that is, to creep into a house in the evening and taking what they can find," or "*bit a lob from a rattler*, alias took a deal box from behind a coach." After a good day, a thief hoped to spend his *crop* (money) at a *case* (brothel or thieves den).

"The Regulator" also offered a physical description of Wild:

What are all that heap of Boys at that Table, that playing at Dice, Swearing, Cursing, and grinning at each other like so many Hell-Cats' and that Man in the silver button'd coat and knotted Peruke, with a Sword by his Side, what does he do amongst them?

Sir, those Boys are all Clouters, alias Pick-Pockets, and that Man in the Silver button'd Coat, is their Thief-Taker, to help them to Money for the Pocket-Books, Shop-Books, or Writing, and other Goods that they shall steal; and I suppose he is now asking them, if they have any such for him at present, or putting them in mind, that he expects to be serv'd by them for the future.

Such daily briefings were reminiscent of Hitchen's own routine. He even details the food and drink served at The Goat and enjoyed by a couple of street thieves. "I see they live well, they have got a Leg of Pork and Turnips, with Pease Pudding, and a Dish of roasted Fowls for their Dinner. I observe they drink Wine and Brandy plentifully." Elsewhere in The Goat, diners enjoy "a Leg of Mutton boyl'd with a Dish of Turnips, and a Goose with a couple of wild Ducks for their Dinner, and now they are smoking their Pipes, and washing it down with good Wine and Brandy."

The Transportation Act didn't really hinder Wild. He made a few adjustments and returned to not accepting rewards and deducting his fees from the thief's share to compensate for his work in piloting the logistics of the transactions. A Second Transportation Act, this one passed in 1719, had further consequences to Wild's business. It focused on the premature homecoming of those sentenced to transportation and offered a £40 reward for their seizure, which allowed Wild to add new employees to the payroll, powerless but to obey his directives.

London was hard, but for many, staying away from home proved even harder. Many fugitives attempted to return. If Wild didn't turn them in for a quick buck, they came to work for him. The sentence of transportation compelled a convict from the country, most often to Virginia, either for seven or fourteen years. The best—or worst—of England's criminals who weren't executed went to America instead, known lightly as "His Majesty's Seven-Year Passengers," an average of six hundred a year from 1719 to 1722, according to historian Bernard Bailyn.

This influx of English jailbirds to American shores later prompted Benjamin Franklin to call this Act "the most cruel insult that perhaps was ever offered by one people to another." In return for this "tender parental concern," Franklin "humbly proposed" that the colonies send rattlesnakes back to England, for it was by the same logic of the Transportation Act that the rattlesnakes "may possibly change their natures, if they were to change the climate."

Despite the effect on the American colonies, it was another windfall for Wild, who now never lacked someone to do his bidding. He held returning transportees in the palm of his hand. They couldn't very well give evidence against him, because as soon as they came forward and revealed themselves in the country, they were essentially hanging themselves.

Wild knew of a felon's reentry almost as soon as his boots touched solid ground. At the harbor, Jonathan Forward kept an eye out and alerted Wild if he spotted any criminals disembarking from a ship. Forward had shipped them out, so he knew. A private contractor, he handled the sentences of transportation for the government, arranging for convicts to be sold to plantations in America for labor. From the state, he received £40 per transportee for the necessary arrangements, and the usual charge to plantation owners was £10 a head.

During the same period as the pamphlet war with Hitchen, Wild had to deal with dissidence from below when two men he occasionally employed took a run at him as well. Edward Felton tried to bring down the boss and was said to have gone nearly insane in the process. William Riddlesden had assisted in the Knap murder case and had shot the fugitive Timothy Dun in the face. When he turned on the thief-taker general, Wild had him transported.

Riddlesden's Bond of Transportation is dated October 26, 1720, and is signed and sealed in red wax by Jonathan Forward. This oversize, arm-length document reads in part that "Riddlesden stood convicted and attained of felony . . . and at a former Sessions he had received Sentence of Death. . . . To whom his majesty had been graciously pleased to extend his Royal Mercy upon condition of Transportation to some part of America for the space of seven years." The bond shows that Riddlesden agreed to "transport himself within the space of six months." As this document illustrates, not only did some transportees return prematurely, but sometimes it was up to them to ship themselves out. As a result, some criminals never left in the first place. Such was the case with Riddlesden, who received sentences of transportation on numerous occasions, with varied results: Sometimes he was pardoned, sometimes he never left, and sometimes he returned early.

In this instance, though, he reached Annapolis in May 1721. From there he made his way to Pennsylvania, where, according to the *American Weekly Mercury*, he turned up with his newlywed wife in Philadelphia. There he rented a house and set up shop as a "Tallow Chandler and Soapmaker, and pretended to give learned Advice in the Law." America clearly didn't suit Riddlesden, who, judging by a September 22, 1721, *Daily Journal* article, again returned to London, triggering a manhunt to transport him again. He was discovered on the road from Newcastle-on-Tyne to London and imprisoned in the Cambridge county jail before finally settling back into Newgate.

The problem with a transportation sentence was that once a convict shipped out, anything could happen. John Meff, for one, spent his time island-hopping in the Caribbean before he returned home. Wild and a turnkey from Newgate nabbed Meff, who was indicted and hanged at Tyburn. Meff is one of nineteen men and women on Wild's "List" apprehended for transportation-related crimes. But Meff was atypical in that he believed America could have changed his life. "If I had been safe landed in America, my ruin might have been prevented: but the ship which carried me and the other convicts was taken by the pirates," he wrote from Newgate, prior to his execution.

After Meff and eight other passengers refused to band together with the pirates, they were cast ashore on a deserted island, where, according to Meff, they would have starved had they not stolen a canoe and paddled to safety. Meff lived in the Caribbean for a "considerable time" until a longing for his family brought him back to England, the only place on Earth where his mere existence was a crime. He picked up thieving again upon his return and ran headlong into Jonathan Wild almost instantly— "Some evil genius attended me."

His trek across the Atlantic, through the islands, and back again had taken it all out of Meff.

I have had enough of this restless and tumultuous world. I am very easy and resigned to the will of Providence, not doubting but I have made my peace with Heaven. I thank God that I have not been molested by my fellow prisoners with the least cursing or swearing in the condemned hole; but have had an opportunity of employing every moment of my time in preparing for a future state.

The author of Meff's entry in *The Newgate Calendar* cited the case as extraordinary. The man was saved from the gallows and granted transportation only to return and begin thieving anew. "One would think there is a fatality attending the conduct of some men, who seem resolutely bent on their own destruction."

Albeit roughly and unpleasantly, Hitchen had exposed many of Wild's practices. The marshal should have expected what came next, but he certainly wasn't prepared. Wild returned the favor with a pamphlet of his own, "An Answer to a Late Insolent Libel, Entituled, A Discovery of the Conduct of Receivers and Thief-Takers, in and about the City of London; . . . Written by C—s H—n." The subtitle alone runs for nearly a page. The pamphlet's authorship was anonymous, but it was obviously Wild's work (written for him by a ghostwriter). Wild charged six pence apiece for his account.

Wild hardly bothered to defend himself. Instead, he focused on the marshal's behavior, and the airing of Hitchen's secrets had quite an effect. Wild took his readers back to his days as the marshal's man. He described in great detail their "Nocturnal Adventures" together. Wild concluded the counterattack with an account of their visit to the Old Bailey molly house, where Hitchen's initial pleasure was quickly interrupted, as Wild described the two making a hasty exit from the molly house after being spotted by some people Hitchen "little expected to meet with in that place." At which point, Hitchen told Wild about another "noted House in Holborn," presumably the notorious Mother Clap's abode on Field Lane. The marshal knew the Holborn locale well and noted that the men within "us'd to Repair, and Dress themselves in Women's Apparel for the Entertainment of others of the same Inclinations, in Dancing &c. in imitation of the Fair Sex."

In Wild's account, the agitated marshal resolved to make the innocent onlookers pay. "I'll be reveng'd of these Smock fac'd young Dogs; we'll secure them and send them to the Compter." Sure enough, the marshal dragged a group of youths in front of the lord mayor the next morning. The young men were still wearing their "Gowns, Petticoats, Head cloths, fine lac'd Shoes, Furbelow Scarves, Masks, and compleat Dresses for Women; other had Riding Hoods; some were Dress'd like Shepherdesses; other like Milk-Maids, with fine Green Hatts." Simply for spotting the marshal in his natural habitat, the youths were committed to a workhouse for hard labor, one of them dying from the punishing conditions after no more than a couple of days.

Wild saved the most damning for last: "Any Gentleman that wants to be Acquainted with the Sodomitish Academy may be inform'd where it is and be graciously introduc'd by the accomplish'd Mr. H——n." The accusation was crushing. Even the allegation could destroy a reputation. Everything else fell away. Hitchen was finished.

It was a self-inflicted wound for the marshal, though. Wild hadn't said a word about it for years, and it could have remained a secret—if only Hitchen hadn't brought the attack. It's also odd that Hitchen would have exposed such a vulnerability to Wild in the first place. He must have trusted his protégé, or perhaps he thought Wild might have been into it—impossible to tell. Either way, it was an enormous risk to share his secrets with the man whom he had versed so well in the art of blackmail. The scorn as well as the punishment for such activities was well-known. Hitchen knew the danger.

The 1707 *Account of the Tryal, Examination, and Conviction of Several Notorious Persons Call'd Sodomites* woefully exposed the criminality of certain sexual acts during this era. On Monday, October 20, 1707—after reports had surfaced that "many Lewd and Scandalous Persons, frequently held unlawful meetings, and wicked conversations in the dusk of the evening near the Royal Exchange, Leaden-Hall Market, Moorfields, White Chapel, and several obscure places, in and about this city"—several men were rounded up and brought in front of the Guildhall Court. Most of the men simply pleaded drunkenness as a defense, but William Marriot made an extremely forthcoming argument—ironically so, because of all the men at the trial, he was quite well-known for attending these "wicked" meet-ups, and described by witnesses as "notoriously addicted to this sort of lewdness."

In his defense, Marriot declared his innocence of sodomy, but spoke in great detail—"only with the hand"—of acts he'd experienced in the past with young men, "foolish customs," he called them. Marriot and the rest of the men were found "guilty of Loathsome Crimes & High Misdemeaners."

Not only had Hitchen's pamphlet failed to dent Wild's esteem, but Wild's countermeasure landed a devastating blow. Hitchen was shocked that his pamphlet had failed to sway opinion against Wild, but he should have known better. "No one but an exceedingly vain man, completely devoid of any sense of humour, would have expected the world to take seriously" what Hitchen had written, according to Frederick J. Lyons. For his part, Wild probably should have shown some restraint. Hitchen's folly only increased Wild's prominence. He hardly needed to bother replying. But the secret of the molly house visit must have been burning a hole in his pocket. Hitchen tried to regain the upper hand, but it was too late for that. The damage was done. If nothing else, the pamphlet war should have sounded a warning to London's young rogues: Steer clear of the thief-taker; his good prices weren't worth it. We can chalk it up as an additional failure for Hitchen that even thieves didn't turn against Wild.

London was about to explode. The South Sea Bubble, an eighteenth-century stock-trading scheme, was about to make and then break the fortunes of thousands, including many of the country's aristocracy. From the South Sea Company stock's collapse came a large number of men and women unprepared for total ruin. A crime wave was about to sweep England.

Defoe (disputed attribution) later described the boiling pot, and how the press and its writers sought to take advantage.

> *On a sudden we found street robberies became the common practice, conversation was full of the variety of them, the newspapers had them every day, and sometimes more than were ever committed; and those that were committed were set off by the invention of the writers. . . . But be that as it will, the real facts were innumerable, and the real robberies actually committed so many, and carried on with such desperate boldness, and oft times with blood, that it became unsafe to walk the streets late at night, within the night or evenings, if the nights were dark, and people were afraid to go about their business.*

Hitchen similarly wrote in "The Regulator" of how tavern, shop, and coffeehouse owners complained of losing business because their customers feared venturing out, "that they may be blinded, knock'd down, cut, or stabbed."

Crime had been bad in the 1670s, as well as following the end of the War of Spanish Succession. But this spate of lawlessness was something else entirely. Wild's Lost Property Office doors were bursting. He was even summoned from time off the clock in Dulwich in the late summer of 1718 when word reached him that a wealthy client had requested his services. In 1720, he opened a second office for a time, back in his old haunts on Lewkenor's Lane, with Mendez running the show there. The same year, after a frenzy of trading activity, the South Sea Bubble burst. Amid the chaos, pilferers bilked the crowds in Exchange Alley, and Wild was called in to solve a case, among others, of two thousand stolen stock receipts.

Since separating with Mary Milliner, Wild had run through a string of relationships. Next on the docket were Judith Nun and Sarah Perrin, alias Gregstone or Grigson. His relationship with Nun was brief, but they did have a daughter together before he transferred his attention to Perrin (with whom he had no children). Both Nun and Perrin were still alive when he began his relationship with Elizabeth Mann, a former prostitute and, arguably, the love of his life. Unlike Nun or Perrin, Mann lived with him. She was a reforming Catholic, who, after being released from the sins of her former life, lived on the straight and narrow until her death circa 1718.

At St. Pancras Church on February 13, 1719, Jonathan Wild wed for the sixth and final time. The bride was Mary Dean, widow of John "Skull" Dean, who was apprehended for burglary in 1717 by Jonathan Wild—hardly a shock—and executed. Whether the arrest was a premeditated move for Skull's wife or merely a coincidence is anyone's guess, but Wild did know the couple, they were in fact neighbors for a spell, before he took up with the widow. Hangman Richard Arnet fittingly presided over the Wild-Dean nuptials, and the ceremony took place at Elizabeth Mann's grave.

Although he would never marry again, his womanizing ways—which caused him great financial difficulty in the years to come—didn't end. The contemporary but anonymous biographer known only as H. D. noted that Wild had "three wives living, and always a Seraglio of Mistresses, no less than half [a] dozen at a time, to maintain according to his rank." Such a stable didn't come cheap.

Not long after his final wedding day, reports surfaced that Wild was on his deathbed. *Applebee's Original Weekly Journal* reported on September 26, 1719, that "Mr. Wild, the famous Thief-taker, lyes past all hopes of Recovery, at his House in the Little Old Bailey." A week later *Saturday's Post* added to the speculation: "We hear Jonathan Wild, the famous Thief-taker, lies a dying."

The culprit of Wild's woes was syphilis. His condition worsened when he tried to remedy the affliction with a concoction made with mercury. But the reports of the thief-taker's demise came prematurely. Whatever afflicted him, he was soon healed, and before October ended, he was back in the papers with an advertisement in the *Post Man and the Historical Account* offering a one-guinea reward for a lost silver pendulum watch. He also threw his hat in the ring to take over for the recently deceased Reverend Paul Lorraine as the ordinary (prison chaplain) of Newgate. A letter in *Mist's Weekly Journal* took exception, declaring that only "a Man of the most exemplary Goodness and Holiness possible" should fill the position of curing souls.

Anything for a pound.

THE FRONTISPIECE FROM THE FIRST EDITION OF
Robinson Crusoe

IX

CRUSOE AND FLANDERS

I was alone, circumscrib'd by the boundless Ocean, cut off from Mankind, and condemn'd to what I call'd silent Life; that I was as one whom Heaven thought not worthy to be number'd among the Living.
—DANIEL DEFOE, *ROBINSON CRUSOE*

In 1714, just after finishing his tenure as the editor of the *Review*, Defoe moved to the four-acre lot at 95 Church Street in Stoke Newington, near where he once attended school. The writer tended the gardens and grounds with a caring touch. His estate contained an orchard, plenty of shade trees, a stable for horses, and other outbuildings. Hackney Brook ran nearby. It was distinctly suburban, but the aging Defoe took no chances. He fitted the doors of the house with the finest latches and bolts on the market. The cutting-edge locks came at a cost, but it was worth it: He had three grown daughters living at home.

Surrounded by a large, tall fence, the house, made of flat, artless brick, felt more like a compound. Only three rows of windows broke the uniformity, denoting the house's three stories. The place reeked of fear. It had many doors, many routes of escape; it was even said to have a crude alarm system by way of a hidden chain in a cupboard. Ropes and ladders would have materialized for covert exodus. One chronicler called the dwelling "a gloomy and irregular pile of red brick—a dreary and pretentious building."

Inside, in the home's large library, Defoe's imagination ran wild. He had been experimenting.

London's crime problem piqued Defoe's interest. Recently, he had gone back to Newgate—as a journalist this time—investigating the case of eighteen-year-old treasonist James Shepheard, who had been denied the customary right to publish his confessions prior to execution. Pamphlets on well-known bandits had been popular since the middle of the seventeenth century. But over time, a shift had occurred. No longer did the stories focus on the victim, God's distaste for the illegal deed, or how to avoid a strike. Now the murderer and highwayman were getting star treatment.

At this point, England's crime literature didn't demand much toil on the part of the writer. The structure was staid and seldom modified. Criminal biographies told rather simple accounts of property exchange. As Lincoln Faller points out, the formula usually involved the "transfer of portable property, usually under threat of violence—and the violence, when enacted, tends to be concrete, direct, a matter of thrusts, cuts, groans. It is almost never emotional, or psychologically induced." In order to get the compulsory redemptive ending right, writers sometimes shoehorned their subjects' lives into the formula, which was more important than faithfulness to fact. Doing so made these tracts no less popular, but in the end, it homogenized them and drained them of realism.

Also appearing during this period was picaresque fiction, adventure novels popular in Spain and France since the sixteenth century. One of the earliest in England was *The Rogue* (1622) by James Mabbe, a translation of *Guzmán de Alfarache* by Mateo Aleman.

Defoe eschewed the romance of the picaresque for reality. He wanted topical stories based on the interests of the people, and the city's violent crime wave had seized popular attention and the writer's imagination. He wasn't interested so much in a specific type of crime as with the adventure in the act of rebellion itself. He later complained that "We take pains to puff 'em up in their Villainy, and Thieves are set out in so amiable a Light," but he knew that when he wrote about crime, it ultimately fell to the reader whether to be scared straight or to cheer the rule-breaker.

Defoe was fifty-eight years old and had a large family, but he didn't play it safe. He gambled again. He looked beyond the tired setup of the criminal story: birth, school, crime, death. As Faller notes, Defoe wasn't afraid to leave "his readers hanging." Sometimes he didn't even supply his narrator with the whole story (as in *Captain Singleton*, when the captain doesn't know the details of his own childhood). As a result, Defoe's characters seem genuine because they don't perfectly caricature thieves or whores. Nobody else was writing like him. While other books blended together, his work stood out.

He blurred the line between fact and fiction, calling his first novel *The Life and Strange Surprizing Adventures of Robinson Crusoe, of York, Mariner ... Written by Himself* (etc., etc., for an additional fifty-three words). In the preface, he kept piling it on: "The Editor believes the thing to be a just History of Fact; neither is there any Appearance of Fiction in it." Defoe took the finished product to William Taylor at the Ship in Paternoster Row. The publisher paid the writer a small amount—"probably a very inadequate sum," according to biographer William Lee—perhaps around £50. For that amount, Defoe surrendered the copyright in the work, as was standard practice at the time. He would see no more money for his efforts. Taylor registered the work at Stationers' Hall on April 23, 1719.

Robinson Crusoe hit the market on April 25, 1719, selling for five shillings a copy. Within two weeks, the first printing had sold out. By the end of the year, it had been reprinted four more times, in addition to the bootlegged editions floating around. These pirated copies sold for two shillings each, and for the discount, readers got a bare-bones version. Nevertheless, even the derivative copies sold quickly. *Robinson Crusoe* was everywhere.

Defoe had a hit on his hands. He hadn't created a literary masterpiece, but he had launched a new style of writing: the first English novel. He had turned criminal biography into fiction. As a result, *Robinson Crusoe* proved popular across all age and income brackets. Credit for the anonymous work went to Defoe without question and the work even garnered him a bit of esteem from fellow writers. Alexander Pope later commented: "The first part of *Robinson Crusoe* is good. Defoe wrote a vast many things, and none bad, though none excellent. There's something good in all he writ." It was kind of Pope to say, but most of the established literary crowd remained unenthusiastic. The novel, this newfangled fiction, was nothing but a fad. It was a waste of time to read something that didn't instruct, or that lacked a moral or religious benefit. (When Henry Fielding took up *Tom Jones* several decades later, the novel was still establishing itself as a genre. Fielding called it a "historic Kind of Writing," and a "new Province of Writing.")

Not surprisingly, Defoe had a sequel out by August of the same year, *The Farther Adventures of Robinson Crusoe*, and a third volume the following August. He didn't get rich from the effort—it's uncertain how much money he made—but it did bring him security, knowing that the public would accept and pay for his future literary endeavors. He could write without financial worries.

It was William Taylor, Defoe's publisher, who truly benefited from the book. He made £1,000 from the immediate release of *Crusoe*, and when Taylor died a few years later, he was worth over £40,000.

Our intrepid novelist soon extended his success in the genre that he had helped birth with *Moll Flanders*, the tale of a sometime thief and sometime prostitute. London's torrent of crime showed no signs of slowing. Robbery begat more robbery. Women with no options turned to the sex trade, and Moll Flanders represented this new face of London. Newgate Prison once again served as inspiration.

As with Crusoe, Moll Flanders is likely a conflation, this time with inspiration coming from more than one of the female prisoners in Newgate, like Calico Sarah and Moll King. Moll King had at one time been a roommate of Wild's former flame, Mary Milliner. King knew London's underworld intimately and worked with Wild numerous times. Defoe exposes the deplorable conditions of Newgate's women's quarters—worse than the men's for squalor and equally as wicked—and in the course of the book, Flanders faces physical attack, the desperation of the Mint, gambling houses in Covent Garden, and the madness of Newgate itself. Flanders stood out as a character and rang with authenticity. Her life was messy, the book was messy—just like real life.

In 1719, nineteen-year-old John Matthews was condemned to be hanged, drawn, and quartered in violation of the Treason Act of 1707 for merely printing a pamphlet. Although now a best-selling author, Defoe also

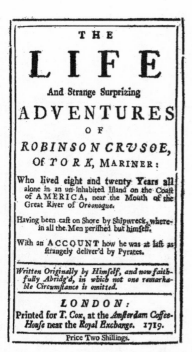

THE

LIFE

And Strange Surprizing

ADVENTURES

OF

ROBINSON CRUSOE,
Of *YORK,* MARINER:

Who lived eight and twenty Years all
alone in an un-inhabited Island on the Coast
of AMERICA, near the Mouth of the
Great River of *Oroonoque.*

Having been caft on Shore by Shipwreck, wherein all the Men perifhed but himfelf.

With an ACCOUNT how he was at laft as
ftrangely deliver'd by Pyrates.

*Written Originally by Himfelf, and now faith-
fully Abridg'd, in which not one remarkable Circumftance is omitted.*

LONDON:

Printed for T. *Cox,* at the *Amfterdam Coffee-
Houfe* near the *Royal Exchange.* 1719.

Price Two Shillings.

THE

FORTUNES

AND

MISFORTUNES

Of the FAMOUS

Moll Flanders, &c.

Who was Born in NEWGATE, and during a
Life of continu'd Variety for Threefcore Years,
befides her Childhood, was Twelve Year a
Whore, five times a *Wife* (whereof once to her
own Brother) Twelve Year a *Thief,* Eight Year a
Tranfported *Felon* in *Virginia,* at laft grew *Rich,*
liv'd *Honeft,* and died a *Penitent.*

Written from her own MEMORANDUMS.

LONDON: Printed for, and Sold by W.
CHETWOOD, at *Cato's-Head,* in *Ruffel-
ftreet, Covent-Garden;* and T. EDLING, at
the *Prince's-Arms,* over-againft *Exerter-Change*
in the *Strand.* MDDCXXI.

THE TITLE PAGE OF THE FIRST
EDITION OF *ROBINSON CRUSOE*

THE TITLE PAGE OF THE FIRST
EDITION OF *MOLL FLANDERS*

remained active as a journalist. If he needed any reminder that his occupation seethed with risk, he only needed to look to Nathaniel Mist, his publisher at the *Weekly Journal,* or *Saturday's Post* (later titled *Mist's Weekly Journal*) where he'd been writing since 1717. The *Post Boy* of February 14–16, 1721, reported that "the Court pronounced Judgment as follows, viz. That he [Mist] stand twice in the Pillory." According to William Lee, after 1715, "with the exceptions of his initials to two translations, and a newspaper, Daniel Defoe never appeared again before the world, as an Author."

Beyond ego, there was little reason to stake a claim—not after all of his arrests. He was older now, comfortable, free from the daily grind of putting together a newspaper all by himself. But he wasn't resting on his laurels. Letters from Defoe to Undersecretary of State Charles de la Faye reveal the writer was back in the spy business, working undercover at Tory newspapers while remaining loyal to the Whigs.

"GIN LANE" BY WILLIAM HOGARTH

THE BLACK LION

Drunk for a penny. Dead drunk for twopence. Clean straw
for nothing.
—WILLIAM HOGARTH, "GIN LANE"

From 1717 to 1723, Jack Sheppard worked diligently for Owen Wood. But as his experience grew, so did his appetite for better work and more money. Wood was a modest man satisfied with small-time jobs, while Sheppard had his eye on larger accounts, including new construction. He was now twenty-one years old and spending his free time in a Newton Street tavern called the Black Lion Alehouse.

Those in Sheppard's era viewed the concept of leisure time for young adults as soul ruining. A young man needed to work long hours or he was certain to fall into mischief. Perhaps this was just a convenient excuse for employers to justify cheap labor, but being out of work drew little sympathy. Peter Linebaugh places Sheppard's "transition from industry to idleness" under the umbrella of three headings: "Bad Company," "Sabbath Breaking," and "Lewd Women." All three converged at the Black Lion. A former button-mold maker named Joseph Hind ran the tavern that catered to rowdy whores and violent thieves. Sheppard joined them with increasing regularity.

In *A Narrative of All the Robberies, Escapes, &c. of John Sheppard*, written by Defoe from Sheppard's perspective, we see one of his rhetorical calling cards: pointing blame at anyone but himself. He and Wood

went on together for about six Years, there happening in that Time what
is too common with most Families in low Life, as frequent Quarrels and

Bickerings. I am far from presuming to say that I was one of the best of Servants, but I believe if less Liberty had been allow'd me then, I should scarce have had so much Sorrow and Confinement after. My Master and Mistress with their Children were strict Observers of the Sabbath, but 'tis too well known in the Neighbourhood that I had too great a Loose given to my evil Inclinations, and spent the Lord's Day as I thought convenient.

That led to Lewd Women.

I may justly lay the Blame of my Temporal and . . . my Eternal Ruin on Joseph Hind, a Button-mould Maker, who formerly kept the Black Lyon Ale-House in Drury Lane; the frequenting of this wicked House brought me acquainted with Elizabeth Lyon, and with a Train of Vices, as before I was altogether a Stranger to. Hind is now a lamentable Instance of God's divine Vengeance, he being a wretched Object about the Streets.

Elizabeth Lyon, with whom Sheppard was smitten, was otherwise known to the customers of the Black Lion as Edgworth Bess. The wife of an absentee soldier, she was heavyset and drank hard. Hind kept her on the payroll at the Black Lion to please the crowd with her wanton sexuality, which she did, to great effect.

Sheppard's affections soon pushed her soldier husband from the picture, but Sheppard's lovesickness didn't come cheaply. Footing the tab for drinks was particularly tough for a young man still stuck in an apprenticeship. As a result, his working relationship with Wood grew strained. Sheppard was young and in lust. He only wanted to find the money to keep up his shenanigans at the Black Lion, where his gaze soon strayed to other young prostitutes, including Poll Maggot, a friend of Lyon's.

Working at the Rummer Tavern in Charing Cross during the spring of 1723, Sheppard saw an opportunity. A couple of silver spoons lay out in the open, taunting him. He needed money for booze and girls, and the spoons were just lying there, a bright, shiny solution to his problems. Into his tool bag they went. It was his first turn as a thief, but he took to it with ease. A couple of spoons may seem like a mild transgression today, but it was a capital offense in 1723.

Sheppard later put this deed and his next transgression into the larger context of what lay ahead: "Unhappy Wretch! I was now commenced Thief, and soon after Housebreaker; growing gradually wicked, 'twas about the latter End of July, 1723, that I was sent by my Master to do a Jobb at the House of Mr. Bains. . . . I there stole a Roll of Fustian containing 24 Yards, from amongst many others, and Mr. Bains not missing it, had consequently no Suspicion."

Suspicious or not, Bains and Wood soon learned about the missing fustian from another of Wood's men, Thomas. Sheppard had failed to unload the fabric for money right away and his fellow apprentice had spotted it in a trunk in Sheppard's lodgings. When Sheppard learned that Thomas had tattled, he strongly denied it, even having his own mother vouch for him. The Widow Sheppard did as her son asked and confirmed the story he had concocted: that he had received the fustian from a Spitalfields weaver. But Sheppard eventually came clean and returned most of the fabric to Bains.

Wood wasn't pleased, but like Jack's mother, he tried to a fault to cover for Sheppard. On one occasion, he even forgave a physical assault during a long workday at the Sun Alehouse in Islington, when a tired and hungry Sheppard lost his temper and struck Wood. On another occasion, Elizabeth Lyon paid a visit to the Woods' home in search of her suitor. The devout Mrs. Wood dropped to her knees and beseeched the young man to come to his senses and rid himself of the harlot. Accounts of what happened next differ. Some describe an affronted Sheppard advising the Woods to stay out of his business, tossing a stick from his third-floor garret that hit Mrs. Wood. Jack's own depiction of this event placed Lyon's husband in Wood's yard, with the stick intended for the soldier but missing its mark. Both interpretations left Mrs. Wood uninjured.

Occasionally the Woods tried to teach Sheppard a lesson, and failed at their task just as often. Sheppard was staying out late, often past midnight.

Wood locked him out on occasion to influence the young man to keep better hours. Each morning, however, Sheppard was asleep in his bed, having climbed up to his window, unlocking it with ease. As eloquently recorded in another contemporary biography, *The History of the Remarkable Life of John Sheppard*, "He made a mere jest of the Locks and Bolts, and enter'd in, and out at Pleasure . . . such was the power of his early Magick."

The affair between Sheppard and Lyon was volatile. His short fuse matched her irascibility. When they came to blows, as they sometimes did, Lyon—described as a "violent-tempered Amazon"—gave as good as she got. Initially racked with guilt over thieving, Sheppard liked to blame Lyon for this false step, which of course only added fuel to the fire of their relationship. The increasing regularity of their fighting helped to ease Sheppard into the arms of other women. His temper may have been quick, but so was his charm. From Lyon, to Poll Maggot, to a host of others, including Kate Keys and Kate Cook, Sheppard kept busy.

It appears Sheppard was a sucker for punishment, however, for while Elizabeth Lyon beat him, Poll Maggot couldn't stand him. According to the *Lives of the Most Remarkable Criminals*, Maggot "had a very great Contempt for [Sheppard] and only made Use of him to go and steal Money, or what might yield Money, for her to spend in Company that she liked better." If Sheppard didn't have any cash, Poll Maggot didn't have time for excuses. "Don't tell me such melancholy Stories," she told Sheppard, "but think how you may get more Money."

Notwithstanding his other dalliances, Sheppard always made his way back to Lyon. When Lyon found herself locked up at St. Giles's Roundhouse—nabbed after filching a cull's ring—it was Sheppard who came to her aid.

Sheppard overpowered the prison's beadle, Mr. Brown, and his wife, snatched the prison keys, and unlocked his lover. When word hit the streets, Sheppard became very popular among the women of town. His feat also made waves among the rabble. "This Action acquired a reputation among the Punks of Drury-lane, beyond any of his Contemporary Prigs," noted *Select Trials*.

On August 1, 1723, Sheppard revisited Bains in White Horse Yard to settle the score over the pilfered fustian. If Sheppard was going to commit a crime, he might as well be richer for it. Near midnight, Sheppard dislodged the wooden bars from Bains's cellar window to gain entry, stole £7 from the businessman's cash drawer, and grabbed £14 worth of merchandise on the way out. When he replaced the wooden bars, he nailed them down with such precision that the following day Bains thought it was an inside job, pointing the finger at a woman lodging in the home. With cash in hand, Sheppard found refuge at the young Poll Maggot's place.

But it was what he did the next day that proved consequential.

In August 1723—just eight months prior to the completion of his apprenticeship, when he could start his own business and earn some real money—Sheppard gathered his belongings from Wood's house and quit.

Now he had more time to spend at the bar—not only the Black Lion, but many different dives, bawdy houses, and gambling houses in and around Covent Garden, the same Drury Lane spots where Jonathan Wild had gotten his London start, and where Wild still had considerable presence. In fact, just down the street from the Black Lion lay the Black Boy, a tavern run by Wild's brother Andrew. If spending his time drunk in a bar was his desire, Sheppard had plenty of company.

The Gin Craze had begun. This rabid addiction to gin—or a bastardized form of the spirit—caused untold problems throughout the eighteenth century. In *London Life in the Eighteenth Century*, historian Mary Dorothy George describes the years between 1720 and 1751 as an "orgy of spirit-drinking." Gin was both highly potent and inexpensive; for thousands of poor men and women, the combination proved fatal.

In 1702, when Defoe made his rambling notes on English tippling in "The True-Born Englishman"—

But English drunkards, gods and men outdo
Drink their estates away and senses too.

and

An Englishman will fairly drink as much,
as will maintain two families of Dutch.

—he couldn't have envisioned just how bad the situation would get. For the most part, Sheppard managed to keep himself upright during his nightly carousing. But as Fergus Linnane explains in *London's Under-world*, "People reeled about the streets or collapsed in gutters at all hours of the day and night. In the middle of the day men, women, and children lay stupefied in the streets in slum areas such as St. Giles and Whet-stone Park. Inside the gin shops unconscious customers were propped up against the walls until they came around and could start again."

What Mary Dorothy George calls "gin-flamed insanity" fueled much of the city's crime now. There is perhaps no better example of this mad-ness than the oft-cited case of Judith Defour, the mother who strangled her infant daughter, Mary, in order to sell the child's clothes for cash to buy gin. According to her confession read in Court, she and another woman "stripp'd the said Child, and ty'd a linen Rag very hard about the Child's Neck, to prevent its crying out, which strangled her." The two women then split the profits and enjoyed a quart of gin.

In a time when waterborne illnesses killed many, and often, most everyone was drinking something alcoholic, but the poor were drinking gin, many times stronger than the usual beer or wine and, in many cases, poisonously lethal. Not even children were safe from its effects, whether of their own volition, or in cases where poor mothers used the liquor to quiet their hungry offspring. As Mary Dorothy George points out, for the poorest of the poor, poverty was both "a cause as well as a result of their craving for gin."

Imported from the Netherlands, gin became popular in the latter part of the seventeenth century. But when English farmers found them-selves with a surfeit of low-quality grain unsuitable for producing beer, or much of anything else, Parliament—which consisted largely of land-owners and gentlemen farmers—looked to make gin a homegrown com-modity. Thus, they passed the 1690 Act for Encouraging the Distilling of Brandy and Spirits from Corn (wheat and grains). The government encouraged production, facilitated sales (no license required), and leveed a high tariff on imports.

The mania of the Gin Craze exploded. A bevy of businesses began selling the liquor throughout London and its suburbs. Since English gin could be sold at such a low price, these vendors—known as dram, brandy, or geneva shops—tended to crop up in the slums and poorer sections of town.

Other retailers and tradesmen, such as tobacconists, chandlers, and fruit sellers, took notice of the spike in demand and began to dabble in the gin business as well. A pint of gin could be had for as little as a penny, and it was so powerful—caused in no small part by the addition of turpentine, a side effect of the unregulated distillation process—many men, women, and children had no problem shelling out a penny to dull themselves for a spell. By the middle of the eighteenth century, almost half of the country's total wheat crop went to make the spirit. Boozing had become an issue of national priority.

Some presciently saw through the economic benefits, like the mercantilist-minded pamphleteer and politician Charles Davenant, who prophesied in 1701, "'Tis a growing Vice among common people, and may, in time prevail as much as Opium with the Turks." Defoe initially supported the economic benefits of using homegrown corn, but in 1726 he sang a different tune, calling these spirit merchants "a collection of sinners against the people."

With the rise in crime, deaths, and even fires—a consequence of unregulated booze making in crowded slums—the government realized by the 1720s that action was necessary. London's leaders met at Hicks Hall in St. John's Street in May 1721 to generate a plan to deal with the mania. The council took up the matter in a series of meetings geared toward finding a "proper method to suppress the Wicked Clubs or Societies of young People . . . and put a Stop to all manner of Vice, immorality and Profaneness." Once the culprits were discovered, the task, according to Edward Southwell, who penned the justices' orders, was to discover "any who are guilty of such impieties, that they may be openly Prosecuted and punished with the utmost Severity and most publick Ignominy which the Laws of the Land can inflict."

The Middlesex justices of the peace presented their conclusions on June 30. They found that most of the trouble was coming "chiefly from the Mascorades and Gameing Houses and from the increase of Play Houses and Publick houses of all sorts in all parts of the Town." It was estimated that as many as one house in ten in "some of the larger parishes" was selling some sort of liquor." Or more sharply put, "Nor is there any part of this Town, wherein the Number of Ale houses, Brandy, and Geneva shops do not daily increase." This, they wrote, was "the principal cause of the Increase of our Poor, and of all the Vice and Debauchery among the Inferior sort of People, as well as of the Felonies and other Disorders committed in and about this town." The meetings failed miserably. The Gin Craze raged for another thirty years.

One of the best illustrations of the devastation comes from the hand of artist William Hogarth. His masterful *Beer Street* and *Gin Lane* prints present a glaring contrast between the effects of the two beverages. In *Beer Street*, we see a city thriving with tradesmen and sign painters bustling about, smiling and well-fed. A blacksmith brandishes a shoulder of mutton. Men and women hold and drink hearty tankards of nourishing ale. Set in the slum of St. Giles, *Gin Lane* gives us a depraved scene of misery and filth. A man battles a dog for a bone. Another man is passed out, dram tipped over, his bones poking through his flesh; if he's not already dead, he's well on his way. Next to him a child falls over a railing into a stairwell from the loose arms of its pustuled and indifferent mother, who is busy taking a pinch of snuff. In the background, a corpse is laid into a coffin. Verse from the Reverend James Townley accompanies the two images:

> *Beer, happy Produce of our Isle*
> *Can sinewy Strength impart,*
> *And wearied with Fatigue and Toil*
> *Can cheer each manly Heart.*

and

Gin, cursed fiend! With fury fraught,
Makes human race a prey;
It enters by a deadly draught,
And steals our life away.

No different from anyone else in this regard, Jack Sheppard "had given himself up to all the sensual Pleasures of low Life. Drinking all day, and getting to some impudent and notorious Strumpet at Night, was the whole Course of his life for a considerable Space." In other words, he, too, was living fast and loose. After leaving Wood, he went southwest with Elizabeth Lyon to Fulham, where they lived as man and wife. There he lived as though he had fulfilled the bond of his apprenticeship, scoring a job as a journeyman under Mr. Panton, a master carpenter. Unluckily, Owen Wood's brother also lived in Fulham, spotted him, and busted the charade.

Back in hot water for fraud and for breaking the bond in the first place, he was taken to the Guildhall to appear before the chamberlain. The chamberlain wasn't in his office, though, so Sheppard and Wood came to an agreement and cut ties once and for all. Here, Sheppard decided to put a life on the straight and narrow behind him for good. He had tried with Wood, and again under Panton—notwithstanding the lie—but to no avail. It was at this point, according to his *Narrative*, that he "then fell to robbing almost everyone that stood in my way."

His spree began in October 1723, when he robbed a Mr. Charles of Mayfair, making off with nine silver spoons, six gold rings, another gold ring with a gem, assorted suits and linens, and more than £7 in coins. With money in his pocket, he and Lyon moved on. The street credibility he'd earned from bullying the beadle at St. Giles's Roundhouse to secure Lyon's freedom allowed him to mix with assorted throngs of London bandits, many of them connected with Wild. Also around this time, Sheppard reunited with his brother Thomas.

Thomas Sheppard was now twenty-six years old and a well-known thief in his own right, of late running with members of the Carrick gang. Thomas twice had been indicted in August 1723 for stealing saws and other tools from carpenters' worksites in Chelsea and Holborn. He went to Newgate for a spell, and then, as Old Bailey records show, he was "burnt in the hand" for his crimes and released. On the outside, Thomas Sheppard called on his brother for a loan of forty shillings and an invitation to sit down for a drink. There was something he wanted to talk to Jack about.

XI

CELEBRITY GANGBUSTER

*I made it my Business to search after the Prisoners; for I had heard
that they used to rob about Hampstead; and I went about it the more
willingly, because I had heard they had threatened to shoot me thro'
the Head.*
—JONATHAN WILD IN THE 1723 TRIAL OF RICHARD OAKEY, JOHN
LEVEE, AND MATTHEW FLOOD

A client had to say hardly more than where he had been robbed before
Wild and his team knew the culprit. Victim of the Rattling Lay near
Aldgate? Obadiah Lemon's crew. Pickpockets near St. Ann's Church
in Westminster? Moll King and friends. Still, his science wasn't always
exact. Defoe later wrote about his own visit with the thief-taker after a
sword went missing.

"I remember I had occasion, in a case of this Kind, to wait upon Mr.
Jonathan with a Crown in my Hand . . . and having made a Deposite, I
was asked . . . where the Thing was lost?" He recalled Wild's show. "At
first he smil'd, and turning to one, I suppose, of his Instruments, 'Who
can this be?' says he, why, all our People are gone down to Sturbridge
Fair."

"The other answer'd, after some pause, 'I think I saw *Lynx* [Samuel
Linn], in the Street, Yesterday.'"

"Did you?" said Wild. "Then 'tis that Dog, I warrant you."

Wild turned back to Defoe. "'Well, Sir,' says he, 'I believe we can find
out your Man; you shall know more of it, if you let me see you again a
Monday.'"

A 1740 AD FROM JOHN APPLEBEE FOR *SELECT TRIALS AT THE SESSIONS-HOUSE IN THE OLD BAILEY* Courtesy of the London Lives Project

"When the Monday came," Defoe wrote, "I was told, they could not see the young Rogue, and they believ'd he was gone after the rest to the Fair, it being about the beginning of September."

Defoe returned to Wild's office after some time had passed. Then again. "I came again and again, but was put off from time to time, and could not at last be serv'd in the Case, it being only a Silver-hilted Sword, which the Thief it seems had found means to turn into Money."

Despite, his failure at restoring the writer's sword, Wild had no shortage of high-profile cases, which usually met with a more satisfactory end. At this point, he was consolidating his power over London's underworld once and for all. Recently he had captured the Spiggot gang, leaving the big gangs of Shaw, Hawkins, and Carrick. Not easy work. For such upheaval, he needed troops. When Wild looked to add to his ranks, he often paid a visit to the Mint in Southwark for extra hands.

In the parish of St. George the Martyr across the Thames in Southwark, the Mint offered sanctuary for those on the run, primarily hard luck debtors, but also wanted felons. A few years before he died in the mid-sixteenth century, King Henry VIII had established a coining mint in Suffolk Place, a mansion on the spot that, when torn down, became the refugee zone. Legal shelters like the Mint had been around for many years. But, according to Frank McLynn, "By 1712 the authorities had effectively clamped down on the misuse of ancient privileges." Many of the old sanctuaries, such as Whitefriars and Alsatia, remained slums riddled with crooks. But the Mint was officially the "last of the 'bastard sanctuaries,'" where debt collectors (known as duns) or peace officers couldn't enter. If a dun did appear, denizens of the Mint were bound by no law as to what they could do to him. This usually consisted of beating the offender almost to death. When a representative from the coroner's office dared enter the Mint to investigate a child's murder, its residents tossed him into the "Black Ditch"—the nearby sewer.

The Mint lay six inches lower than the Thames. Human excrement and pollution settled there, infesting its inhabitants. The place was marked by dirt, hunger, and violence. Luxurious it wasn't. Because of its sheltered status, the Mint attracted outlaws of all types. Thieves often congregated there to plan their next heist. A person was free to come and go as he pleased—just as long as he could outrun the duns waiting outside the gates. Respite came only on Sundays, when debts legally couldn't be collected. Minters sometimes took a chance and fled the asylum on Sundays in order to scare up funds.

Wild always kept his ranks fresh. In his business, he couldn't afford to be caught unprepared or without the proper numbers, regardless of the fact that the diminished supply was a result of his habit of offering up his own workers to the hangman at Tyburn for reward. Near the Mint, on Red Cross Street, stood the Duke's Head, a pub where Wild drank with friends and stabled his horses. Here Wild found good earners. Hardened criminals were easy to spot, and Wild recruited them, of course, but he saw beyond the riffraff. Mixed in with the Mint's criminal element was a veritable army of poor foot soldiers: down-on-their-luck and misfortunate men and women eager to make a dime if given the chance.

Wild staffed his corporation precisely. He was a connoisseur, patient. If he saw a tradesman contemplating his options at the Mint, he understood the man needed time, the opportunity to get hungry. Only then did Wild consider adding him to his force. He wanted them desperate. During recruiting trips, Wild often used liquor as a tool, according to clerk and author H. D., who described the recruitment process: First, Wild got friendly with the gin sellers and the publicans at the local taverns, getting a rough sketch of the patrons' plights from the barkeeps. When properly versed in their woes, he contorted his personality and put on a smile. Wild bought a few rounds. He lent an ear and listened. He got the drunks drunker. He was compassionate as ever. Finally, he offered the desperate man a penny in his time of need. A small advance and a piece of advice— *Come steal with me and be poor no more.* The tiny investment rarely failed to pay off. Wild examined his books and found an opening someplace for his new henchman to steal.

Such was the case with a destitute former cheesemonger whom Wild lured at the Mint, as described above, handing him half a pound in alms upon their meeting. On the cheesemonger's first outing, he secured a nine-guinea payday, pilfered from a man on horseback. The freshly branded highwayman returned to Wild and quickly discovered the unfair economics of the situation. Wild took seven guineas for himself and left his worker with only two—and he did so without the pleasantness and understanding that the cheesemonger initially had met. The time for shenanigans had passed. Wild held the man's life in his hands now, and could turn him over to the hangman for theft at any point.

But from Wild's perspective, this small cut of the proceeds was better than nothing. Because of him, this penniless, pathetic soul now had two guineas. We know the cheesemonger felt differently, because after a few more heists and lopsided splits, he went it alone, cutting Wild out entirely. The country boy had no idea.

Wild fumed over the cheesemonger's lack of ethics. "I am serv'd by a parcel of Rascals when I have put Bread into their Mouths, but I'll hang him if there was not another Rogue left in England," he said.

Now versed in the ways of the street, the cheesemonger thief went on a robbery spree, each time failing to pay his monetary respects to his benefactor. Wild had created a monster. He had no choice but to hunt him down and end it. Wild quickly landed a few leads and set out on horseback to scour the countryside. Before long, he spotted a man on horseback—the cheesemonger. He had found his mark.

Seeing Wild come his way, the thief drew his pistol. "Jonathan," he said, "you have led me here into a damn'd Trade, which I am weary of, and now I've got Money in my Pocket, I am resolv'd to go over to Holland, and try to put my self into some honest Business, by which I may get my Living, without Fear or Danger."

Wild listened intently. Facing a gun didn't scare him. He had armed himself, "as thick as an Orange with Cloves." But now it was time to put on his "Fox's Skin," time for the easygoing fast talker to make an encore. He continued to listen to the cheesemonger's plea while inching forward toward his target. Beneath his large coat, he held a pistol of his own. The discussion continued, back and forth—but only until Wild knew he had his prey in a sure shot.

Wild drew his pistol swiftly, pointed it at the cheesemonger's face, and unleashed a flurry of bullets. He then flew on him like a "Tyger," finishing the job like a "fierce butcher." Wild relieved the dead man of his money and restored the balance of his power. The cheesemonger never had a chance.

The government closed the Mint down in 1723, its inhabitants given a clean slate to get them out. The *Weekly Journal* described the amnesty day, as thousands of "Minters" littered the road, like "one of the Jewish tribes coming out of Egypt." The exodus wasn't without its spirits, though, the report noting "an ass loaded with geneva"—or gin—accompanying the men and women.

William Spiggot didn't go quietly. Charged with robbery, the twenty-nine-year-old gang leader famously refused to enter a plea until pressed by four hundred pounds of stones, and only then after more than half an hour, with "Blood being flush'd and forc'd up into his Face, and pressing as violently against the Veins and small Tendrills." Officials gave Spiggot a few days to recover before they killed him properly at Tyburn.

Before he swung, though, Spiggot did cop to his crimes, advising the ordinary of Newgate that he had committed around a hundred highway robberies, his locale of choice being Hounslow Heath. His capture and hanging landed a death blow to his gang. Wild caught its last free member, William Colthurst, shortly thereafter. Only three large gangs remained in London: the Hawkins, Shaw, and Carrick groups. If Wild wanted to control the London underworld, he needed to end the big three, and he spent the majority of 1721 attempting to do just that.

The Hawkins gang, a group of highwaymen, was the smallest of the three. Twenty-eight-year-old John Hawkins, an enormous man and a one-time butler, led the group. As a butler in the comfortable home of a distinguished family, he became taffy (fat) by drinking and eating more than his fill. Like many highwaymen, Hawkins first gambled then frittered his money away, until he found himself out of collar (unemployed). He continued to gamble, however, until he had nothing left to wager. At that point, few options remained but to get a horse and a couple of pistols and turn to the highway. No matter how much he robbed, though, he gambled more, losing enough to ensure that he was always broke.

Hawkins's brother William also belonged to the gang, as did Ralph Wilson and James Wright. Hawkins later wrote that Wilson, another degenerate gambler, was too dumb to know the difference between loaded dice and true ones, or about other gambling "bites," such as the "Slip" and the "Palm." Not surprisingly, Wilson seldom came out ahead, either, entering the highwayman's trade a starving man. Asked if he had the mettle to bear arms, Wilson answered, "Yes, as well as any Man, for the Want of Money has made me ready for any Thing." Wilson later bemoaned his decision to his confessor: "No Life is so gloomy as that of a Robber! He's a Stranger to Peace of Mind, to quiet Slumber! and is made a Property of by every Villain who knows his Circumstances. This is a Hell to one who has had any relish of a more generous Way of living. But I was enter'd, and knew not how to retreat."

The year prior, at the Queen's Head Tavern, Wright and Wild, both brandishing pistols, had locked horns in a scrum that went unsettled until Quilt Arnold and a pair of bodyguards gave their boss—who was hanging onto Wright's chin with his teeth—the advantage he needed. Wright's apprehension unnerved the rest of the group. Would he talk? It took only one man to start talking, and the rest invariably fell. More often than not, the first one to talk was safest. Many bandits devoutly followed the adage, "Save yourself now rather than worry about it later." But James Wright never said a word. He did his time.

William Hawkins, on the other hand, could hardly keep his mouth shut when pinched with Butler Fox in September 1721. He gave up everyone in the gang, including his own brother, John. The Hawkins gang had taken down a couple of high-profile targets, Lord Bruce and the Earl of Burlington, but instead of bringing the fruits of their labor to the Lost Property Office, they exported their goods to Holland. With

William Hawkins's directions, Wild seized Butler Fox at Fox's home. In court, Wild described the apprehension.

"The prisoner at first was very obstropolus, and swore he would not go with me; but I pulled out a Pistol, and swore as fast as he, that if they made any more Resistance, I'd fire among them; and with that, he grew quiet as a Lamb."

Butler Fox pleaded to the thief-taker: "For God's Sake, Mr. Wild, tell me how the Case is—"

"Ay, you Rogue," Fox's wife interjected, "this is your Friend Hawkins's Doings."

"'Tis even so," Wild confirmed. "Your Friend Hawkins has impeached ye."

Soon, practically every member of the Hawkins gang was squealing on one another, until finally, there was no one left. When John Hawkins was detained in May 1722 for robbing the Bristol mail coach, Ralph Wilson turned up to give testimony against him. When Hawkins was found guilty, the highwayman initially showed only contempt for the turncoat: "I expect to die, but yet I would not change Conditions, with the Villain that has sav'd his own Life, by swearing away mine, for I prefer Death to a Life saved in such an infamous Manner."

John Hawkins later tried to forgive his accuser, once a friend, and imparted that he did so freely. But as his execution drew closer, John Hawkins eventually took to panic and wept. "Lord Jesus, come quickly!" Hawkins pleaded moments before he dropped from the Triple Tree. The Lord didn't grant his request. He suffered mightily as he hanged, his breath refusing to leave him. Officials placed his body, "hang'd in Irons on a Gibbet," on Hounslow Heath in a display of deterrence.

Of all the gangs in London, the Shaw gang was among the bloodiest. James Shaw, a no-nonsense murdering kind, led the crew of about thirteen footpads. In the summer of 1721, Shaw, along with James Reading and "Long Isaac" Drew, robbed, beat, and killed one Philip Potts near the Tile Kilns in St. Pancras. The assault was savage even by the day's standards: With Reading's help, Shaw brained Potts with a wooden staff. The three men made off with a silver-hilted sword, a silver watch, and the remnants from Potts's pockets.

The Shaw group's downfall also began with a single arrest. After that, Wild hardly had to lift a finger; the crew eagerly betrayed one another, essentially doing Wild's job for him. First it was William Burridge for highway robbery. Burridge gave up Reading and another member named Wigley. Reading already had a reputation as a rat, so the rest of the gang nervously went into hiding. Wild waited. The snakes were rattling, scared. Sure enough, another Shaw member, Nathaniel Hawes, offered Wild information on his running partner, John James. So it went, down the line. One gangster after another busted because of the group's own self-inflicted disloyalty.

Informants were the double-edged scourge of a criminal partnership. Running with a partner made it easier to get a lot of jobs done, but it also left a thief exposed to loose talk. Nonetheless, many criminals wanted a collaborator for exactly that reason: having someone to betray if trouble arose, preferably someone younger and dumber. They called it "squeazing the chats," one associate ratting on another, who had been kept in the dark, and therefore couldn't do the same.

By the time ringleader James Shaw was caught, the reward for his capture had grown to £140. Wild's testimony at his trial highlighted the backstabbing of the thieving trade. "The Prisoner, Shaw, being apprehended for robbing Mr. Hungate, he thought likewise to save himself by impeaching Drew; but Drew going first before the Justice, impeach'd Shaw; For, says he, *there's no other Remedy, and if I don't leave off this Trade, I shall come to be hang'd.*" The Constable at Shaw's trial added, "When Shaw was taken he said, he was a dead Man. I asked him, if he could not save himself by being an Evidence? And he answered, *No, Long Isaac has sworn against me already, and I know he will hang me.*"

He wasn't wrong. Shaw swung at Tyburn on February 8, 1722.

In Wild's pursuit of the Shaw gang, it becomes clear just how muddied the line was between criminal, informer, and prosecutor (the one levying the charges in court).

After Wild busted William Burridge, the two became partners of a sort in running down the rest of the Shaw crew. Blood money certificates show that Burridge and Wild did a few jobs together, sharing the reward in some cases. Wild spent a lot of his time simply turning one thief against another. Professional perjurers had been hanging around the courtroom for years. They were known as "straw men," a piece or two of straw in the buckles of their shoes indicating that they were willing to testify for money.

One of Wild's regular informers was William Field, who he'd met during his days in the Wood Street Compter. Field had come up in the streets under Hitchen, as one of the marshal's mathematicians, before offering the Court of Aldermen information on Hitchen's shenanigans. Under Wild's guiding hand, Field's duplicitous word supported guilty convictions for James Dalton and a host of others, during a few months in the winter of 1720.

In the case of John Hawkins, the court explained its reasoning for allowing such shady characters to testify. In his 1722 court appearance, Hawkins tried in vain to have Ralph Wilson, a man of such "notorious an ill Character," discredited. The Court responded:

> *There is no doubt but he is an ill Man. His own Evidence declares it. He confesses he was concerned with you in robbing the Mail; but yet he's a legal Witness. The Wisdom of the Legislature has found it necessary to admit of the Evidence of an Accomplice, without which it would sometimes be difficult to discover and convict the Persons concern'd in a Robbery. You are not however try'd upon his single Testimony, but what he swears is corroborated in several Circumstances by the Evidence of others.*

Rapping (perjury) wasn't actively punished. Witnesses lied and then lied some more. When they were caught, nothing happened. Everyone moved on. If perjury had been discouraged more stridently, Wild's scheme of filling the courtroom with informers wouldn't have worked nearly as well. Of course, Wild was a wholehearted perjurer himself, which judges at the time either didn't see or overlooked. Will Field, meanwhile, went into the receiving business, but his courtroom stories were far from finished.

On July 22, 1722, the *Daily Journal* reported the arrest of "Major Kerrick, the chief of the street robbers." The news marked the fall of the Carrick gang, and also, an unofficial crowning. Wild had done it: He had knocked out all comers.

The Carrick gang consisted of more than thirty footpads, a large portion of their ranks having come from Ireland. With their chief locked up, Wild tore apart the Carrick gang. In a two-week span, from late July to early August, he rounded up over twenty of their number.

Twenty-seven-year-old James "Valentine" Carrick had paid his dues on the street. Eschewing his well-to-do family for the military, and then the life of a street robber, Carrick oversaw the most vicious gang in London. His nickname, "Valentine," was self-titled, a nod to his attraction to the opposite sex. As a young ensign in Spain, he had developed a carnal appetite for lewd women, and was said to have "delighted" in sexual pleasures until just moments before his execution. He was arrested, along with John Molony (alias Malhony), for assaulting William Yonge on the highway on July 1, 1722.

According to his own testimony, Yonge was riding in a sedan chair from the Bedford Head Tavern in Covent Garden when three assailants struck late on a Sunday night. One of the men set his pistol against the chairman's ear.

"God damn ye, set down, or I'll shoot you through the Head," the assailant said.

Yonge testified that the bandit, a "little, fair Man, in a black Coat, and a light Tye Wig; and I verily believe Carrick is the same Person," then turned to him.

"Your Money, Sir, I am in haste," the assailant said.

When Carrick gave his account in court, he wanted so badly to verbally spar with Yonge and catch him in a lie that he unwittingly placed himself at the scene of the crime.

"Pray, Sir, which Side of the Chair was I on when you say I robb'd you?" Carrick asked.

"On the left Side," Yonge answered.

"Now that's a Lie, for I was on the right Side."

His defense was pronounced "frivolous."

Carrick made himself comfortable at his hanging on July 18, 1722. He "laughed and smiled upon all whom he there knew; gave himself genteel Airs in fixing the Rope aright about his Neck, and as he constantly took Snuff during Prayers in the Chappel, so at the Tree he had continually some pretty gesture or other when the People were silent and expecting of something from him."

Wild took home at least £900 in reward money for bringing down the Carrick gang and that represented just one avenue of his moneymaking pursuits. His receiving business was clearing upwards of £300 a year. He had come a long way since his debtor days in the Hole at the Wood Street Compter.

By 1721, he was also seizing thieves all across England—in Bristol, Dover, Gravesend, Maidstone, and Oxford—through an extensive web of agents. The *Daily Journal* reported on November 2 of that year that "They write from Bath and Bristol, that their Roads are much infected with Robbers, and that application having been made to Jonathan Wild, that Gentleman has resolved to take a tour of those cities, as soon as his Equipages can be got ready." His commissaries sent him intelligence and looked out for wanted men and women. As Gerald Howson points out, this geographic expansion really did make Wild the thief-taker general of Great Britain and Ireland.

Even more impressive than his wide net was the fact that each time he made an arrest in a distant English town, the press reported it. Wild never missed an opportunity. He had made himself a celebrity, one of the newspaper era's first. Even his wife's health made news.

Wild began his days at seven a.m. with a "pint of sherry and bowl of thick chocolate, which he ate with a spoon." When his reception area had filled, and only then, the thief-taker emerged from his chambers. By eight a.m., his home was teeming with highwaymen, thieves, and lackeys, all elbowing among lawyers, clients, and victims of theft from the opposite end of the spectrum. Attired in his calamanco nightgown with a turban around his head, Wild conducted business all morning.

After he had heard all the requests, he retired to the back parlor to meet with his lieutenants, Quilt Arnold and Abraham Mendez, to consult the books and determine their course for the new day. For the five hundred or so thieves working under him, these discussions were a matter of life and death. If a thief had been slacking or deceptive with his accounts, Wild and his men determined at this morning meeting whom to offer up for Tyburn at the next Sessions at the Old Bailey. Having made their list, the men constructed the appropriate plans to carry out their task—whether to "Hang or Save," as one contemporary biography put it.

Plates and pictures elegantly furnished Wild's home, which bustled with a valet de chamber and servants—transportation returnees—waiting on him and even dressing him. He now walked with a silver staff with a crown handle and had a coach and six for transport. He hosted haughty dinners and parties, inviting an esteemed list of alderman, magistrates, and noblemen. The extravagant feasts seldom featured fewer than five courses.

His performance, while commendable, wasn't flawless. Philip Stanhope, the Fourth Earl of Chesterfield, noted that Wild mixed with the elite of London with an "awkward familiarity." After all, he still had an unrefined Staffordshire accent, and in his home he displayed the bloody keepsakes of his unique industry: a footpad's pistol, a piece of hangman's hemp, and more. Wild's collectibles gave silent witness to his mettle, while his turban and wig hid other souvenirs—the silver plates in his head thanks to his now twice-fractured skull. True war scars.

In addition to his new and proper home, Wild had also acquired an import-export ship, and spoke of having country acreage where he killed the deer for his King's Head gatherings. He also had the stable at the Duke's Head on Red Cross Street in Southwark. With all of the loot he and his corporation were accumulating, he needed space to store the goods, so he had a warehouse in Newington Butts in Southwark, and another on Chick Lane north of Smithfield, called the Red Lion Tavern.

In 1844, more than a century after Wild's death, the Red Lion Tavern was demolished, but not before its interior revealed an intriguing glimpse into Wild's business. According to Peter Cunningham's *Handbook of London: Past and Present*, inside the tavern lay a maze of "trap-doors, sliding panels, and cellars and passages for thieves," with many of the secret channels connecting to the chandler's shop adjacent, where one of Wild's men could complete an escape.

Before being razed, the Red Lion had been a lodging house, but it never stopped sheltering thieves and whores. Just three years prior to its demolition, the Red Lion had concealed an escaped convict named Jones for almost six weeks—even though officials had inspected the house thoroughly on numerous occasions. Subterranean passageways and hidden niches within the Red Lion allowed both murderers and the murdered to remain concealed for great lengths of time. In 1844, inspectors unearthed a skull and bones from the basement of the Red Lion Tavern.

The Victorian rediscovery of these "two strangely constructed houses . . . excited alike the attention of Royalty and parties moving in the higher walks of life." Tickets to view the Red Lion and chandler's shop were sold, and Prince Adolphus, the Duke of Cambridge, brought a "distinguished party" for an entertaining review of Wild's old warehouse. The chandler's shop posed as a front, which stirred no suspicions, but "Immediately behind the counter were the trap-doors, one of which was used as means of escape, and the other opened into secret drawers, or a depository for stolen articles," according to *Lloyd's Weekly*. False staircases, escape chutes, and myriad hiding places were astonishing enough, but stranger yet, someone was still hiding in the cellar at the time of its demolition. A chimney sweep named Williams gave up his hideout as the buildings began to crumble around him, emerging from the earth like the ghost of one of Wild's victims, rising from the crypt.

Wild understood that it wasn't just what he did that mattered, but also, what people *thought* he did. The press rarely failed to report his arrests, whether by his own prompting or not. His name had escaped the advertisements section. Now legitimate news reports focused on him, and a massive number of them at that. The blood money certificates show that he often received the reward money for bringing a highwayman to justice along with two, three, or four accomplices, but they of course never spoke of their exploits to the media. Wild may have had to split the bounty, but he received all the glory.

Even rumor played a part in managing his image. Duncan Campbell, a famed deaf and dumb soothsayer, spread word that Wild's dominion over the thieves of the land had come from his knowledge of the secrets of the black arts (Satanism). Wild actually encouraged the rumor. He understood that gossip could work in his favor; it drew gasps from the superstitious, but it also filled simpletons with fear—always a useful tool.

Perception was everything. When Wild fraternized with justices of the peace at the tavern, it looked to his underlings like the justices were in the bag. They strived to make him money and stay in his good graces. "His business in all Things," he often said, was "to make Fools of Mankind."

In 1720, the Privy Council had been looking to stem the rash of robberies on the highways. They turned to Wild, who advised that the answer to solving the problem was a matter of paying him more—£100 more. The Council agreed. A Royal Proclamation, which went into effect in 1722, increased the reward for highwaymen apprehended within five miles of London to £140.

A poet, going by the initials N. P., and describing himself as "many Years his intimate Acquaintance," observed in *Weighley, alias Wild: A poem*, "Here he played his Card very well, he impos'd on the Government, under the Notion of Serving the Publick." But as the poet noted, "Now the Price of Blood was rais'd, and some body must perish." Wild promptly delivered at least three robbers for the increased reward.

He was a man of action. He produced results.

Jack Sheppard escapes from St. Giles's Roundhouse

XII

CLEVEREST OF ALL

Sheppard was now upon his wicked Range in London.
—*THE HISTORY OF THE REMARKABLE LIFE OF JOHN SHEPPARD*

Jack Sheppard met his older brother for a drink at a tavern in the fall of 1723. Thomas wanted Jack to join him in a partnership. They drank on the matter, and both agreed that the Sheppard Brothers would make a fine team. The city was theirs for the taking.

For their first score, they made off with cash and clothes from an alehouse in Southwark. Thomas kept all the loot. *Select Trials* referred to Jack as "generous" in this matter. Far more troubling, Thomas fenced the goods through William Field, which could only mean that Jonathan Wild knew of their dealings.

In February 1724, generous Jack saw exactly where he stood with his big brother. The Sheppard alliance was beginning to flourish, and after a couple of large heists, Jack netted his first profit from the business relationship. They took Elizabeth Lyon with them, broke into the house of Mary Cook, a Clare Market linen draper, and procured £55 worth of property. On Valentine's Day, they robbed William Phillips on Drury Lane, as well as a lodger named Mrs. Kendrick.

It wasn't long before Thomas was guilty of another misstep, getting pinched while attempting to fence the loot. Once more imprisoned at Newgate, Thomas showed his true colors, and how little blood meant to him. He ratted on his brother and Lyon to save himself. Jack became a fugitive, his life worth £40 to anyone who laid hands on him. The search commenced. Jack and Elizabeth found refuge at the Queen's Head on

King Street in Westminster and bided their time. Sheppard knew £40 would attract attention.

He had been spending time with Thomas's acquaintances, mainly remnants from the Carrick gang, like James "Hell & Fury" Sykes and Joseph "Blueskin" Blake. He also found time for Lyon and Maggot. But he occupied himself in hiding with the patience of a grounded child. He missed the adrenaline of his recent capers. He fancied the mad, drunk conversations of the pub. He was bored. So when he ran into Sykes, who invited him to a game of skittles at Redgate's Victualling House, Sheppard weighed his options: Accept an offer from a relatively new acquaintance, a "brutal and foul tempered" footpad, or piss the time away shut in with Lyon.

Sheppard wanted to have fun. Plus, he was a hell of a skittles player.

A tavern game, skittles was played in or out of doors, depending on geographic traditions, on a skittle ground or skittle alley. Some taverns developed a recreation area beside the establishment in the open air or as an attached structure. The game derives from an earlier diversion called kittle-pins, comparable to bowling. Nine wooden pins lined up in threes to form a diamond, faced the shooter, who threw a wooden disk called a cheese, or else a ball, to knock them down. Gambling played a part in the game, of course, but sometimes just to the extent that the loser bought the next round of drinks. Many men rushed to the skittle grounds straight from work to get a game in before heading home. Others skipped their labors altogether. Some accounts describe players who didn't stop to eat a proper meal but instead dined at the skittle grounds. Games could last from dawn to well after midnight.

Then as now, gambling offered a great diversion for low- and high-brow alike. Card games, such as basset, faro, hazard, loo, ombre, and piquet, made or broke many a man. At some houses, people of quality wagered tens of thousands of pounds, a life's fortune won or lost.

"Betting was universal," notes Jack Lindsay in *The Monster City*. "Wagers were laid on all sorts of events, horses, prize-fights, cockfights, footraces." Little lay outside the lines of proper taste for a friendly wager. "Everyone betted on the turn of [a] coin, the cast of a dice, the sex of an unborn child; and gambling was not unknown in church." If all else failed, a wealthy man could always bet "on the speed of his footman in Hyde Park," according to Lindsay.

The lower class wagered just as often. Henry Fielding's *An Enquiry into the Causes of the Late Increase of Robbers* devotes an entire section to the subject under the heading "Of Gaming among the Vulgar; a third Consequence of their Luxury." Fielding wrote, "This Vice is the more dangerous, as it is deceitful, and contrary to every other Species of Luxury, flatters its Votaries with the Hopes of increasing their Wealth; so that Avarice itself is so far from securing us against its Temptations, that it often betrays the more thoughtless and giddy Part of Mankind into them; promising Riches without bounds."

People wagered on bull baiting, bear baiting, bear wrestling, cockfighting, and other animal conflicts, as well as speed contests like horse racing. Men fought with their bare hands in prizefighting, where gambling further roused the crowd. (Onlookers sometimes joined the fray, landing a few swings on their fighter's opponent if the contest was in doubt.) Most rings weren't elevated, making spectator participation that much easier. Women duked it out as well. Female participants had to hold coins in their hands so as to determine the winner—first to drop the coin lost—and also to prevent eye gouging and hair pulling. Challenges appeared in the newspaper, such as when Ann Field of Stoke Newington, a mule driver, called Elizabeth Stokes of London to a brawl. A *Daily Journal* advertisement documented the acceptance, Stokes's agreement reading in part: "as the famous Stoke Newington ass woman dares me to fight her for £10, I do assure her I will not fail meeting her for the said sum, and doubt not that the blows which I shall present her with, will be more difficult for her to digest than any she ever gave her asses."

The best-known fighter from this era was James Figg, an acquaintance of Jack Sheppard.

A one-time fencer—"the Atlas of the Sword"—he had turned his attention to the ring in 1718, at age twenty-three. The six-foot heavyweight became modern boxing's first champion. A 1718 *Daily Courant* ad promoted one of Figg's earliest bouts: "At the Boarded House in Marylebone-Fields, on Wednesday next, being the 23rd of April, will be perform'd a Tryal of Skill, between Thomas Lewis, Master of the Noble Science of Defense, and James Figg from Thame in Oxfordshire, Master of the said Science. Note, The Prize will be fought Wet or Dry."

The following year, Figg opened his famous English School of Arms and Art of Self-Defense academy on Tottenham Court Road (later moved to Oxford Road). Figg's academy modernized many aspects of the sport, such as an elevated ring, a wooden-railed ring enclosure, a referee (outside the ring), and rules to declare a victor (last man standing). Figg did well enough for himself that Hogarth featured him in the second painting of *A Rake's Progress*, and poet John Byrom memorialized him in "Upon a Trial of Skill," which began:

> Long was the great Figg by the prize-fighting swains
> Sole monarch acknowledged of Marybone plains.

Sheppard was itching for a drink when he ran into Sykes in April 1724. Sykes said he was looking for a fourth for a game of skittles, and skittles was Sheppard's game. He could sling with the best of them.

For Sheppard it wasn't just about the game. He yearned for some companionship other than Lyon's. He enjoyed crowds, the bantering patrons of a boozing ken. The bounty had been placed on his head for only a few days, but when Sykes asked him to join him for a game at Redgate's Victualling House, Sheppard could hardly conceal his desire. When Sykes said there were a couple of "Chubs that we might make a Penny," Sheppard now had a financial incentive to boot.

A proven athlete, Sykes had made the papers as a running footman in 1719. One article noted that Sykes was so fast that he could outrace horses over a two-mile course. Inside Redgate's, Sykes bought the first round, and as the game began, Sheppard let down his guard. He was out in the open, and anyone could have recognized him and aimed for the bounty on his head.

No one got the chance. Sykes had plans. The invitation was a ploy to get Jack to Redgate's. Jack had picked the wrong man to trust. As he took his turn at the wooden pins, into the pub entered Constable Price from Seven Dials. With Hell & Fury's direction, the constable corralled Sheppard and hauled him before magistrate Justice Parry. Sheppard was charged for the Cook and Phillips break-ins and incarcerated at St. Giles's Roundhouse—the same prison where he'd bullied the beadle and ousted Lyon almost a year prior.

Sheppard was slated to appear before the court first thing in the morning. He planned to miss the appointment.

Because the beadle had a history with Sheppard, he locked the prisoner in the most secure cell, on the top floor of the two-storied St. Giles. But the beadle didn't search Sheppard thoroughly, if at all. Sheppard had a razor in his pocket—not much to the average person, but to him, a tool of great value.

He took stock of his cell. The door was thick, and he lacked the necessary instruments to work the lock. The windows were barred. He looked to the ceiling. Naturally agile, he displayed a deft athleticism when it came to climbing. He also had the necessary pluck. The roof it was.

With his razor, Sheppard cut one of the wooden spindles off a chair in his cell. Now he had two tools. He pulled the mattress beneath his target area to catch falling debris and dampen the noise. With the spindle and razor, he dug his way out from above, penetrating the ceiling to reach the roof tiles. Within a couple of hours of being locked away, he could see the night sky. It was nine p.m.

The streets below bustled. As he made space to pass through the roof, a tile or brick tumbled down the sloping roof and plunked a pedestrian. The onlooker cried out "Prison break!"—which pushed Jack into double time. He tossed the remaining tiles, raining them down on the pedestrians below, and emerged from the top of the prison with a bed-sheet and blanket. He dashed across the roof and dropped down the backside of St. Giles from a rope made of linens. He touched down amid the headstones of the neighboring churchyard just before the beadle reached his cell.

Sheppard hopped the churchyard wall, but instead of running from the scene, which would have elicited a chase, he joined the throng in front of the prison, everyone still hollering to alert the prison's keepers. As Sheppard recalled, "All staring up, some crying, there's his Head, there he goes behind the Chimney." Some say that Sheppard himself joined in, pointing to the roof to announce that he'd spotted the escapee, but either way, he was free. He fled through the crowd as they gaped at the London sky, waiting for a body to appear.

"I was well enough diverted with the Adventure, and then went off about my business," he said.

Sheppard had barely escaped before he returned to his pilfering ways. What else could he do? He was a thief now. He had no other occupation.

On May 19, 1724, Sheppard was hanging out with a footpad named Benson when the two came across a cull arguing with a whore about a pocket watch that she'd attempted to steal from him. Sheppard and Benson saw an opportunity. Benson tried for the watch, but the man cried "Pickpocket! Stop thief!" The two men sped to escape, charging through Leicester Fields. Benson made it through the crowd, but a sergeant of the guard from Leicester House snatched Jack and turned him over to a constable. Sheppard spent the night at St. Ann's Roundhouse, a prisoner anew.

The next morning, Lyon came to visit him, but she aroused suspicion, so she too was locked up as a possible accomplice. Justice Walters transferred the pair to the New Prison at Clerkenwell (today Islington) to account for the Cook and Phillips robberies once again. At the New Prison, Sheppard and Lyon played husband and wife, and therefore were allowed to share a cell. Sheppard's reputation drew the attention of fellow thieves and many so-called "cracksmen," who visited him to share their kind words and, more importantly, saws and files and the like. Sheppard had no intention of making his stay a lengthy one.

Sheppard did have an additional card up his sleeve. He could always rat on a few of his cronies, which in this case, he did. But he provided information so minimal and of such poor value that officials nullified the deal. The next stop would be Newgate if he didn't come up with a new plan—and soon.

Captain Geary, the keeper at the New Prison, learned of Sheppard's recent history. To ensure against a similar breach, Geary had Sheppard and Lyon put away in a sturdy pen called the Newgate Ward, and for good measure he fit Sheppard with chains and heavy weights.

Sunday evening, May 24. Sheppard still hadn't budged. He was in a tight spot. The New Prison was tougher to crack than St. Giles, and he had to break Lyon out, too; no small task. The tools from the stream of visitors made releasing himself from his shackles easy. He cut through the iron links and then focused on the window, where iron bars and a sturdy wooden beam blocked passage. He used his saw to take out an iron bar, leaving the wooden muntin beam, nine inches thick and solid oak. In his box of contraband tools, he had a gimlet. His carpentry skills now served him well. If he bored enough holes into the wood, he could weaken it.

He created an opening wide enough to slip through, but he needed to get Lyon's ample figure out the window and down a distance of twenty-five feet to the yard below. He directed her to shed any unessential clothing, which he used to assemble a rope—in this case, petticoats tied to blankets. He secured the line around her waist and lowered her slowly. Then he tied the rope to one of the iron bars in the window and followed her down.

"But where are they Escap'd to?" asks Sheppard's *History*. "Why out of one Prison into another. The Reader is to understand, that the New Prison and Clerkenwell Bridewell lye Contiguous to one another." In other words, their descent had landed them in the neighboring prison yard. Now they had to ascend an imposing twenty-two-foot wall in the dead of night, at two a.m. Then atop the wall they had to overcome a *chevaux de frise*—a barrier of crisscrossing iron spikes and barbs.

In the darkness, he dropped to his hands and knees to inspect the base of the wall. At the wooden gate, he discovered he could make use of the bolts and hinges to secure his feet, and then use his gimlet to dig holes into the wood above for hand- and footholds. In this fashion, he climbed the twenty-two-foot gate. He balanced, he steadied. Foot after hand, he climbed to the top, sat on the gate, and looked down—but there was no time to rest. He tossed the blanket rope down to Lyon. One pull at a time, he hauled her to the top. When Lyon lost her footing against the gate, he had to hold the rope, supporting the full weight of his paramour in midair. Both at the top of the gate, Jack eased Lyon down on freedom's side and followed her. Scaling the wall had taken just ten minutes.

Sheppard's life featured many acts for which he would be remembered, but in some circles this New Prison escape transcended all else. Simply put, the feat was miraculous. Even the keepers at the New Prison were so impressed that they preserved the instruments of his escape to display the art of the act.

The people at large didn't know Sheppard's name, but by twice freeing himself from bondage, he had become a hero to criminals citywide. As author Horace Bleackley wrote, "The underworld of London began to regard this redoubtable Jack Sheppard as the cleverest of them all."

He may have had a growing inclination to work alone—considering what his brother and other thieves had done for him—but his rising stature meant that veteran thieves and newcomers alike now sought him out as a partner. Being in demand gave Sheppard the upper hand, and he worked with notorious thieves William Blewit and Edward Burnworth, as well as novices. Two such greenhorns were Charles Grace, a cooper, and Anthony Lamb, a mathematical instrument maker's apprentice, whom Sheppard knew from the Black Lion. Grace and Lamb requested Sheppard's expertise in June 1724 to take down a lodger staying at Lamb's master's home on Wych Street in the Strand. A sucker for compliments, Sheppard agreed to direct the heist. Lamb gained them entrance to the house, and once inside, Sheppard stationed Grace beside the sleeping lodger with a pistol to his head. With his underlings in place, Sheppard lifted cash and goods worth £300.

Afterward, Grace, who needed his share of the money to quench the refined tastes of a whore, disappeared. Sheppard also made a clean getaway. But Anthony Lamb was picked up almost immediately for the robbery. Without much prodding, Lamb gave a thorough account of the heist, and subsequently received a sentence of transportation. Yet another felony connected to Sheppard's name.

But it wasn't for nothing; it was a good score. Part of Sheppard's haul included a luxurious paduasoy suit worth £20, attire fit for a gentleman. He had it tailored and wore it with the pride appropriate for a man of his growing reputation. It was the first sign that Sheppard's accomplishments were going to his head.

Far from running scared, Sheppard ventured to his old haunts, "like a dog to his vomit," to the neighborhood where his thieving began. On July 12, Sheppard targeted the very man who had saved him from a childhood spent in a workhouse. He set out to rob the kindly William Kneebone.

To pull off the job, Sheppard paired up with the bridle-cull (highwayman) "Blueskin" Blake. Blake was a bit older than Sheppard and had been thieving since childhood. *The Newgate Calendar* recorded that Blake had "been a thief almost from the cradle," and that "his habits of vice increased with his growing years." As a boy, Blueskin went to school for nearly six years, but he showed little propensity for education. Nevertheless, it was at school that he met William Blewit. Through Blewit, Blake was introduced to Jonathan Wild and entered the thief-taker's junior league.

Young Blake picked pockets on London's streets, focusing on pedestrians around Lincoln's Inn Fields. By age fifteen, Blake knew the interiors of the city's array of prisons and workhouses. But he was never more than an ordinary thief. For him, it was a matter of quantity. He stole plenty.

Blake grew into a man of disheveled brawn. He was never a gentleman of the road, but rather a coarse, rugged, unkempt highwayman. On one occasion, after he stopped a coach from Hampstead and met with obstinacy from a woman in the carriage, who declared that Blueskin was sure to hang for the deed, he flew off the handle.

"You double Pox'd Salivated Bitch," he said. "Come, no dallying, deliver your Money, or else your life must be a Sacrifice to my Fury." Then he ordered the woman, a bawdy house operator named Mother Wybourn, to strip naked.

As the years passed, Blake robbed with Richard Oakey and John Levee and drifted into the Carrick gang. He amassed a pretty penny from his multitude of robberies, but apparently lost a great deal at the gaming tables with Carrick. Through it all, Blueskin remained interlinked with Jonathan Wild. In 1723, Wild arrested Blake after a fierce struggle that left Blake with a saber gash. Yet, in prison Blake received from Wild an allowance of three shillings and sixpence a week, and the thief-taker picked up the bill to have him stitched up as well.

A year later, in July 1724, Blake stood with Jack Sheppard, looking at William Kneebone's draper shop across from St. Mary's Church in the Strand.

We don't know the impetus for Sheppard's sudden betrayal of Kneebone. We do know, however, that Kneebone was ready for it. Someone had tipped him off that Sheppard had targeted his abode. The warning made little difference, nor did his preparations: "Having heard that two of my Neighbours' Houses had been robbed, and receiving some Intimation that mine was marked down for the next, I took particular Care to see all my Doors and Windows fast, before I went to Bed: Notwithstanding which, it was broke open that very Night."

At midnight, Sheppard and Blake entered the home through the rear cellar by cutting through a set of oak bars. Sheppard later revealed that he'd worked on the wooden bars over a two-week stretch, whittling through the wood a bit at a time. They moved from the cellar to Kneebone's workshop, and then throughout the house. Sheppard opened every lock and bolt in his path. He and Blake robbed with ease for nearly three hours. By night's end, they made off with 108 yards of woolen cloth and an assortment of smaller items, all worth about £50.

Dawn revealed the deed to Kneebone. "I was call'd up about four in the Morning, and found my House broke open. The Bar of my

Cellar-Window was cut, the Bolts of my Cellar door were drawn, and the Padlock wrench'd off."

Sheppard and Blake transferred their spoils to a rented stable near the Horse Ferry in Westminster. They then made a deadly mistake: They brought the woolen cloth to William Field to fence. Field's family and Blake's both hailed from Wapping, and Field occasionally boarded at the Rosemary Lane home and brandy den of Blueskin's mother. Sheppard and Blueskin briefed Field on the details of the Kneebone robbery.

Incensed at Sheppard's betrayal, Kneebone called on Jonathan Wild to rectify matters.

A depiction of Wild seizing Sheppard
by George Cruikshank
from William Harrison Ainsworth's Jack Sheppard: A Romance

XIII

WILD VERSUS SHEPPARD

He [Wild] was the uncrowned king of Newgate prison. Both felons
and turnkeys trembled at his nod.
—HORACE BLEACKLEY AND STEWART MARSH ELLIS, *JACK SHEPPARD*

Sheppard had once attended one of Wild's mid-morning prig assemblies
at the King's Head in the Old Bailey where the thief-taker held court in
his robe and slippers. "I was indeed twice at a Thief-Catcher's Levee, and
must confess the Man treated me civilly; he complimented me on my
Successes, said he heard that I had both [a] Hand and Head admirable
well turn'd to Business, and that I and my Friends should be always welcome to him; But caring not for his Acquaintance, I never troubled him,
nor had we any Dealings together." Despite being treated courteously,
elsewhere Sheppard offered his less than flattering thoughts on Wild's
trade:

> *I have often lamented the scandalous Practice of Thief-catching, as it is*
> *call'd, and the publick Manner of offering Rewards for stolen Goods, in*
> *Defiance of two several Acts of Parliament; the Thief-Catchers living*
> *sumptuously, and keeping of publick Office of Intelligence: these who*
> *forfeit their Lives every Day they breathe, and deserve the Gallows as*
> *richly as any of the Thieves, send us as their Representatives to Tyburn*
> *once a Month: thus they hang by Proxy, while we do it fairly in Person.*

Now, with the Kneebone robbery, the lives of Jonathan Wild and
Jack Sheppard finally collided. Kneebone approached Wild with details

of the crime the following morning. The homeowner had a suspect list of one, and Wild put the wheels in motion to deliver Jack Sheppard. But as he often did, first he went public with information about the robbery.

An advertisement appeared in the *Daily Post* on July 17, five days after the break-in, putting forward a £20 reward for anyone willing to report on those responsible. At first glance, it was just another of Wild's business ads. But behind the scenes, Wild had been chomping at the bit to place it. He'd been looking for justification to bring Sheppard in for some time.

From the beginning, Sheppard had roused Wild's attention. The housebreaker was strong, crafty, and wanted no part of Wild's criminal machinery, having shunned all of the thief-taker's advances to work under him. Sheppard's continued independence was bad for business. It needed to be stopped, and Wild had every intention of doing just that. All the while, Sheppard did what he did. He stole. If caught, he escaped.

As the young thief's reputation grew, his independence propelled him to the top of Wild's wanted list. He had partnered with Blake and others, so Sheppard had no problem working with a companion—he just didn't want anyone ordering him to do so, or bossing him around. He wandered across gang lines, but he never formally joined one. Still, Wild worried that the popular young thief might take a shot at picking up the pieces of the Carrick gang by grabbing James Carrick's open spot at the top as its leader. But Sheppard had no such intentions.

Instead, Sheppard and Blake began running as highwaymen following the Kneebone robbery. On July 19 and 20, they committed a couple of low-profit heists along Hampstead Road. John Pargiter, a chandler, was deep in his cups when Sheppard and Blueskin confronted him leaving a Hampstead inn. Sheppard relieved the drunk of three lousy shillings, and Blake closed the matter by pistol-whipping Pargiter into a ditch. Sheppard helped Pargiter out of the ditch and saved him from possibly drowning in the mud before they departed the scene.

The following day, the embarrassed chandler pointed the finger at a couple of soldiers in the area that night. The Brightwell brothers, besides being soldiers in the Grenadier Guard, were men of high character and great sobriety. According to the *British Journal*, one was even educated in Latin and "Roman Antiquities." The brothers ultimately were acquitted, but not before one of them caught gaol-fever. He died less than two weeks later.

Sheppard and Blake committed their final act on the highway on July 21, again for little gain. It was Sheppard's last performance as a highwayman, though not for lack of effort. He'd made a bold push to become a gentleman of the road. He armed himself to the nines, with pistols, rope, and gag, but ultimately his bid fell flat. He laid blame for this failure on Blueskin. Once again, the young thief must have wondered why he ever bothered to take a partner. Said Sheppard later, when describing his collaborator: "He was concern'd along with me in the three Robberies on the Hampstead Road besides that of Mr. Kneebone, and one other. Tho' he was an able-bodied Man and capable of any Crime, even Murder, he was never Master of a Courage or Conduct suitable to our Enterprizes." Sheppard illustrated his point:

> *The last Summer, I hired two Horses for us at an Inn in Piccadilly, and being arm'd with Pistols, &c. we went upon Enfield Chase, where a Coach pass'd us with two Footmen and four young Ladies, who had with them their Gold Watches, Tweezer Cases and other things of Value; I declar'd immediately for attacking them, but Blueskin's Courage dropt him, saying that he would first refresh his Horse then Follow, but he designedly delayed till we had quite lost the Coach and Hopes of the Booty.*

Blake may have been a bull-hearted wimp, but Sheppard never cut it as a highwayman, either.

With Sheppard bumbling around on the road, Wild focused on his girlfriend, Elizabeth Lyon, well-known by now as the woman whom the gallant Sheppard had carried to freedom. (More than a century later, author Alexandre Dumas *père* enshrined this tactic for detectives in *The Mohicans of Paris*: "Cherchez la femme!" *Look for the woman!*) Wild found Lyon without much trouble at a brandy shop in Temple Bar, and she held up no better than anyone else previously associated with Sheppard. She disclosed that her beau was at Blueskin's mother's house on Rosemary Lane.

A couple hours after Wild had taken Lyon into custody, Quilt Arnold found Jack in a bedroom at Mother Blake's house, as expected. Sheppard had no intention of being retaken after such a brief liberty. He pushed his pistol into Arnold's chest and fired without hesitation. But the pistol misfired. Sheppard's tracker didn't return the favor. Instead, Arnold secured him and called for a nearby magistrate to arrest the thief.

The incident marked a crossing of the line. When Arnold entered the bedroom, it was kill or be killed. Sheppard had pulled the trigger. He understood his position completely. He knew what lay ahead.

News of the event obviously landed in the press, marking Sheppard's first such exposure. Amid the shaky spelling and details—not to mention the reporter's confusion of the two Sheppard brothers—we see Wild receiving credit for a capture made by one of his agents. From the *Daily Journal*, July 25, 1724: "Yesterday one Shepheard, a notorious Housebreaker, who lately made his Escape from New Prison, and had impeach'd his own Brother, was committed to Newgate, having been retaken by Jonathan Wild; he is charged with several Burglaries, &c."

Here was the firing salvo. The thief's thief, a burgeoning hero of the prig class, stood poised to become a popular hero to the general public. Sheppard was the picture of vitality: young, strong, and healthy. He had a childlike smile, liked to crack jokes, and had an esteemed reputation among London's whores. Readers naturally would look for a foil, and here he was: Jonathan Wild. The thief-taker understood the significance of Sheppard's popularity. He needed to have Jack Sheppard put down, and fast.

Wild, now age forty-one, wore the countenance of a much older man. Author Richard Holmes calls the Wild of 1724 "an older, hard-bitten figure." He walked the city streets packing pistols. He lingered across the street from Newgate Prison with his silver staff in hand like a gravedigger in a cemetery. From a distance, with hat and wig, Wild blended in with his contemporaries. However, up close and exposed, he was the image of the perfect brute. His bald head was covered in silver and scars; his whole body gave proof of his mettle: seventeen different wounds by way of gun, sword, and dagger. Gout hobbled him, and a limp stuttered his gait.

In August 1724, the aging Wild met poet and playwright John Gay in Windsor. Gay hadn't yet written *The Beggar's Opera*, but four years later, this popular work cemented the thief-taker's image for generations. *The Flying Post or Weekly Medley* later gave an account of the meeting between the notable men, stating that Gay and an associate found Wild alone at a tavern. After mutual recognition, effusive conversation ensued. Gay pushed wine on Wild, who "discours'd with great freedom on his profession, and set it in such a light, that the poet imagin'd he might work up the incidents for the stage."

Sheppard's brother had betrayed him. His girlfriend had given him up. His cronies were practically running over one another to turn on him. Now it was time for the rat. When Wild needed information to secure the conviction on behalf of Kneebone, he called an old pal. William Field came running.

Did Field know anything about the robbery? By chance, he did. He had been down at Sheppard's Westminster warehouse just the other day, in fact. He had so much information that he could probably put himself at the scene and profess his own involvement. An accomplice turning on his cohorts would lock the case down for the wily old thief-taker.

Field had been handling stolen loot for Thomas Sheppard, Blueskin Blake, and Hell & Fury Sykes, among others. He also kept busy by appearing in the courtroom on behalf of Wild, appearing at the Sessions House to give "evidence" against a host of thieves. It's estimated that the serial impeacher was responsible for the death sentences of between fifteen and thirty people. His name and signature also appear on a blood money certificate under Wild's signature; Field received a £5 share for the capture of a housebreaker in Southwark.

Sheppard never held a high opinion of Field, who he felt lacked the grit to steal for himself. But Sheppard assumed they were "all of a piece." Wrong again. Sheppard had botched the Kneebone robbery mightily. First, he had wronged a man who had tried so hard to help him in years past. Sheppard should have known not to rob someone who would be so insulted by the act that he would stop at nothing to see justice done. Sheppard had also wildly misplaced his trust in Will Field, even underestimating Field's willingness and gumption to steal himself.

Sheppard explained what happened next: "In a Day or two after, to the great Surprize of Blueskin and my self, we found the Warehouse broke open, the Cloth gone, and only a Wrapper or two of no value left; we concluded, as it appeared after, that Field had plaid at Rob-Thief with us." After hearing about the inventory at the Horse Ferry warehouse, Field slipped out after dark, secured the stolen woolen cloth, and hurried the Kneebone evidence over to Wild. Everything was set. Field was ready to cop to having been a part of it, and the city's eminent sleuth had the merchandise to prove it.

Kneebone paid his former ward a visit in his cell and demanded an explanation. Sheppard admitted to it all, though he pointed the finger for masterminding it elsewhere. Ill company was the blame. Sheppard was transferred the next day, July 24, from the New Prison in Clerkenwell to Newgate Prison.

Newgate hadn't changed much since Defoe's days there twenty years earlier, which he described in *Moll Flanders*. "'Tis impossible to describe the terror of my mind, when I was first brought in, and when I looked round upon all the horrors of that dismal place . . . the hellish noise, the roaring, swearing and clamour, the stench and nastiness, and all the dreadful afflicting things that I saw there, joined to make the place seem an emblem of hell itself, and a kind of an entrance into it."

Newgate Prison was the oldest, biggest, and most ominous in London. It was also believed to be the most secure.

XIV

THE TRIAL OF JACK SHEPPARD

*Sheppard, the notorious housebreaker, who lately escaped from
the New Prison and was retaken by Jonathan Wild and committed
to Newgate, attempted to escape from the gaol a day or two ago;
several saws and instruments proper for such a design being
found about his bed, he is since confined in an apartment called
the Stone Room, kept close and sufficiently loaded with irons to
prevent his designs for the future.*
—ATTRIBUTED TO DEFOE, *APPLEBEE'S ORIGINAL WEEKLY JOURNAL*,
AUGUST 1, 1724

Newgate was one of the two western gates in the walls that encircled the
Roman settlement of Londinium. In time, its gatehouse became Newgate Prison, a jail for felons and debtors. The Old Bailey (from the Old
French *baille*, meaning "defensive wall") emerged from a medieval expansion of the prison, but burned down in the Great Fire. It was rebuilt in
1673, tall and foreboding in unadorned brick. The courthouse building
connected to the southern end of Newgate Prison by a tunnel, which ran
past the old Roman wall.

Sir Peter Delmé, the distinguished lord mayor of London, sat at
the bench along with the aldermen, all elegantly bedecked. Sir William
Thompson, the recorder, ran the show. Sheppard sat in the large room
with dignitaries behind him and accuser and witnesses facing him. A mirror placed above the dock—to allow light from the windows to illuminate
the scene—reflected Sheppard's pug face to the spectators of the court.
Thompson announced the three indictments against young Sheppard:

THE CONDEMNED HOLD OF NEWGATE PRISON, ONE OF THE SAFEST
CELLS IN ALL OF ENGLAND, AND THE DEAD MAN'S WAITING ROOM

the Cook, Phillips, and Kneebone robberies. The first and second were dismissed quickly for lack of evidence.

Sheppard spoke without fear when the judge called his name on Thursday, August 13, but no amount of bravery could hide the resentment that faltered his speech and made him stutter. The proceedings moved ahead with the Kneebone indictment, in which Sheppard was charged with stealing 108 yards of woolen cloth, two silver spoons, and other goods from the home of his former benefactor on the night of July 12, 1724. According to the law at the time, the aggrieved party served as prosecutor, and the prisoner wasn't allowed counsel. Sheppard sat alone in the dock at the center of the Sessions House.

Kneebone commenced with his description of events, displaying more disappointment than ill will: "I went to see him there [Newgate] and asked him how he could be so ungrateful as to rob me after I had shown him so much kindness. He confessed he had been very ungrateful in doing so, but said he had been drawn into it by ill company, and then he gave a particular description of the manner of his breaking into my house."

Thief-taker Wild testified next:

The prosecutor came and told me that his house had been broken into and he had lost a large quantity of woolen cloth. That he suspected the prisoner was concerned in the fact because he had committed several rogueries thereabouts, and he desired me to inquire after the goods. I promised to do him all the service I could, and accordingly, understanding that the prisoner was acquainted with Joseph Blake, alias Blueskin, and William Field, I sent for Field, who coming to me I told him if he would make an ingenuous confession I believed I could prevail with the Court to admit him as evidence. Then he discovered the prisoner and gave an account how some of the cloth they stole was disposed of; by which means the prisoner was apprehended and part of the cloth was found.

And finally Field: "The prisoner told me and Blueskin that he knew of a ken worth milling—that is, a house worth breaking—for he said there was something good to be got in it."

Sheppard fumed. Field continued.

Blueskin and I disapproved of the design, because we did not think it could be easily done, but the prisoner told us that it might be done with all the pleasure in life, for he had lived with the prosecutor and was acquainted with every part of the house and would undertake it himself if we would but stand where we were and give a good look-out. We agreeing to this, he cut out the bar of the cellar and window and so got into the shop and brought out three parcels of cloth, which we carried away.

Sheppard seethed. He understood Wild's performance, and Knee-bone had every reason to take offense. But as for Field—Sheppard could barely control his contempt. Never mind his own guilt, Field was portraying himself as though he had had the guts for banditry and been there in the thick of it. When it came time for his defense, Sheppard attempted a character assassination of the witness, his resentment prevailing. As he later remarked of the peacher, "I told him all the particulars of the story, never dreaming the rascal would make such an ill use of the confidence I put in him." In his *Narrative*, Sheppard wished that "Field may repent and amend his wicked Life, for a greater Villain there is not breathing."

Sheppard's defense was pathetic at best. The crowd in the courtroom unanimously predicted the outcome. The jury deliberated and returned in no time, having found Jack Sheppard guilty as charged. It was hard to find otherwise; after all, the defendant had failed to prove or even state his innocence. But Sheppard no doubt planned to obtain his freedom later.

The next day, Jack Sheppard was sentenced to death.

Newgate officials remained on edge as they waited for the recorder to issue his "Dead Warrant." In the meantime, prison staff kept a vigilant eye. Newspaper accounts of Sheppard's previous two escapes were on everyone's lips, the turnkeys included. The prison keeper, William Pitt, was laid up and away, so Bodenham Rouse, a prison worker with nearly twenty-five years' experience, took charge. Turnkey Rouse staffed the prison with his most trustworthy lineup: Alston, Ireton, Langley, and Perry.

In late August, Rouse and his staff received news that they could drop their shoulders: The Dead Warrant included Sheppard's name. His date of execution was set for Friday, September 4, along with Anthony Upton and Joseph Ward. Now Rouse could move Sheppard to the Condemned Hold, the dead man's waiting room, one of the safest cells in all of England, and known as the "stone jug." But Sheppard's demeanor gave them pause. He laughed, he bantered, he was relaxed. When told to ready himself to meet his maker, Sheppard demurred.

"Yes, so my great Lord and Master says; but, by God, I'll do my best endeavors to make him a false prophet."

Another prisoner, Lumley Davis, on the other hand, had been teetering back and forth. He had designs for his own escape, but he was also clinging to the slight chance of a pardon. When his chances of amnesty momentarily improved, Davis was buoyed. When a pardon was just as quickly denied one last time, Davis surrendered—to God, his soul; then, to Sheppard, all of his tools for escape.

At one end of the Lodge at Newgate lay a bar where prisoners and turnkeys alike enjoyed drink; on the opposite side stood a large and sturdy door with iron spikes at its top, which separated the lodge from the hatchway. The hatchway connected to, and was open to, the Condemned Hold, allowing for prisoners to enter when they had visitors. On Friday, August 29, less than a week until his day of reckoning, Sheppard went to work in the hatchway and began filing through one of the spikes. In the distance, westward, Sheppard knew that the man who supplied the tools for his freedom was swinging from the Tyburn Tree as he steadily sawed and filed away.

By Monday, August 31, Sheppard's work on the spike was nearly complete. He didn't slow even for visitors. He continued to saw while Lyon came for a visit, bringing Poll Maggot along as well. They talked to him and kept watch all afternoon. By six that evening, Sheppard had done it. The spike above the door finally gave way. The resulting gap offered just enough space for him to slither through.

At the bar, turnkeys drank beer served to them by the Widow Spurling. A large porch obscured their view to the hatchway. At the very moment that Sheppard made his move, the turnkeys later admitted, incredibly, that the topic of their conversation as they drank at the bar was Sheppard's remarkable Clerkenwell escape. They had no idea that he was in the process of surpassing that event.

Once above the door, Sheppard called on Lyon's heft to aid him. His lover obliged, and along with Maggot, the women pulled their man through the opening. Disguised in a woman's nightgown—which helpfully covered the fetters around his legs—he hobbled right through Newgate's front door. The three hurried into the street, where Sheppard quickly jumped into a hackney coach at the top of Old Bailey Street.

And just like that, he was gone. Sheppard had done it again.

Newspapermen converged on Newgate to observe the scene of Sheppard's latest caper. No one had ever managed such a feat, escaping from the Condemned Hold in broad daylight, turnkeys in the room, and then walking out the door. Wagstaff, the ordinary of Newgate, gave a brief description of the events.

> *He got loose from his chains, by an almost impracticable, and unheard of contrivance and invention; and, who has often said, that there was neither lock nor key ever made, that he should make any difficulty to open (for he could open keys as well as locks) Him! (Whom well guarded and strong prisons cannot contain, and who is now upon his wicked and bloody ramble in the world.) We hope the public will contribute the upmost to defend themselves against.*

The jailers, disgusted and embarrassed, wasted little time in mounting a search. The *Post Boy* reported on September 8, "Yesterday, several Persons went Post out of Town in quest of John Sheppard the Condemn'd Malefactor." Alston, Ireton, Langley, and Rouse launched their pursuit, while Wild initiated his own in a separate direction. He started again with Elizabeth Lyon. With Sheppard nowhere to be found, Wild settled on having Lyon locked up.

For the most part, the relationship between Sheppard and Lyon—which shot from one extreme to the other at any given moment—centered on crime. Sheppard knew she didn't always have his best interests at heart, but neither could he extricate himself from her orbit. "I have sometimes procured her liberty, and she at others has done her utmost to obtain mine, and at other times she has again betrayed me into the hands of justice." His final summary? "A more wicked, deceitful, and lascivious wretch there is not living in England. She has proved my bane."

In the hours immediately following his escape from the Condemned Hold, Sheppard headed not to Lyon—where he knew he would be vulnerable—but to Blackfriars Stairs to spend time with another prostitute.

He and Lyon never saw each other again.

From Blackfriars Stairs, Sheppard met up with friend and butcher Will Page. They knocked back a few drinks at the White Hart, after which Sheppard finally removed the chains from his legs with a saw. In the days ahead, Sheppard and Page went to Warnden in Northamptonshire to hide out at the home of some of Page's relatives. They wore new blue butcher's smocks, the escapee portraying himself as a butcher's son from Clare Market.

In that first week of September, a hailstorm damaged hop crops in Winchester, and high winds contributed to the drowning deaths of two men and two women at sea in Long-Reach. A turpentine fire nearly destroyed Mr. Dodd's Oil Shop at the Olive in Fenchurch Street. In Edinburgh, a drunk Scot watched an Irishman bugger his wife, whom he then forgave for adultery. A week later, French cook Louis Varny, described as "disorder'd in his Senses" by the *British Journal*, slit his own throat, then jumped from a third-story garret onto a street in Pallmall. The fall "dash'd out his Brains." Captivating yarns all—but nothing seized the public's attention like the jailbreaker.

Friday, September 4, was to have been his execution day. In Tyburn, in the middle of the road, Ward and Upton hung lifeless from the Triple Tree. That same day, a mysterious letter appeared in the *London News*, purportedly written by Sheppard and addressed to the famed hangman, Jack Ketch.

John Ketch, a seventeenth-century executioner, had earned notoriety by botching the beheadings of William Russell and James Scott, First Duke of Monmouth (also the first illegitimate son of King Charles II), who had instigated the Monmouth Rebellion to depose King James II. Ketch died in 1686, but the name stuck. Subsequent men who took the role of executioner also took the name. The position of the common hangman was filled by ex-cons who were pardoned to take the job. Some continued their criminal ways, such as John Price, who held the post of

Jack Ketch in 1718 and was condemned the same year for the murder of Elizabeth White.

The letter from Sheppard to Ketch in the *London News* reads, in part:

> *To show you that I am in charity I am now drinking your health and a bon repos to poor Joseph [Ward] and Anthony [Upton]. I am gone a few days for the air, but design speedily to embark, and this night I am going upon a mansion for a supply. It's a stout fortification, but what difficulties cannot I encounter, dear Jack. You find that bars and chains are but trifling obstacles in the way of your friend and servant.*

The letter was signed "John Sheppard," and coolly mentioned his whereabouts as "my residence in *Terra Australis incognita*"—Latin for "unknown southern lands." The French flair and this hint of Latin cast damning doubt on the authenticity of the letter.

A postscript to the letter mentions Mr. Applebee, for whose *Original Weekly Journal* Defoe was writing at the time. In his biography of the writer, William Minto observes that "In connexion with *Applebee's* . . . Defoe went some way towards anticipating the work of the modern Special Correspondent. He apparently interviewed distinguished criminals in Newgate, and extracted from them the stories of their lives." Following Sheppard's escape, Defoe, now in his mid-sixties, kept a keen eye on his movements. He was always looking for news, and at the moment, the escape artist *was* the news. Defoe had found the perfect subject.

Page was broke. Sheppard was both broke and bored. His stay in the country was nearly as tough on him as the Condemned Hold. He needed excitement. Why live if not well? The duo left the Northamptonshire countryside—the law on their tail or not—determined to pass time in the city for a spell.

Sheppard and Page had been casing a watch shop for nearly an hour. It was almost nine p.m. on September 5. They'd been chatting to the shop boy on each pass, gibing him for letting his master keep him so late. "Well done, my lad, now I like you," Sheppard said tellingly to the boy as he was putting up his tools for the night.

Page was no criminal. A respectable young man from Clare Market, the son of a butcher, his only vice was his devotion to his childhood friend. Page was enamored with Sheppard, particularly after the prig's latest escape from the Condemned Hold. Page was a hanger-on. But the fondness was reciprocated. Sheppard called him a "trusty comrade," and in fact, Page may have been the only truly loyal friend Sheppard ever had. In a world in which thief turned on thief and not even lovers could be trusted, Page demonstrated a steely devotion. So when Sheppard put his hand through the window of Martin's Watch Shop on Fleet Street, Page stood lookout as his friend snatched three silver watches. The watchmaker, until now, had been confident that the location of his shop—only a block from Newgate Prison—would dissuade such unlawful attempts. Sheppard took little heed.

Sheppard quickly unloaded one of the watches for a guinea and a half and devoted the rest of the evening to bouncing around his old haunts in Drury Lane and the Seven Dials. He had drinks with friends at Black Mary's Hole. At the Cock and Pye Alehouse, he reconnected with an old acquaintance, a barber, and had brandy and oysters. Page stood watch at the door. Sheppard's anonymity had dissolved. People recognized him left and right. Merchants in particular only too happily cried out upon spotting the young thief, as a cobbler on Bishopsgate Street did. (One establishment, the Black Jack Tavern, was renamed "The Jump" in canting circles after Sheppard was said to have made a daring leap from one of the tavern's windows to escape Wild's men.)

With a price on his head and Wild nipping at his heels, Sheppard knew it was time to go. None too soon, either. He narrowly escaped a brush with Ireton, the Newgate man, as he made his way from Drury Lane. Loyally—although perhaps foolishly—Page went with him.

Wild was turning over every flat and shop in the city. He also continued to work Lyon for information, although even if she'd wanted to rat on her man, she didn't know his location. Despite the thief-taker's determination, it was the keepers of Newgate—so ridiculed by street singers for their lapse in watchfulness—who worked day and night to save face. They were the ones to first ascertain Sheppard's whereabouts: Finchley Common.

An armed posse set out from Newgate on the morning of Thursday, September 10—three in a coach, three by horseback—all determined to bring the bandit to justice. History doesn't record who saw whom first. Langley was checking on an isolated cottage, and Sheppard and Page came outside for a look, both still wearing their blue smocks and white aprons.

"There's a stag!" Sheppard shouted to Page, and the pair took off running. Langley jumped from his horse and snagged the slow-footed Page. Sheppard dashed into high-grassed farmland nearby. Langley pointed his comrades in Sheppard's direction and frisked Page, whose pocket gave up a chisel. Alston jumped his horse over a fence and led the charge into the meadows, but Sheppard had disappeared.

The hunters regrouped and targeted a farmhouse near Brown's Well. They combed the main house and the outbuildings, but Sheppard was nowhere to be found. Beside themselves with frustration, they nearly gave up their quest . . . when inside a stable the farmer's daughter spied Sheppard's toes poking out from a pile of hay. If not for the "mean girl," Sheppard would have escaped. Surrounded, he had to make a split-second decision: fight or submit. With a circle of pistols facing him, he opted for the latter. *Applebee's Original Weekly* presented Sheppard in a less than heroic light in this moment: "Pistols presented to his Head, he begg'd them, for God's Sake, not to shoot him on the Spot, trembled, was in great Agony, and submitted."

Alston was the first one on him as he surrendered. A search of the prisoner's person revealed a knife and two silver watches, one hidden in each armpit, the leftover bounty from the Martin heist.

Once in custody, shocked by the sudden turn of events, Sheppard surprised everyone with uncharacteristic silence. The Newgate men, having succeeded in their quest, found a drinkery on the Common and, prisoners in tow, stopped for a swig of liquor to celebrate. Sheppard read the sign above his head as he entered the establishment: "I have brought my hogs to a fair market." After a brandy, Sheppard regained his composure. The men talked and enjoyed one another's company. Spying eyes wouldn't have been able to discern the adversarial nature of the group. After drinks, the men took a coach and four back to London.

By two p.m. on September 10, Sheppard was back in the Condemned Hold at Newgate Prison, "his old mansion." He was chained to the floor, his feet cuffed together, but his good spirits had returned. In fact, the whole prison buzzed. Turnkeys puffed with pride. Inmates proudly shared space with the great Jack Sheppard. The "Te Deum" rang out through the Lodge.

The escape, chase, hunt, and capture had stirred the passions of the city. According to Sheppard's *History*:

> *His Escape and his being so suddenly Re-taken made such a Noise in the Town, that it was thought all the common People would have gone Mad about him; there being not a Porter to be had for Love nor Money, nor getting in an Ale-house, for Butchers, Shoemakers and Barbers, all engag'd in Controversies, and Wagers, about Sheppard. Newgate Night and Day surrounded with the Curious from St. Giles and Rag-Fair, and Tyburn Road daily lin'd with Women and Children; and the Gallows as carefully watch'd by Night, lest he should be hang'd Incog.*
> *. . . In short, it was a Week of the greatest Noise and Idleness among Mechanicks that has been known in London, and Parker and Pettis, two lyricks, subsisted many Days very comfortably upon Ballads and Letters about Sheppard.*

Jonathan Wild, however, didn't join in the festive mood. He was kicking himself for losing out on the exposure that Sheppard's recapture brought. While the roust was going down in Finchley Common, Wild had run down a bogus lead and ended up in Sturbridge. Wild's error elicited guffaws from the prisoners of Newgate. According to author Christopher Hibbert, "At least one prisoner literally laughed himself sick."

One other man shared in Wild's cheerlessness. Will Page, after a brief stay in Newgate, was indicted for the Martin theft and for perverting justice by assisting in Sheppard's run. The famous jailbreaker declared his childhood chum's innocence on all counts, but Page was found guilty and transported.

JACK SHEPPARD IN CHAINS IN NEWGATE PRISON
Frontispiece to Daniel Defoe's 1724 narrative of Sheppard's life, published by John Applebee

XV

MR. APPLEBEE'S MAN

Newspapers became less political, and their circulation extended from
the coffeehouses, inns, and ale-houses to a new class of readers. . . .
He [Defoe] converted them from rabid party agencies into registers
of domestic news and vehicles of social disquisitions, sometimes grave,
sometimes gay in subject, but uniformly bright and spirited in tone.
—WILLIAM MINTO, *DANIEL DEFOE*

Applebee's Original Weekly Journal had covered Elizabeth Lyon's capture. "On Tuesday Night his [Sheppard's] Wife was Committed to the Compter for assisting him in his Escape; having been apprehended and taken that Day by Mr. Jonathan Wild." Then on September 12, it reported that "Sheppard took to the Hedges" before his capture at the farm in Finchley Common. All the papers in town devoted copy to the escape and recapture, the *Daily Journal*, *Weekly Journal or Saturday's Post*, and *British Journal* all covering the affair. The *Evening Post* even featured Sheppard's story on the front page.

But the *Applebee's* articles by Defoe—who, like all other reporters and columnists at the time, didn't get a byline—give inside information, including insight from the prisoner himself on his escape. The toast of Newgate, Sheppard apparently discussed his latest escapades with "a Divine and several Gentleman." He was described as "composed and cheerful," and quick to divulge the intricacies of his efforts.

Applebee's had been reporting on Sheppard since August 1724, and continued its accounts almost weekly through November, with a total of sixteen articles on him. The story, which developed in regular installments, satisfied readers' growing interest while still leaving them wanting more. London now had Sheppard mania.

Wild had a history of exploiting the press to further his criminal enterprises, and now Defoe recognized that criminals had much to offer to his journalism. Trolling Newgate Prison for stories only reinforced this understanding. Defoe was staying out of trouble, but those around him weren't so lucky. His son Benjamin served jail time in 1721 for seditious libel (as had his father in 1703), and Nathaniel Mist of the *Weekly Journal or Saturday's Post* ran up a tally of at least fourteen arrests for his paper's attack's on the government.

Mist's imprisonment in 1720 had led to Defoe's employment with Applebee, his first article in the latter's journal appearing on June 25, 1720. Here Defoe finally cleared himself of politically driven news. As Maximillian Novak explains, "*Applebee's Weekly Journal* was intended more for the entertainment of its readers than for their edification, and specialized in accounts of criminals and in light material," and biographer James Sutherland calls Defoe's addition of the "non-political essay" to the six-page weekly paper one of his greatest innovations.

Starting at *Mist's* and continuing at *Applebee's*, Defoe wrote about highwaymen and thieves like Jack Sheppard, debtors, quack doctors, stock-jobbers and the South Sea Bubble, freedom of the press, gambling, the plague, and even fashion. Most of these contributions came in the form of a letter, where, as Novak observes, the author employed a "lighter touch." Although his stories weren't uniformly cheery. Novak points out "essays on suicide and painful deaths, on the sufferings of the poor, and on ingratitude."

Defoe even developed a knack for reporting on nothing, when there seemingly was no news. Sutherland describes Defoe's strategy for dealing with a dry spell:

> *When he could think of nothing better he wrote letters to Mr. Mist or Mr. Applebee (Mr. App.) from imaginary spinsters recounting their emotional troubles, or from married men complaining about their wives. It can hardly be claimed he raised the intellectual level of the weekly newspaper; but he undoubtedly humanized it, and under his*

guidance Mist's *and* Applebee's *gradually captured a far wider and less educated public than had ever before been reached by an English newspaper.*

Also, because he had no byline, no dog in the fight, he didn't have to waste his efforts defending himself in print as he once did. He didn't need to protect his name, and as a result, his imagination flowed.

Most times, however, as with his novels, the secret of his authorship rarely lasted. When he was discovered, it didn't come without controversy. He has been accused of playing both sides of the fence. His work for Mist's opposition paper didn't stop him from launching the Whig-leaning *Whitehall Evening Post* at the same time. It's unlikely that his political preferences fluctuated with each passing season, so what were his true intentions? Was he a rascal or a ringer? Was he getting one over on the city? Was he a moralizer, or a man without conscience? A spy for the government added to a newspaper's payroll to quash or soften inflammatory stories, or a hired gun brought in to write for the publisher's viewpoint, and nothing more?

When Mist twice had to stand in the pillory in February 1721, Defoe, certainly empathetic, came to his defense. At odds politically, they both adhered to the principle of moving papers for money. Defoe offered his views on Mist's punishment in an introductory letter in *Applebee's*, in which he expressed sympathy with "A Brother Journal Man," and wrote of liberty and freedom of the press. He advised his readers and fellow writers to

> *remember, that the Press and the Pit are alike open, and stand very near together. The Press is open, that is true; and the Prison is open, that is true; Guardez Vous, Mr. App; write warily, write cautiously. But you will say, What must a poor Printer do? Must he turn his Tale as the Weather-cock of State turns? And when the Wind blows a Whig Gale from Court, turn Whig; when it blows a High Church Gale, face about to the High Church; and in times of the unsteady Gales, trim and look every Way, and no Way, all at once? What must he do? No, no, Mr. App! be honest and be wise; be steady to yourself.*

He urged "Men of Scribble" to "Leave off the Comment, and keep to the Text (*Facts*)." Once again, he pointed to others while bending his own rules. But maybe Defoe was coming up with something new again.

He once fictionalized the accounts of prisoners—prostitutes Moll King and Calico Sarah for *Moll Flanders*, or the orphaned thief in *Colonel Jack*—but now he used the lives of criminals for his nonfiction. In the evolving story of Jack Sheppard, Defoe chose not to invent but rather report. He still used all of his authorial experience to his advantage. Defoe was dabbling in what today we would call literary journalism, employing fiction techniques to enrich true stories. Tom Wolfe, who later styled the genre "New Journalism," defined the hallmarks of this new form: "1. Scene by scene construction, 2. Use of dialogue, 3. Third person point of view, and, 4. The use of status symbols." Joseph Addison, Richard Steele, and Ned Ward stand alongside Defoe as the founders of literary journalism. Defoe had struck at something original.

Defoe's interest in criminals may have been further spiked by the fact that much of the action was taking place in his old neighborhood. Wild and Sheppard were his geographical brethren, their dramas unfolding on the streets in which Defoe had grown up. Defoe was born in St. Giles, Cripplegate, the location of Sheppard's Roundhouse escapes, around the corner from Wild's first shop in Cock Alley. He had hobnobbed with King William III and Robert Harley, First Earl of Oxford, but Defoe never forgot where he came from, or the life of the common man. He wrote to enlighten, to elucidate what was going on in the world for his countrymen.

At home in Stoke Newington, he was an attentive and loving father. His son-in-law Henry Baker described him as

> *a gentleman well known by his writings, who had newly built there a very handsome house, as a retirement from London, and amused his time either in cultivation of a large and pleasant garden, or in the pursuit of his studies, which he found means of making very profitable. He was now at least sixty years of age, afflicted with the gout and stone, but retained all his mental faculties entire.*

His happiness and satisfaction came, in no small part, from *Robinson Crusoe*. For the first time in his life, Defoe was financially secure. The fruits of all those years of writing had come to bear. Now he received advances from publishers when embarking on book projects. He had made it.

Despite the country scene of a patriarchal graybeard in his gloaming, Defoe still had a great deal of energy in him. Besides *Mist's* and *Applebee's*, he also wrote for the *Whitehall Evening Post* and *Mercurius Politicus*, and he helped Baker get the *Universal Spectator* off the ground. When he wanted to dig into a longer project, he wrote a pamphlet or novel, often choosing from the subjects he covered in his journalism. He concentrated on a topic exhaustively for a spell, gave it a full treatment, and then returned to his reporting.

Through the title character of his 1722 novel, *Colonel Jack*, he offers a glimpse into how he obtained his material.

> *In this way of talk I was always upon the inquiry, asking questions of things done in public, as well as in private; particularly, I loved to talk with seamen and soldiers about the war, and about the great sea-fights or battles on shore, that any of them had been in; and, as I never forgot anything they told me, I could soon, that is to say, in a few years, give almost as good an account . . . as any of those that had been there. . . . By this means, as young as I was, I was a kind of an historian.*

Colonel Jack depicts a boy with no surname—"a dirty glass-bottle-house boy, sleeping in the ashes, and dealing always in the street dirt"—and his entry into the world of crime, from pickpocket to highwayman. By 1724, it was in its third printing. When Jack Sheppard came rambling through the same Rosemary Lane as Colonel Jack had, Defoe saw life reflecting his art. As author Richard Holmes writes, "it was a story just waiting for any journalist, novelist, playwright—or biographer—to seize."

John Applebee had a keen eye for sales, so it's no surprise that he staffed Defoe as one of his writers. Applebee, a printer and bookseller, had a long history in the London press and, working out of Blackfriars, had recently cornered the market in criminal biography. He published a range of rags and pamphlets on popular criminals: their lives, confessions, and dying speeches, as well as accounts from the ordinary of Newgate. Applebee pushed it all. Until this point, the ordinary, in addition to caring for an inmate's spiritual life, also had claim to money earned from stories by the condemned. Popular prisoners' accounts sometimes fetched upward of £25, and yearly compensation for the ordinary during this period could reach £200.

When gathering information, the ordinary sometimes played detective, trying to elicit information on further crimes, some yet unsolved, or the identity of a criminal's consorts. For example, from the account of Mrs. Knap murderer William White, the ordinary wrote:

> *I mention'd to him (as I was desir'd) several Robberies, and some Murthers, that of late have been committed, and not yet discover'd; and I ask'd him particularly, whether he knew any thing of the breaking [in at] Sir Henry Hicks's Coach-house at Low-Layton in Essex and taking some Coach-glasses thence; and his Answer was, That himself was not (nor knew any one that was) concern'd in any of those Facts.*

The ordinary sought a confession so the condemned could cleanse himself of crime and ready himself for the afterlife—but no doubt it was just as often for the sake of a good ending. Author Andrea McKenzie notes that, "Clergymen and enterprising pamphleteers vied for the exclusive possession of the 'lives,' 'confessions,' and 'last dying words' of the most famous criminals of the day."

Defoe knew as much. In *Moll Flanders*, he described the ordinary as a well-oiled sot, "whose business it is to extort confessions from prisoners, for private Ends, or for the farther detecting of other offenders." In the book, the mere presence of the ordinary nauseates Moll.

> *The ordinary of Newgate came to me, and talked a little in his way, but all his divinity ran upon confessing my crime, as he called it (though he knew not what I was in for), making a full discovery, and the like, without which he told me God would never forgive me; and he said so*

little to the purpose that I had no manner of consolation from him; and then to observe the poor creature preaching confession and repentance to me in the morning, and find him drunk with brandy by noon.

Applebee squeezed his way into the ordinary's action, and there he remained for some time. He had a stable of writers at his disposal, his garreteers, given entry to the prison and always at the ready to put a prisoner's story to paper. If need be, Applebee greased palms and paid a prisoner or a prisoner's family for the rights to the tale. In 1721, he had a hit with his true confessions broadsides series. By midcentury, more than a thousand prisoners, male and female, had told their stories—on broadsheets for two pence, pamphlets for six. Applebee's business model proved a success.

If Reverend Wagstaff—a journeyman ordinary filling in for Thomas Purney, the prison's official chaplain, who was ill—could get Sheppard's life story, then, more power to him. Applebee would surely publish whatever Wagstaff could scrape together for his *Ordinary's Account*, but this time the chaplain had his work cut out for him. Sheppard couldn't stand Wagstaff, or any of the other "gingerbread men," as he called men of the cloth. He saw through their offers to save his soul as interest in the cash that such a story would bring. For his part, the formidable Wagstaff didn't care much for the thief, either, calling him "inhuman" and "barbarous."

Then a journalist came to see Sheppard. Working on behalf of Applebee, Defoe visited Newgate to hear Sheppard's tale. Christopher Hibbert writes that no one was better suited for the task than Defoe. "When he came to talk to Jack in Newgate, he came as a man who had been imprisoned himself, who had been bankrupt and wronged and misunderstood and lonely. He came as a writer who was interested in the man of action rather than in the man of ideas. He was concerned only with those who had lived hard."

The battle for Sheppard's story had commenced.

BLUESKIN BLAKE ATTEMPTING TO CUT THE THROAT OF
JONATHAN WILD
Courtesy of the British Museum

XVI

BLUESKIN'S PENKNIFE

In his limitless ambition and boundless confidence he [Wild] was overreaching himself. He selected his victims without regard to their capacities for revenge or their popularity.
—CHRISTOPHER HIBBERT, *THE ROAD TO TYBURN*

In his September escape, Sheppard had enjoyed ten days of freedom before being recaptured. Now, in October, he remained securely locked up inside Newgate Prison. His summer running partner, Blueskin Blake, remained at large, however—wanted but not yet apprehended for the Kneebone robbery.

Because the robbery had caused such fervor around town, additional consequences awaited Blueskin Blake. He and Wild, after a long history together, were at odds. Blueskin long since had ceased bringing his stolen goods or details of their whereabouts to the Lost Property Office for Wild to manage. Wild wasn't going to protect Blake on this one. Quite the opposite.

On October 2, Wild and his team pinned Blueskin down at a dwelling in St. Giles. Quilt Arnold led the attack, followed by Wild and Abraham Mendez. Arnold described the raid. "Going to his Chamber-door, I bid him open it, but he swore he would not, and so I burst it open. He drew a Penknife, and swore he would kill the first Man that came in: 'Then I am the first Man,' says I, 'and Mr. Wild is not far behind, and if you don't deliver your Penknife immediately I'll chop your Arm off.' Then he threw the Knife down, and I apprehended him."

Wild, Arnold, and Mendez walked Blueskin past Kneebone's house on the way to Newgate. "There's the Ken!" Wild said, pointing out the cause of Blake's predicament.

Blake understood his position. "Say no more of that, Mr. Wild, for I know I am a dead Man; but what I fear is, that I shall afterwards be carried to Surgeons' Hall and anatomiz'd."

"No, I'll take Care to prevent that, for I'll give you a Coffin," Wild said.

H. D.'s eighteenth-century biography of Wild records that he often begrudged surgeons who looked to tear apart the bodies of his acquaintances—even if it was Wild who had delivered them to the gallows. All condemned men feared the Surgeons' Hall. Since 1540, the Barber-Surgeons Company had the right to seize four bodies a year from the gallows for the purpose of dissection. (During this period, the official remedy for countless afflictions was bloodletting, which made the tools of the barber valuable to the surgeon, and vice versa. The company's two vocations weren't separated until 1745.) But a coffin could fend off body snatchers at the Triple Tree. Men and women who couldn't afford one, or who didn't have friends or family to protect their corpses, could be taken off to the Surgeons' Hall for medical practice.

In William Hogarth's *The Four Stages of Cruelty*, the last engraving, *The Reward of Cruelty*, illustrates what became of a body if surgeons took hold of it. One doctor rifles through the stomach, ripping the intestines from the abdomen, while another doctor pokes his blade around in the eye socket. At the foot of the dissection table, a dog gnaws at the dead man's discarded heart. Skull and bones stew in a cauldron over a fire.

This wasn't the first time Wild had arrested Blueskin, who had worked in the "Corporation" since he was a boy. Wild had detained him in 1723, probably as a ploy to get Blake to rat out three of his cronies, Matthew Flood, John Levee, and Richard Oakey. Blueskin did Wild's bidding, and his testimony helped to send the three men to Tyburn. For his efforts, Wild cut Blake out of the £420 reward that he received, a piece of which the highwayman was no doubt expecting.

Blake and Wild had a long, strange relationship. In the past year, Wild had gifted Blueskin with a musketoon, while Blake had endeavored to remain in good standing with the thief-taker by presenting Mrs. Wild with a gold watch snaked from a gentlemen exiting Salter's Hall.

Blueskin remained loyal to Wild to a fault. He gave evidence against his running mates at Wild's discretion, including information of late from twelve separate robberies. In the bargain, two of his oldest associates, Edward Polit and William Blewit, took the fall on his account.

This type of wheedling didn't sit well with Jack Sheppard, who, despite partnering with Blake, rightly thought him a "worthless companion" and "a sorry Thief." In his *History*, Sheppard spoke out against ratting, which "had made dreadful Havock among the Thieves" and caused "the depravity of the Brethren in that Respect."

The problem for Blueskin was a lack of options. Despite his history with his benefactor, he held no great love for Wild. It was a relationship of necessity. To endure as a thief for as long as he had, he needed help from the top more than anything else. Defoe later wrote about the attitude among thieves like Blueskin, who chose to take something rather than nothing from Wild. "The young Generation of Thieves, who as we may say liv'd under him, were always kept low and poor, and could not but subsist but by the Bounty of their Governour; and when they had a Booty of any Bulk or Value, they knew not what to do with it, but to deposite it, and get some Money for the present Use."

On the day of his trial, Blueskin finally raised the courage to stand up for himself. Perhaps it was his recently acquired lover, a fiddle-loving young woman from Islington, who gave him the strength to go against the thief-taker, or maybe it was as he said—nothing more than a spur-of-the-moment decision.

At noon on October 14, Wild floated around the bail dock, a waiting area for prisoners prior to trial, ready to attend the latest Sessions at the Old Bailey to give his testimony against Blueskin. He swilled wine from a flask and was forthcoming and easygoing, if not a little curt, with the thieves whose time had come. He spotted a former Carrick man, Simon Jacob. He laid it out for the prig, pondering his life in terms of reward money.

"I believe you will not bring £40 this time, I wish Joe [Blake] was in your Case, but I'm afraid he's a dead Man," said Wild.

The comment didn't go undetected by Blueskin, who approached. Wild offered him a drink. They shared some wine. Sheppard had already been tagged for the Kneebone robbery, so maybe there was still a chance. If the thief-taker spoke on his behalf at trial, surely Blake might come off with a sentence of transportation, his life spared. He offered the idea to Wild.

"I cannot do it," Wild said, "You are certainly a dead Man, and will be tuck'd up very speedily." Then he added, "I'll send you a good Book or two, and provide you a Coffin, and you shall not be anatomized."

Blake snapped. He pulled out his penknife and launched himself at Wild. He seized the thief-taker by the neck and slit his throat—a deep, angry cut that opened him clean to the windpipe. Wild fell in a bloody heap. A turnkey wrangled Blueskin under control before he could strike again. But the mighty slash fell short, just missing the windpipe. Wild survived.

Several factors saved Wild's life. The instrument of assassination was too dull. A penknife was small and easy to conceal, but as its name suggests, it was intended only to sharpen quill pens. Wild's attire further thwarted Blueskin's bid. The *Evening Post* reported that before penetrating the skin, the knife first had to pass through Wild's shirt of "Muslin Stock," which was "twisted in several Plaits round his neck." Finally, the response to the attack was surprisingly quick. Had the wound been left unattended much longer, Blueskin's attack would have succeeded. But three surgeons happened to be at the Justice Hall, and they quickly treated Wild. Wild recovered in bed for the rest of October.

At Blake's trial, the would-be assassin cursed the blunt penknife. He remarked that if he had succeeded he would have left the world a happy man. He rued that he couldn't toss Wild's head "into the Sessions House Yard among the Rabble." When later questioned by Ordinary Purney on what had provoked the attack, Blueskin answered that it was Wild's flippant disregard for his plea for transportation. According to the Ordinary of Newgate's Account: "He answer'd that none prompted him to that Assault, but a sudden Thought that Moment enter'd into his Mind, or else he should have provided a better Knife, which would have cut off a Head directly."

William Field made an encore appearance at the Old Bailey as a witness to the Kneebone robbery. He mustered some dialogue to bolster his fictional participation in the heist, which contradicted his previous testimony. Field described himself as a timid, unwilling participant who didn't know Sheppard well, or much about Kneebone's shop. He said that he had told Blueskin as much. According to Field's testimony, Blake answered: "Blood, nor I neither; but Jack Sheppard does, for he has liv'd there, and he'll undertake it, and we shall have nothing to do, but to help to carry off the Goods, or else I should be as unwilling to venture as you."

Blueskin was found guilty of the Kneebone robbery and sentenced to hang.

Wild lived, but his veneer of invincibility did not. Blake proved it was possible to harm the scourge of London's underworld, and he had done so in public. Wild ruled, but one cut of Blake's knife had changed everything. Nobody knew the intricacies of their backstory. In fact, the prevailing perception had it that Blueskin was close to Sheppard. If Blake didn't go quietly, neither would his comrade.

The *Daily Journal* published news of the attack the following morning, October 15, and by the weekend, the *London Journal* reported that "The Villain triumph'd afterwards in what he had done, swearing many Oaths, that if he had done his Business he should have died with Satisfaction."

Misinformation spread in the rush to get the story. Most notably, Blake had been accredited with being a highwayman of great skill, which of course he wasn't. Nonetheless, the lore about him grew. Those who witnessed the savagery couldn't believe the wound wasn't mortal. As a result, balladeers composed verse as though Wild's death was imminent. Jonathan Swift may have hated Defoe, but he quickly got in on the criminal action with "Blueskin's Ballad." The second stanza reads:

When to the Old-Bailey this Blueskin was led,
He held up his hand, his indictment was read,
Loud rattled his chains, near him Jonathan stood,
For full forty pounds was the price of his blood.
Then hopeless of life,

He drew his penknife,
And made a sad widow of Jonathan's wife:
But forty pounds paid her, her grief shall appease,
And ev'ry man round me may rob if he please.

In the end, Wild's wife wasn't made a widow, and a sharper knife would have made all the difference.

The year 1724 hadn't been a good one for Wild. In June, he had petitioned the Court of Aldermen for the Freedom of the City of London, an old medieval honor that conferred freedom from serfdom, and thus stood as a mark of the city's respect. Wild still held no official position, so having something in writing wasn't a bad idea.

He addressed his "Humble Petition" to the lord mayor and Court of Aldermen. It named a dozen criminals for whom he'd gone to "great trouble and charge in apprehending and convicting divers felons for returning from transportation." Added to this was a gentle mention of the fact that he had "never received any reward or gratuity for such his service," and that he was "very desirous to become a freeman of this honourable city."

The record of the Court of Aldermen notes Wild's petition, as well as their response: "The Consideration thereof is adjourned till another time." Wild never received the Freedom of the City of London. But *Applebee's* reported on June 6 that he was awarded a "very handsome Sum" for his apprehension of premature transportation returnees, maybe as a consolation, and "'tis hoped that Mr. Wild will double his Diligence for the Future."

Meanwhile, Sheppard continued to stew. A new death warrant couldn't be issued until it was proved that the Sheppard arrested at Finchley Common was the same Sheppard previously convicted. He waited for the new Sessions to commence. In the interim, he and Wagstaff reacquainted themselves and began their battle anew. The prison's turnkeys, on the other hand, were far more hospitable to Sheppard—particularly when they found visitors clamoring at the door, eager to unload a few coins in exchange for a glimpse at the slippery young bandit.

An unprecedented stream of people visited Sheppard. They gave money and other small items to him. Instruments of escape kept popping up inside Sheppard's cell: hammer, chisel, files. Because he was allowed to hold his Bible, that's where he hid a small file. But this and the rest of his contraband were all uncovered eventually. Wagstaff spied the file concealed within the scriptures. He asked Sheppard how he had come into possession of the file and other instruments, and the prisoner replied tersely, "Ask me no such Questions. One File's worth all the Bibles in the World."

When queried about his accomplices, it was more of the same: A perturbed Sheppard gave no information on others, expressing his belief that it would only contaminate him with guilt. His bravado delighted London. Each day his legend grew.

Sheppard was moved from the Condemned Hold to the prison's strong room, "the Castle," until the next Sessions. Located on the third floor of the four-story prison, the Castle measured twenty feet by ten and had a single iron-barred window. Sheppard was fettered with irons. His feet were padlocked to a bar in the floor. But each night, unknown to his jailers, Sheppard freed himself to stretch his legs and get some exercise.

On October 7, he was caught in his cell, wandering the room in an apparent reconnaissance mission, free of the padlock and chains. The Castle was considered impenetrable, but the sight of Sheppard roaming the room freely gave his jailers pause. *Applebee's* covered the story: "John Sheppard, the Malefactor, found means to release himself from the Staples fixed in the Floor of the Apartment called the Castle." After a search of the prisoner revealed no instruments of escape, the head keeper "intreated him to discover by what Magick Art he had thus got himself from the Staples. He reached forth his Hand, and took a Nail, and with that, and no other Instrument, unlocked himself again before their faces. Nothing so astonishing ever known!"

Astonishing, yes, but not smart. He shouldn't have shown off for the prison's keepers. But apparently he hadn't thought much of his accomplishment. "There is scarce a Smith in London" who couldn't do the same, he said. As a result, he was placed in handcuffs and weighed down with heavier restraints. A fail-safe padlock fortified the irons. The metal bondage applied to Sheppard was hitherto unseen in the annals of London jails.

Kneebone paid Sheppard a visit. The appalling sight of his former ward chained down in his cage brought tears to Kneebone's eyes. Sheppard likewise cried. Kneebone attempted to intercede on Jack's behalf to lighten the prisoner's load. He was denied.

When word of Blake's attack on Wild made it back to the prisoners in Newgate, the prison fairly shook with excitement. Wild had been in many street fights, but never such a public strike like the Blueskin assault. Wrote Defoe, "Those audacious Criminals exclaim'd against him, as a Man who had the first great Encourager of their Villainies, or at least had been instrumental to draw them into the very Practice itself; in Revenge for which the said Blueskin bid fair for giving Jonathan his quietus in the very Face of Justice."

The mood was shifting. Public interest was swaying. The memory of the South Sea Bubble was fresh. The Earl of Macclesfield was about to become immersed in scandal; in less than a year, he would be convicted of swindling £100,000 in bribe money, only to receive a slap on the wrist, his fine paid largely by the King himself. The establishment was losing favor, and people were lining up to pay to see Jack Sheppard.

In his cell, Sheppard had few options. He alternated between lying on his back on the cold stone floor and sitting in the uncomfortable chair. The handcuffs rubbed his wrists raw. He appeared miserable, but visitors continued to flock. They tossed him silver and copper coins, although as he later said, "I wanted still a more useful Metal, a Crow, a Chissel, a File, and a Saw or two, those Weapons being more useful to me than all the Mines of Mexico."

The Sessions began. The turnkeys kept busy with escorting and guarding prisoners to and from the Justice Hall at Old Bailey. Despite their divided attention, they knew that Sheppard was locked securely in the Castle.

XVII

The Castle

I found there was not a moment to be lost; and the Affair of Jonathan Wild's Throat, together with the Business at the Old Baily, having sufficiently engag'd the Attention of the Keepers, I thought then was the Time to push.
—Daniel Defoe, *A Narrative of All the Robberies, Escapes, &c. of John Sheppard*

At two p.m. on October 15, under-turnkey William Austin came to the Castle—along with a few other officials, including Captain Geary from the New Prison—with Sheppard's dinner. Sheppard was in good spirits and friendly with the men. They chatted. Sheppard asked Austin if he could call on him again that evening to save him from the boredom of isolation. Austin said he was much too busy. No, he wouldn't have the chance to return until the next morning. Come early, Sheppard told him, again expressing his loneliness.

The men inspected Sheppard's restraints again, deemed them secure, and left. It was almost three o'clock. This was the moment. He'd have more than enough time. As nineteenth-century prison inspector and author Arthur Griffiths noted, "Released thus from all surveillance, time was all that Sheppard needed to effect his escape."

He took to his task immediately. The October sun would set just after five p.m., so he had only a couple of hours of daylight at his disposal. First, he released himself from the handcuffs; whether he accomplished this feat again with a nail or used some other method, he never divulged. With hands free, he set to work on his legs, still chained together and

SHEPPARD'S ESCAPE FROM THE CASTLE

padlocked to a bar in the floor. He opened the padlock without trouble and then used all of his strength, utilizing the leverage of his weight to twist the chain until it snapped. He took one of the chain links that had broken loose, as well as the padlock, for the next stage of his plan. Every step of the way he stockpiled similar debris to use as valuable tools. He tied the clanking bands and leg chains to his calves with his stockings to silence them.

From his earlier investigations of the Castle's layout, Sheppard had decided to escape upward as he had done from St. Giles. But first he needed to remove the iron bar blocking passage through the chimney's flue. He attacked the wall above the fireplace, about six feet above the floor, intent on reaching the bar from the outside. Using the broken link, he gored through the plaster and opened a hole in the wall to expose the end of the bar. With the padlock, he hammered the bricks surrounding the bar, pounding, scraping, clawing. One brick after another fell to the floor. He loosened the iron bar and then removed it. It measured two and a half feet long and one inch in diameter. He added the bar to his inventory of tools.

Sheppard climbed up the flue until he hit the ceiling above. With the iron bar, he pounded a hole into the room above, known as the Red Room. No one had set foot in it since a group of rebels had been locked away there in 1716. In complete darkness, he reached out for the walls, groping along, searching for the door. Along the way his foot kicked a large nail, which he added to his supply of tools. Once at the door, he went to work on the lock. As Sheppard later remarked, "The Keepers say the Door had not been unlock'd for seven Years; but I intended not to be seven Years in opening it." He loosened a nut to expose the inner workings of the lock and exited the Red Room, creeping along in a corridor leading to the chapel.

The new moon offered safe passage but no light; Sheppard only had his sense of touch. He heard the bells of St. Sepulchre's Church ring eight o'clock. He slowly progressed through the ancient prison, toward the roof. Five additional doors stood between him and freedom. In the darkness, he tenaciously bored through plaster, brick, stone, and iron. Doors and walls, locks and fillets. Along the way, he grabbed more bits and pieces, always anticipating his next move. He found the door to the chapel, bolted from the opposite side. He broke through the wall beside the door to reach around to open the lock on the other side. In the chapel, he found and took an iron spike. There was a door to exit the chapel, doors in the hallway, doors to reach the roof—a prison of doors. He thoroughly surveyed each one, top to bottom, for the most effective solution. Six doors in all, formidable and stout.

It was almost nine p.m. when he reached the roof.

Once he made it to open air, he realized that he needed a rope. In his rush, he hadn't remembered to bring his blanket with him. He turned around. Back into the prison he went, back through the maze of broken doors, once again in darkness. It took only minutes, but Sheppard's nerves were riled. The thought of getting caught while breaking *into* prison—after all he had accomplished, after six hours of work—knotted his stomach with dread. He crept along.

Back down the chimney of the Castle he went and grabbed his blanket. He climbed back up, retracing his steps and reemerging on the leads with much relief. He secured the spike from the chapel between some bricks. He tied his blanket to the spike and slid down the outer wall of Newgate Prison. He dangled, then dropped to an adjoining house, landing on the roof. The streets below were still alive, shops still open. He had to be careful.

On the roof, he found an open attic door. He quietly descended the steps into the family home of a turner named Mr. Bird. Down one flight, then another; all was well. He reached the top of the stairs leading to the ground floor.

Clink! His fetters knocked together.

"Lord, what Noise is that?" a woman downstairs asked, alarmed.

"Perhaps the Dog or Cat," a man answered.

After a beat of silence, the Birds returned their attention elsewhere. Sheppard decided to halt his flight and lay low for a spell. He retreated to the garret for a well-deserved rest.

After two hours, a refreshed Sheppard returned to the second floor to listen to the inhabitants below. The family was stirring about still, but he went for it. He bounded down the stairs, flew through the door, and didn't look back.

He walked toward the St. Sepulchre's watch-house and eyed the hour. It was just after midnight. The whole affair had taken approximately nine hours. He still wore the blue butcher's smock from his earlier travails, and over it he sported a large coat. He turned down Snow Hill. Through Holborn and onto Gray's Inn Lane he walked. Five miles north, in the open fields of the country, he found an empty farmhouse in the village of Tottingham. It was two a.m. His legs and ankles were battered and swollen, his body spent. He collapsed.

But he had made it.

"I was once more, contrary to my own Expectation and that of all Mankind, a Freeman," he said in his *Narrative*.

He awoke in the farmhouse after only three hours, his ankles aching, his flesh lacerated. He needed to rid himself of his chains. Not only were they heavy and painful, but they also marked him as a prisoner.

At eight a.m., Austin was the first to reach the Castle to witness the scene of Sheppard's destruction. A mountain of bricks greeted the turnkey. He couldn't fathom what had happened. He bounded down the stairs to inform his colleagues. Upon reaching the Lodge, words failed him; he couldn't explain what he'd seen. It took a couple of bolts of Holland gin for Austin to convey the news.

That morning, officials ordered an immediate search of Newgate, combing every nook and cranny of the prison. The investigation led the group of keepers and turnkeys, stupefied, to a blanket dangling from the roof. Prisoners had escaped from Newgate many times, true, but never from the Castle, and never so heavily burdened with manacles. Never like this.

The keepers were dumbstruck. Viewing the trail of structural carnage, they feared that "the Devil himself" had aided the convict in his escape. William Pitt and Bodenham Rouse feared for their jobs, and had to appear before the Lord Mayor of London and Recorder Thompson to prove that they or their staff hadn't abetted the jailbreaker.

In the days following Sheppard's disappearance, London newspapers swelled with details of the great escape, and noted the twenty-guinea reward for his capture. The *Evening Post* ran a physical description of him: "He is about 22 years of age, about 5 feet 4 inches high, very slender, of a pale complexion, has an impediment or Hesitation in his Speech." It was an unanticipated turn in the captivating cat-and-mouse chase building for weeks, and the story made front-page headlines: The renowned thief-taker general, squared off against a plucky thief and escape artist of unrivaled skill, whose trusty sidekick, Blueskin, had perpetrated a grisly attack on the man of law. As Richard Holmes points out, "It could be seen as a duel between crime and justice, rebellion and authority, youth and age, or freedom and oppression."

Journalists, Daniel Defoe among them, hurried to the prison to see the escape scene for themselves and to interview the stunned turnkeys. The reporters received open access to the grounds and witnessed the debris from his feats of demolition: manacles, chains, bricks, mortar, locks, and padlocks all left behind.

On Saturday, October 17, the *Weekly Journal or Saturday's Post* offered the following jaw-dropping story.

> *On Thursday Night, John Sheppard escaped again from Newgate, though he was double ironed, Hand cuffed, and chained down in the Room, called the Castle, yet he found Means, in a very surprizing Manner to free himself from the Staple to which he was chained: Afterwards he broke down the Wall of the Chimney, and got into several Rooms, broke through six Doors, on which were five strong Locks and a Bolt, and thereby getting upon the Leads of the Gaol.*

The London public read the astonishing news at their breakfast tables or in coffeehouses. Nothing like this had ever filled the pages of a newspaper before. The story was happening almost in real time, the skilled scofflaw once more among them, back on the streets.

On those same streets, writers and balladeers conjured up testimony to Sheppard's might. One Grub Street poet hurried out "An Epigram on John Sheppard's Last Miraculous Escape," which read in part:

Samson of Old was a Strong Man, 'tis true,
But Samson was a Boy, bold Jack, to you:
When once Confin'd and Chain'd, he never fled,
But pull'd his Prison-Walls upon his Head;
With Malice in his Heart, his Strength he tries:
And, to destroy his Keepers, with them dies:
But you have shewn Superior Strength and Brains.

Even King George I himself kept tabs on Sheppard's saga, demanding all incoming news on the escapee. While the feat surely intrigued the King personally, the escape marked yet another stain on Prime Minister Robert Walpole's growingly unpopular and corrupt regime.

Sheppard's achievement proved no less damaging for Jonathan Wild. Whenever someone challenged his power and won, it was bad for business. Sheppard was on the loose yet again, doing what he pleased, and Wild, relegated to his bed, was in no condition to do anything about it.

The city of London took note. Sheppard's notoriety had soared in just a few short months. His earlier endeavors from St. Giles and the New Prison at Clerkenwell had drawn little fuss. The press at the time merely listed his name alongside Ward and Upton. He was just another thief in a country full of them. He was all the more forgettable to readers for his common name. In fact, a Captain John Shepherd had given the name its infamy at the time, after he was charged with murdering Robert Mayer on the high seas.

Now things were different.

Among the classifieds in the newspapers during the week of October 20 ran an advertisement for a pamphlet published by John Applebee in Blackfriars. "The History of the Remarkable Actions and Life of John Sheppard," on sale for one shilling, has long been credited to Daniel Defoe. If not wholly his work, he at least had a hand in it as a collaborator. Richard Holmes notes that some of the passages were so rich in description that "It would have taken a shrewd onlooker—a novelist or biographer—to catch the moment." As the advertisement noted, it contained information gleaned from interviews conducted with all of the principals of the case: shop owners, justices of the peace, prison officials, and the ordinary.

It offered a backstory on the thief and a longer read than any of the previous articles. Other pamphleteers looking for a piece of the profit issued a flurry of similarly themed pamphlets, but Applebee owned this story. Thanks to Defoe, the rag offered the most vivid and detail-packed coverage of Sheppard's previous escapes. The pamphlet has the ring of an "exclusive." Applebee's team had the inside scoop, and the public ate it up. It was printed three times in as many weeks, spurring even more intense interest in Sheppard, who, the pamphlet reminded readers, was "gone once more upon his wicked range in the world."

The "History" furthered Sheppard's image as a cocky outlaw. It drew readers into his world, into his cell, where he let loose with boastful, memorable statements. In one scene, a representative from the lord mayor's office inquired, "Which was Sheppard?" and Jack retorted, "Yes, Sir, I am The Sheppard, and all the Goalers [jailors] in the Town are my Flock, and I cannot stir into the Country, but they are all at my Heels *Baughing* after me."

In the papers, strange letters purportedly by Sheppard popped up. Apparently, the fugitive had time to write to everyone: his mother, turnkey Austin, hangman Jack Ketch again (where he mentions Wild and his "mortal Aversion to Hemp," meaning the hanging rope), and even a letter to Blueskin in the *Daily Journal*: "Jonathan recovers; curse on thy little dull clasp knife; must I be plagu'd to finish what you so clumsily begun." In another, "Sheppard" distinguishes John Applebee by name in an alleged cover note hand-delivered to the publisher's maidservant:

Mr. Applebee,

This with my Kind Love to you, and pray give my Kind Love to Mr. Wagstaff; hoping these lines will find you in good Health, as I am at present; but I must own you are the Loser for want of my Dying Speech;

But to make up your Loss, if you think this Sheet worth your while, pray make the best of it. Though they do say that I am taking among the Smugglers, and put in Dover Castle, yet I hope I am Smugglers still. So no more, but your humble Servant,

John Sheppard

And I desire you would be the Post Man to my last Lodging. So farewell now, I quit the English Shore.
Newgate Farewell.

Near the end of the month, *Parker's London News* published a letter from Sheppard to his mother that author Christopher Hibbert thinks "more likely to be genuine than any other of the letters which were at the time published." The letter again mentions Applebee's name when Sheppard directs the Blackfriars publisher to pay his mother the eight pence per diem Sheppard was to receive "for my Memorandums." It's the mention of Applebee's name in a letter published by *Parker's* that enhances the authenticity of the dispatch. If the letter was faked, why insert a rival publisher's name?

In the note to his mother, Sheppard mentions his good fortune at having successfully completed his escape and saved his life. "I hope the Grace of God I shall keep myself from any more of such heinous Crimes, and from the Hands of my Enemies." If authentic, the letter is prescient in noting his enemies. Wild was healing by the day, and Arnold and Mendez remained on the hunt. Sheppard needed to take every precaution lest he join his associates, nearly every one of which was either dead or in prison.

All over London, in the press and on the street, speculation ran fast and loose. He was spotted across the country. He was captured. He was stealing. He sought a job at a brewhouse on Thames Street. Rumor had it that he was in Canterbury. Any robbery brought Sheppard's name to people's lips. From the *London Journal*: "The description the man gives of the Person who robbed him, squares exactly with that of the dexterous Sheppard, who is generally believed to be in London playing his old Game."

So where was he?

By seven a.m. on the morning following his escape, the English rain came to Tottingham. Jack rested. He knew few people would be venturing outside. He counted the money from his time in the Castle when visitors had tossed him coins: around forty shillings. He went into the village to purchase supplies. Hiding his fetters under his coat, he entered a chandler's shop, staffed by an aging blind woman. He inquired about a hammer to work on his restraints, but to no avail. He bought bread, cheese, and beer and was on his way.

Saturday, he lay low. On Sunday, the owner of the farmhouse spotted him.

"For God's sake, who are you?" the man asked.

Sheppard knew this question would come and had rehearsed his answer, saying that he was "an unfortunate young man who had been sent to Bridewell about a Bastard Child, as not being able to give Security to the Parish, and had made his escape." Locked up for not having parents or anyone else to pay for his freedom, he had escaped. Who wouldn't have done the same?

The tale worked well enough, although the man still didn't like the way Sheppard looked and told him as much. In the end, the landowner sympathized with the young man's professed predicament and allowed Sheppard to stay.

Later that Sunday, Sheppard secured a smith's hammer for twenty shillings from another man in the fields to whom he had told his bastard-son story. Now rid of his manacles, it was time to head back to the city.

He found a place to eat in Charing Cross. Outside, he ripped and dirtied his clothes to portray himself as a vagrant. Inside, he ordered a roast veal dinner. He delighted in the meat, but appreciated even more what he overheard from the other patrons. A dozen people in the joint were all chatting about the great Sheppard escape. There was plenty of praise, but he also heard advice. The latter all went unheeded. His mother would soon beg him on hand and knee to get out of town. He told her he would, but as he later admitted, "I cannot say it was in my Intention heartily so to do."

The press and the public took it for granted that he had disappeared. That's what anyone else in his place would have done after four escapes. A fifth surely would be pushing it. One pamphlet from the period assumed that he had gone, "Unless the young Refugee should be out in his Politicks, and stay too long too near Home, and, not Foreclose the Equity of Redemption, by a speedy Transportation of himself out of these his Majesty's Dominions."

Enjoying his own celebrity seems to have been worth more to Sheppard than his freedom. After all, what fun is it unless people know what you've accomplished? Whether or not that's what drove him back to the city, he certainly relished his notoriety once he'd arrived.

The next day it was more of the same. He walked into a Piccadilly alehouse on Rupert Street. As chance had it, a woman unknowingly engaged him in a conversation about the jail-breaker *Sheppard*. He played the devil: He opined that the law was too strong, and that the authorities would take Sheppard again in no time. The woman appeared troubled by his words, cursing Sheppard's pursuers and betrayers. Sheppard tells what happened next: "I stept towards the Hay-Market, and mixt with a Crowd about two Ballad-Singers; the Subject being about Sheppard. And I remember the Company was very merry about the Matter."

Now he knew that he was the most famous man in the city. He had no desire, after his accomplishments, to ride off into the sunset and live a quiet life in the country.

On Tuesday, October 20, Sheppard decided to find a place in which to lay his head on a more permanent basis, so he sought refuge in a doss-house near Leicester Square in Newport Market, an area of butchers and meat purveyors. He rented a garret there and, once settled in, sent for Kate Cook. She came and brought a friend, another doxy, Catherine Keys.

In the days ahead, when he wasn't spending time with the two Kates, he was running the streets of his youth, Spitalfields, Drury Lane, and Lewkenor's Lane. He jumped right back into the flow. By month's end, he grew dismayed at the blue butcher's smock, which he had worn thin. He hadn't changed his clothes in over a month. At a pawnshop at the sign of the Four Balls in Drury Lane, owned by the Rawlins brothers, a display of smart new clothes in the window caught his attention.

Sheppard waited until after dark and then slipped into the shop to help himself to some finery. As he was heisting the goods, he heard hushed voices from the room opposite the door. The Rawlins brothers knew they had an intruder; they could act at any moment. Sheppard evened the odds by pretending that he had a partner. He growled instructions at an imaginary colleague, "loudly giving out Directions for shooting the first Person through the Head that presum'd to stir." The Rawlins brothers lacked the stomach for confrontation. Sheppard walked out with a new wardrobe and other accoutrements valued at £60.

By Halloween, Sheppard had been free for sixteen days. That morning, he began drinking early. Thanks to the Rawlins brothers, he had a new costume: black suit, ruffled shirt, periwig, silver-hilted sword, gold watch, a carnelian ring, and a diamond ring. He later noted immodestly of his Halloween wardrobe, "I made an extraordinary Appearance; and from Carpenter and Butcher was now transform'd into a perfect Gentleman."

The outlaw was pushing his luck. What he had gained from the Rawlins heist only emboldened him further. He lunched with the two Kates on Newgate Street, just feet away from the prison. Following their meal, they took a hackney coach through the arch of the gateway, past the prison, below the very spot where Sheppard had slid down the wall in his escape. He wasn't acting the part of a fugitive—not one who was going to remain free for very long, at any rate.

XVIII

FORLORN AT THE TRIPLE TREE

Hangman, hangman, hangman,
slack your rope awhile.
I think I see my father
ridin' many a mile.
Father, did you bring any silver?
Father, did you bring any gold,
or did you come to see me
hangin' from the gallows pole?
—REFRAIN OF "THE MAID FREED FROM THE GALLOWS POLE"

By the time Sheppard met his mother at Sheer's Alehouse on Maypole Street, he was thoroughly drunk. Inside Sheer's, Sheppard bought his mother a glass of brandy and drained the greater part of three quarterns himself. Mrs. Sheppard beseeched her son to flee the country. Sheppard made a hollow promise and left for more drink. Halloween night gave Sheppard a chance to showcase his intemperance. After leaving his mother, he bounced from boozing ken to boozing ken. As the night grew late, he met up with Moll Frisky, a woman described as a "Female of the Hundreds."

Francis Place later wrote about Sheppard as if he was a sot, and William Makepeace Thackeray considered him nothing more than a "scoundrel." But in prison alcohol flowed like water, and we have no reports of him abusing drink in prison, unlike others. Maybe he understood the gravity of each of his imprisonments: He needed to escape to stay alive.

JACK SHEPPARD 1724, IN NEWGATE PRISON, BY SIR JAMES THORNHILL

Halloween was something different. His overindulgence appears more a matter of circumstance. He liked to drink, sure, and even binge on occasion, but getting tanked wasn't an everyday occurrence. His desire to be around people had propelled him into the nightlife. He liked to talk, and sometimes when he drank, he went for it hard. On Halloween, it appears that he wanted to patronize as many alehouses as he could for the simple joy of hearing his name.

But booze was about to lead to his downfall.

In Drury Lane, he and Frisky stopped off at the shop of Nicks, a butcher, to soak up some of the alcohol. He haggled with Nicks over the price of some beef ribs. After coming to terms, the jaunty Sheppard, a nice drunk, invited Nicks for a drink. Sheppard was buying. By midnight, he sat at Mrs. Campbell's chandler and dram shop, sipping brandy with Frisky and Nicks. Sheppard was no longer merely loaded; he was legless. When friends recognized him, they couldn't believe his audacity—to sit there in the open, and tanked to boot. They advised the wanted man to pick up and go.

Sheppard continued to sit and drink. A work boy from the Rose and Crown across the street recognized him and told his boss, Mr. Bradford, who also worked as a borough officer, and as such had a duty to report fugitives. Bradford called in a watchman and a constable, who took Sheppard without so much as a fight. The escapee had in his possession two loaded pistols, but he never attempted to draw them. It was a pathetic end.

Here's how Sheppard remembered it: "At length my Senses were quite overcome with the Quantities and Variety of Liquors I had all the Day been drinking of, which pav'd the Way for my Fate to meet me; and when apprehended, I do protest, I was altogether incapable of resisting, and scarce knew what they were doing to me."

They threw him inside a hackney coach to Newgate once more. But now something inside of him stirred. The booze's effect shifted. They had captured him virtually comatose, but the commotion shook him out of his stupor and triggered a response. "Murder," he yelled from the coach, "help, for God's sake, rogues, I am murdered, and am in the hands of blood-hounds, help for Christ's sake."

By the time the coach reached Holborn, word had spread that the famed Sheppard was being brought to jail. The news brought thousands into the streets. Sheppard called out for help. No one came to his aid. The gawkers had come to gawk, not to liberate a wanted man.

The morning papers of Monday, November 2, ran news of the Sheppard recapture, of course, but also an advertisement of note. "Lost, the 1st of October, a black Shagreen Pocket Book, edged with Silver, with some Notes of Hand. The said Book was lost in the Strand, near the Fountain Tavern, about 7 or 8 a Clock at Night. If any Person will bring the aforesaid book to Mr. Jonathan Wild, in the Old Bailey, he shall have a Guinea Reward." Wild was back. The Fountain Tavern was an infamous brothel. Wild had the pocketbook. Advertising embarrassing goods, one of his oldest tricks, never grew stale.

A week later, Wild appeared in the papers again, this time in conjunction with the Sheppard recapture. But the thief-taker hadn't recovered enough to resume his duties at the Old Bailey as a witness for the prosecution. He remained absent during Sheppard's November court appearances.

Wild directed his attention elsewhere for the rest of 1724 anyway. He was about to become embroiled in a much more dangerous battle. He and an old thief he employed to head his ship of stolen goods, Captain Roger Johnson, were digging in against a waggon-lay practitioner (plunderer of wagons) and tavern owner named "Country Tom" Edwards and Edwards's friend, Thomas Butler, a thief who had worked on and off under Wild's supervision. The story went that Edwards and Johnson had a mutual disdain for one another. When Edwards grabbed Johnson one day in the Strand and called on a constable to have him arrested, Wild intervened and instead had Edwards arrested. It was on that day that Country Tom "vow'd revenge."

Edwards received assistance in going after Wild and Johnson from a most surprising source. A letter buried in a collection of state papers, stamped *Paper Office: 1766*, today stored at the National Archives in Kew, offers clues. The book's title page reveals that it contains: "Cases within the Act passed the 17th of October 1722 for suspending the Habeas Corpus, Entitled An Act to empower His Majesty to secure and detain such person as his Majesty shall suspect are conspiring against his person and Government. High Treason. Suspicion of High Treason." The book contains a letter pertaining to Wild, addressed to the recorder of London and signed by the secretary of state for the Northern Department, Charles Townshend. The latter politician appealed, on behalf of King George I, to have a prisoner named Butler bailed from Newgate in order to provide evidence in a case of importance involving "a most notorious and dangerous Offender." Thomas Butler had served as an underling to Wild, and Wild himself was the offender in this case.

Throughout his career, Wild hawkishly kept his own books and lists, but now his name had been recorded in the King's secretary's book of deeds. The thief-taker general had come to the attention of the heads of state.

At Newgate, Sheppard was secured under 300-pound weights and twice bonded around each leg to keep him in place. He copped to the Rawlins robbery. Officials also remanded a man and woman for the same crime, no matter that Sheppard had sworn he'd acted alone in the treachery. The Castle was still in disrepair, so prison officials locked him inside the Middle Stone Room, the dungeon next door. To avoid a repeat scenario, they put two guards on him at all times. He wouldn't have an inch of freedom this time.

Attorney General Sir Philip Yorke, First Earl of Hardwick, had orders to put this episode to an end. On November 6, Yorke had received official word from the King in a letter from Thomas Pelham-Holles, secretary of state for the Southern Department, to have Sheppard executed. It read:

Sir:—His Majesty being informed of the very extraordinary escapes that John Sheppard, a felon convict, has twice made out of Newgate, and how very dangerous a person he is, has commanded me to signify to you his pleasure that you do forthwith cause him in the proper course of law to be brought before the Court of King's Bench, to the end that execution may, without delay, be awarded against him; and, that he may be the more securely kept, His Majesty would have you move the Court that he may be remanded to Newgate, to remain in custody there until his execution.

I am Sir,
Your most humble servant
Holles Newcastle

On Tuesday, November 10, Sheppard arrived at Westminster Hall in a guarded hackney coach just after eleven a.m. The news of his appearance at the King's Bench had already spread among the masses, and crowds had begun to form. Inside, Attorney General Yorke did as ordered and pushed for expedience in the prisoner's execution, ordering a writ of habeas corpus and writ of certiorari. The court heard the particulars of the case and witnesses' testimony. Sheppard pleaded to have his petition to the King read aloud, which was permitted. They understood his desire for pardon, but the court asked a simple question: If he was so worthy of clemency, why had he repeated the same crimes time and again? According to newspaper accounts, Sheppard responded by pleading "Youth and Ignorance, and withal his Necessities, saying he was afraid of every Child and Dog that look'd at him, as being closely pursu'd; and had no Opportunity to obtain his Bread in an honest Way, and had fully determin'd to have left the Kingdom the Monday after he was re-taken in Drury Lane."

Sheppard seemed to be making headway. He was told that he could save himself, but only by giving up those "who abetted and assisted him in his last escape." He told the truth. "He averred that he had not the least assistance from any person but God Almighty." But, according to the court, uttering the Lord's name in reference to his crime desecrated the commandment on blasphemy. Two steps forward, one step back.

In a final bid to prove he had acted alone in his escape, he offered to exhibit how he had performed his "art," and show the court how he removed his handcuffs. The court demurred and pronounced a sentence of death. Jack Sheppard was to be hanged in six days, on Monday, November 16.

He exited the Hall. The crowd had multiplied. In the commotion at Westminster Hall Gate, a constable's leg was broken. Several other injuries were reported. According to the *Weekly Journal or British Gazetteer*, "He was remanded back to Newgate through the most numerous crowds of people that ever were seen in London, and Westminster Hall has not been so crowded in the memory of man."

The following morning, Sheppard's appearance at Westminster Hall graced the front page of the *Daily Journal*. But not all who read it were entertained. For many Londoners, the story had deeper ramifications, making waves among the propertied class in particular. In their view, Sheppard needed to be stopped. The letter from the King to Attorney General Yorke had been long thought out. Among Yorke's papers is confirmation that the English government was well aware of Sheppard as far back as the beginning of August 1724. After all, a prisoner repeatedly escaping His Majesty's prisons doesn't go unnoticed. By November, it must have been driving the government mad that Sheppard hadn't swung yet. It was stirring the masses, giving other thieves cause, and law-abiding subjects pause. In *The Life of Lord Chancellor Hardwicke*, George Harris states that following Sheppard's original press coverage on August 29, "We afterwards have an account of Sir Philip Yorke and his colleague going down to Windsor, for the purpose of calling His Majesty's attention to matters of the highest importance connected with Sheppard." Namely, the thief's execution.

After his latest death sentence, Sheppard was called to a private meeting by Thomas Parker, First Earl of Macclesfield, and lord chancellor of England, the bilker caught with £100,000 of other people's money. In other words, another thief. Parker didn't swing at Tyburn, though. He merely lost his job in May of the following year. But when the time came, balladeers took notice of the inconsistency. "An Epistle from Jack Sheppard to the Late Lord Chancellor of England" appeared as a broadsheet, its words sung to the tune "Which Nobody Can Deny." It goes in part:

Since your Curiosity led you so far
As to send for me to the Chancery Bar,
To show what a couple of Rascals we are,

Which no Body can deny.
Were your virtues and mine to be weighed in a Scale,
I fear, honest Tom, that thine would prevail,
For you broke through all the laws while I only broke jail,
Which no Body can deny.

Back at Newgate, Governor Pitt, the man in charge, declared the state of matters quite clearly: "It is your business to make your escape, if possible, and mine to take care you shall not."

"Then let's both mind our own business," Sheppard said.

After his hangover wore off, Sheppard had been kind and gracious with all who came to his cell, Ordinary Wagstaff included. When fellow inmates asked him how he was "boned" (caught), he answered amicably, filling in the details of his apprehension the best he could. He was cheerful because he believed he'd do it again. He never doubted that he'd escape, even if it took until execution day. He was certain he could give them the slip.

The bare-knuckle boxing champion James Figg came for a visit at the Middle Stone Room, and the two men had a spirited conversation. Sheppard commented that he wished he'd challenged the boxer to a good-hearted scrap. Figg enjoined the jailbreaker that, if indeed he made the march to Tyburn, he should stop at the boxing academy on Oxford Road along the way. Figg promised to have a drink waiting for him.

On Wednesday, November 11, Sheppard was moved back to the Condemned Hold, albeit a bit more fortified a chamber than it had been during his last visit. Not only was his earlier route above the door no longer accessible, but officials had also upgraded security guidelines.

More visitors followed. Country bumpkins and noblemen alike paid the gate fee—now four shillings—for a glimpse, all enduring the miserable setting and abominable stench that famously characterized the Condemned Hold. An actor set to play him in an upcoming Drury Lane theatrical production stopped by to do research for his role. It's also believed that a young William Hogarth paid a visit to Sheppard, who is recognized as the inspiration for the painter's *Industry and Idleness* series. Wise visitors pressed a cloth drenched with vinegar to their noses to mask the foul air. If a visitor might have pull, Sheppard never failed to ask him or her to put in a good word for him with the King, maintaining hopes for a royal pardon.

Sir James Thornhill, the leading portraitist of the day, had had a hand in decorating the dome of St. Paul's Cathedral and worked as serjeant painter to the crown. Thornhill also visited and sketched Sheppard. The prisoner sat at a table, cross-legged, still attired in his stolen black suit. Thornhill depicts Sheppard's youth, his wide, prominent eyes, as well as his large handcuffed hands set against a child's body. When asked for his opinion of the distinguished painter's initial efforts, Sheppard told the painter that his pencil work made him look too old, "whereupon, some Amendments were made to it," according to the *London Journal*.

Of course, journalists also came, including a return appearance by Defoe to gather the details of Sheppard's latest escape. Perhaps it was at this point—the details shrouded in mystery—that they reached an agreement. If the condemned man made it as far as Tyburn, Sheppard agreed to perform some gallows advertising to promote an upcoming pamphlet telling his story. In exchange, Applebee promised to provide the coffin and hearse.

More sightseers came and went. One of them secretly passed a gift to Sheppard. The infamous prison breaker now had possession of a sharp knife.

As had happened before when Sheppard was at large and unaccounted for, haphazard suppositions again were made, this time erroneously stating that Sheppard had completed a fresh escape. News of Blueskin Blake was more definitive.

As a prisoner at Newgate, Blueskin had a late surge in the guts department. Sheppard may have thought him worthless, but Blake made a series of ballsy moves. While in the Condemned Hold—before Sheppard arrived again—Blake; his cellmate, Abraham Deval, in for counterfeiting a lottery ticket; and a youngster named Julian the Black Boy tried to saw through their iron fetters and burst through the wall of the Condemned Hold the night before their execution. Their efforts were thwarted.

In the cart, on his way to Tyburn on November 11, Blake still didn't give up. While Deval caused a commotion and diverted attention, Blake unleashed his hands by biting at the cord binding them. His hope was to cut himself free and jump from the cart. Once again, the bid was prevented.

All of his efforts snuffed, Blueskin opted to drink. When the hanging procession stopped at Griffin Tavern in Holborn, Blake drank so much that by the time he reached the "three-legged mare" at Tyburn, he was thoroughly stewed. As Ordinary Purney described it, he was so "disguised in Liquor" that he was unable to deliver his dying speech coherently. He reeled and faltered. Perhaps in lieu of a speech, we can remember him for his unending lack of remorse when it came to his action against the thief-taker general. His failure to kill Wild was said to have driven him to tears at the chapel on the morning of his death. But as Blake liked to say, "The Greater the Rogue, the greater the Luck."

Julian the Black Boy was hanged as well, his corpse "carry'd off by the Surgeons, being almost torn in pieces by the Mobb who opposed them."

A legend had haunted the halls of Newgate since the thirteenth century. In a time of great hunger, the prisoners had devoured a German scholar locked up on charges of sorcery. Author Catharine Arnold describes what happened next: "Shortly after the scholar had been killed and eaten, a hideous black dog—with eyes of fire and jowls dripping with blood—appeared in the dead of night and proceeded to exact a terrifying revenge." Over the centuries, the Black Dog had visited the condemned on the night before their executions, "its appearances accompanied by the sound of dragging footsteps and a nauseating stench, like the smell of death." For the unfortunate soul who laid eyes on the dog, it meant only one thing—death was imminent.

Since 1605, custom held that on hanging eve the bellman rang his bell to deliver "pious admonition" from the wall of the neighboring St. Sepulchre's Church. "You prisoners that are within, Who, for wickedness and sin, after many mercies shown you, are now appointed to die tomorrow in the forenoon; give ear and understand, that tomorrow morning, the greatest bell of St. Sepulchre's Church shall toll for you." Then came a visit from the sexton of the church, who rang a handbell at the window to get the attention of the condemned:

All you that in the Condemned Hold do lie,
Prepare you, for tomorrow you shall die.

November 15, 1724, was the dark night of the Black Dog for Jack Sheppard. In the Condemned Hold, no one had called for Sheppard all day. When the bell tolled, it was only Sheppard and the French barber and wife killer, Lovi Houssart, occupying the cell. Nothing better to lift the spirit of a doomed man than a razor-trained throat cutter. Houssart, who apprenticed to be a surgeon, also appears within Secretary of State Townsend's letters. The King was "unwilling that so notorious and barbarous a crime should upon any Account whatsoever go unpunished," Townsend wrote. If the "poor people" prosecuting Houssart should fail, he commanded officials to take the "Prosecution into your hands." Sheppard and the murderer got along famously. The ordinary of Newgate wrote of Houssart that

> the person with whom he seem'd the most pleas'd was John Sheppard; and while they were in the Condemn'd-Hold, they were sometimes very Merry and Jocose together. It appear'd plainly that he was not then making any preparation for Death, from several Expressions which I heard proceed from him; for Instance, when a great Number of Sparks from their Charcoal Fire issued swiftly forth, he wish'd (to Sheppard) they were all of them Bullets, that the Prison might be beaten about his Ears, he might dye like Sampson.

Sheppard was running out of time and options. He was fettered like an animal, but he remained undeterred. He turned his attention to the forthcoming trek to Tyburn. He plotted escape procedures for virtually each step of the death march, up to and including his final moment. He even took the wildly optimistic measure of arranging for friends to hurry him off to a waiting surgeon, who—as John "Half-Hanged" Smith had done in 1705—would restore life to him.

After hanging for several minutes (reports vary from five minutes to two hours), Smith was cut down. He later gave an account of his ordeal, noting that

> *when he was turned off, he, for some time, was sensible of very great pain, occasioned by the weight of his body, and felt his spirits in a strange commotion, violently pressing upwards; that having forced their way to his head, he, as it were, saw a great blaze or glaring light, which seemed to go out at his eyes with a flash, and then he lost all sense of pain. That after he was cut down, and began to come to himself, the blood and spirits forcing themselves into their former channels, put him, by a sort of pricking or shooting, to such intolerable pain, that he could have wished those hanged who had cut him down.*

He was then bled and tucked into a bed, where his life began anew.

Of course, Sheppard hoped it wouldn't come to that. With that in mind, he focused on the moment that his irons were removed and replaced with cord—which precedent suggested would occur—as his best opportunity for flight. He concealed the knife that he had guarded in secret for days in the lining of his coat, near the buttons, directing the face of the blade away from his body.

He waited for morning.

On November 16, crowds gathered before dawn. Two and a half miles lay between Newgate and Tyburn, and the trip usually took at least a couple of hours, with all the stops for drinks. At Sheppard's Tyburn Fair, scaffolds were erected with grandstand seats priced high for the event.

Many professions were given a special day off work—no small gesture, since there weren't many other than Easter, Whitsunday, and Christmas.

The scalper Mother Proctor sold the best seating—known as "Mother Proctor's Pews"—and could pocket upward of £500 on a good hanging day. All available spots were occupied quickly. The air was cold, but it was worth it for the majority of onlookers, who would get their first glimpse of Sheppard. Imagination was about to give way to flesh and blood.

In the days leading up to the execution, London publishers had pushed Sheppard's story for all it was worth. That morning, the *Daily Journal* had devoted its front page to the thief's march. "John Sheppard's Last Epistle" called on Sheppard's people to make the scene:

> *To the Hundreds of Drury I write,*
> *And to all my Filching Companions,*
> *The Buttocks who pad it all Night,*
> *the Whores, the Thieves, and the Stallions.*

Estimates put the crowd—spurred by this and earlier newspaper accounts—at 200,000 strong.

The great number of spectators came as no surprise to London officials. Authorities had expected a crush of people and staffed the event accordingly. According to the November 16 edition of *Parker's London News or the Impartial Intelligencer*, constables and headboroughs in Westminster were under orders to "preserve the Peace this Day, when Sheppard is to be executed; and the Sheriffs have also order'd an extraordinary Number of their Officers to guard him to Tyburn, he is to be carried thither in his Hand-cuffs and Fetters." No one bothered to inform Sheppard that his handcuffs would be staying on his wrists.

He was taken to the press yard to begin his journey just before eleven a.m. He was still wearing his black suit when a smith began removing the fetters from his legs. Sheppard expectantly awaited the removal of his handcuffs. His plot was about to commence. But to Sheppard's great surprise, Undersheriff Watson informed him that the bondage around his hands would stay as it was, an uncustomary turn. Sheppard employed his gilded tongue to persuade his jailers, but there was nothing Watson could do even if he'd wanted to; Sheppard was to die this day. Security would not be breached. Those were the orders.

Suddenly, Sheppard flew into a bloody rage. A great row ensued, only reinforcing the decision to keep the cuffs as they were. By "Main Force" the prisoner was subdued and brought under control. Sheppard's display also roused suspicion. Undersheriff Watson searched him and screamed when the knife in the prisoner's coat opened a bloody gash in his finger. The jig was up.

As the knight of halter secured the noose to the prisoner, Sheppard offered his apologies, and all was forgiven. His anger subsided, and his grand plan squelched, he explained to his jailers for the sake of conversation what his strategy had been. If protocol had followed and his handcuffs had been replaced with rope, he would have leaned forward in the cart and splayed the cord with the concealed knife. When the cart had reached his home turf at High Holborn, where he'd expected to find friendly faces awaiting him, that's when he would have jumped. He would have ditched the cart, slithered down the slight passage of Little Turnstile, and made his disappearance through Lincoln's Inn Fields.

It was worth a shot. Nothing ventured, nothing gained. The officials had won the round, however. With Sheppard's stammer, it was hard to stay cross with the youngster. All laughed.

He took a seat in the tumbrel by Wagstaff and behind the uniformed Jack Ketch. The march to the bloody meadow began. Past St. Sepulchre's, the bell tolled, alerting the city that another man or woman was on the way to the gallows. Up Holborn Hill and through the London streets the procession moved, some on horseback, others on foot: peace officers, city marshal, Undersheriff Watson, soldiers in red coats, javelin men, and a number of constables. In the cart, Wagstaff nagged Sheppard for any last details that might abet his literary plans.

Eyes peered from the main thoroughfare and the city's cross streets. Inside and out, houses on the route swelled with spectators looking through windows or from the rooftops. The wealthy enjoyed beer and wine. The poor soaked in their gin and toasted the unlucky center of attention. Men shouted their support, and young ladies tossed nosegays. Many found it surprising how young the prison breaker appeared. He didn't look like a rogue or criminal; they saw a mere kid.

Sheppard held his head high, but he never stopped conniving. The day hadn't gone according to plan; still, he remained on the lookout, vigilant for escape. Who had come to lend a hand? He didn't know whether allies would spring him or he'd seize a spur-of-the-moment opportunity. Newspapers later noted his peaceful state. "His behaviour was modest, but his concern seemed less than could be expected from one under such fatal circumstances," according to the *London News*.

Near the Church of St. Giles-in-the-Fields, one of Sheppard's former associates reached the tumbrel and whispered in the prisoner's ear. Was this his break? Sheppard let out a chuckle but made no effort to flee. Keeping the message to himself, he continued inching toward the Deadly Nevergreen. At ease, he told Wagstaff, "I have now as great satisfaction at heart, as if I was going to enjoy an estate of £200 a year."

As the cart reached Marylebone Fields at Oxford Road, Sheppard once again saw a familiar face. James Figg, as promised, was waiting for him with a pint of warm sack. The procession halted. Figg handed out wine to the officials, and Sheppard received permission to toss one back with his pal. Other friends stopped by for a last drink and toasted the boxer and thief.

North of Hyde Park, past the intersection of Oxford and Edgware Roads, the convoy's lead horse approached Tyburn. Past the gallows lay the tranquil countryside, open sky, and rolling hills, but around the Triple Tree itself settled dirt and filth, a laundry line of soiled linens covering bodies of all sizes. These spectators had been waiting for hours. The show finally arrived. The rabble swilled gin. Nobles filled the grandstand. Aficionados of executions who never missed a hanging beheld the proceedings. The crowd parted for the death cart, which halted underneath the large hanging beam.

Underdressed for the cutting air, Sheppard tried not to shake. This was it. Nothing left to do. The matter now lay beyond his hands. His friends would decide whether he lived another day. Could they carry off his resuscitation instructions? A house had been prepared nearby for the procedure: They were to swathe the body in warm blankets, apply friction to stir circulation and recharge life, then administer a good bleeding.

Sheppard stood to deliver his speech. He confessed to a pair of crimes of which he had previously been acquitted—the Cook and Phillips robberies—and used the occasion to sully William Field's name anew, declaring once and for all that the snitch hadn't been present for the Kneebone robbery. Accounts reported, "He behav'd very gravely," and "spoke very little."

All around him was the commotion of a festival. A crush of humanity sang, danced, ate, drank, and brawled. Belying the prescribed effect of public executions, pickpockets ran amok at the hanging of a fellow thief. Hawkers sold fruit and various wares, including bogus pamphlets labeled as Sheppard's "Last Dying Speech and Confession."

With everyone's attention focused, Sheppard clarified the matter. He called out for Mr. Applebee. The publisher approached the cart and took papers from the prisoner. Sheppard spoke strong and clear; he wanted his legion of fans to know that this was the story of his life and his last dying confession, which the good Mr. Applebee was going to publish. As per the agreement, Applebee had arranged for an undertaker with a coffin to transport Sheppard's body for burial at St. Sepulchre's churchyard.

But was it really Applebee, or Applebee's man, Defoe? The person's identity has never been established clearly. Many have pointed to Defoe and not the actual publisher, since Sheppard knew the writer by the Applebee name. Others have indicated that Defoe, at age sixty-three, and not in good health, couldn't have suffered the cold and crowds, even for such a good story. If it was Defoe, it certainly wouldn't have been out of character. As John Richetti notes, "Both as an author and as a political agent, Defoe made the assumption of false or alternate identities the very essence of his working method."

Whoever the man was, it was a genius moment of advertising. But as with all good marketing plans, it had gray areas. The autobiography of Jack Sheppard, *A Narrative of all the Robberies, Escapes, &c. of John Sheppard*, came not from the prisoner's hand but from his mouth. Defoe had written the work based on his visits to Newgate.

It was left to Sheppard to signal when he was ready to die. A white handkerchief was the designated cue. When he pulled the cloth from his head over his face, the hangman would send the horse and cart away, leaving Sheppard to hang. The anxious crowd hushed in expectation. His handcuffed hands rose to his face. He took hold of the white cloth, the horse bolted, and his body swung.

Death did not come easy for Jack Sheppard. He swung and swung but would not die. It was a long, drawn-out strangulation. Minute after minute, he remained alive. The crowd shared in his agony. Rich and poor, enemy and ally—all felt for the youthful figure, struggling and in so much pain. It was observed that Sheppard died with "much Difficulty, and with uncommon Pity from the Spectators."

For twenty minutes, he swung. After the twitching mercifully ended, a soldier rushed forward, sword in hand, and cut Sheppard's body down.

Chaos erupted.

Sheppard's body still had life in it. There was still hope. But in the confusion, two factions emerged: the group he had organized that was to bring about his resurrection, and innocent onlookers who took it upon themselves to keep his body from the anatomists. A battle for the body ensued. Sheppard's posse mistook the coach hired by Applebee for one belonging to the dissectors for conveyance to Surgeons' Hall. They broke the carriage to pieces and pelted the driver with rocks. The body floated along the shoulders of the mob, pulled and grabbed, thrashed and clawed. After ten minutes, the battle for possession extinguished any life that remained in the hanged man.

> *Hard Fate at Tyburn's Triple-Tree he swung,*
> *But whilst alive was rescu'd by the Throng;*
> *On Thousand and Ten Thousand Heads he rid,*
> *And by his Friends ill Conduct, not the Hangman dy'd.*

The mob had "kill'd him with kindness."

Sheppard was dead. There would be no encore.

Once the melee had subsided, the victors of the prize carried Sheppard's body toward the Barley Mow Tavern in Long Acre, Covent Garden. But the fight was far from over. The desire to keep surgeons from the body prompted members of the same team to fight one another in a prolonged stretch of confusion. A riot broke out in Long Acre. As the body rested at the Barley Mow, the hunt turned to war. People threw brickbats, rocks, and anything else they could hurl. Looting took place. The number of wounded mounted. Officials literally read the Riot Act (of 1714), but it had no effect. Finally they had to call in the cavalry, a company of foot guards from the Prince's Guard. As author Charles E. Pearce commented, "Surely no malefactor, and he a common house-breaker, was ever so honoured as to have a company of the Guards attend his funeral!"

Hours passed before the hysteria subsided. Officials granted a name-less gentleman the right to take possession of the body. Finally, at ten p.m., the bruised corpse of Jack Sheppard was laid into an elm coffin with a velvet pall. Escorted by the Guards, their bayonets fixed, it was brought to St. Martin-in-the-Fields churchyard and lowered into the earth. The black suit that he had been wearing ended up in the hands of Jack Ketch, a perquisite of the hangman's post.

Unlike *The History of the Remarkable Life of John Sheppard*, released with-out information on the great escape from the Castle, the timing of *A Narrative* was a thing of beauty. The advertising had been precise. For several weeks, it had been on notice as "soon to be published" in the newspapers, and the publicity campaign was sustained straight on to the gallows. The day after the hanging, November 17, the *Daily Journal* further aided the pamphlet's cause. "When he arrived at the Tree, he sent for Mr. Applebee, a printer, into the cart, and in the view of several thousands of people, deliver'd to him a printed pamphlet, Entitled, *A Narrative of all the Robberies* . . . N.B. The said Narrative is now publish'd by John Applebee, Printer, in Black-Fryers; and sold by the Booksellers of London and Westminster."

Priced at one shilling, the pamphlet sold quickly and abundantly. In a month's time, it was in its eighth printing.

Applebee had nailed it. He and Defoe had created the celebrity crim-inal. As Philip Rawlings observes, "To a large extent Sheppard's fame was a product of newspaper reporting—perhaps the first instance of newspapers building up a popular image of an individual."

Two weeks after Sheppard's death, a pantomime titled *The Harlequin Sheppard* took the stage in Drury Lane. The discarded leg irons from Sheppard's final escape were found later that November after a search of his rented garret in Newport Market. The discovery also unveiled an iron crowbar and handcuffs, among other items, including much of the bounty from the Rawlins robbery. As a result, charges were brought against the two Kates.

At their trial on December 4, Kate Cook attempted to distance herself from Sheppard. According to Old Bailey documents: "Yet she pretended to be ignorant of his ever being in Newgate, tho his twice escaping from thence had been the common Discourse of the whole Nation." But as the following exchange illustrates, the court remained unconvinced.

> Court: *You had known him above two Years, and believed him to be a very honest Man? Pray, did you never hear that he was condemn'd, and, that he broke twice out of Newgate?*
> K. Cook: *No really, not a Word.*
> Court: *That's a little strange, considering your Acquaintance with him.—I believe, but few in England, besides yourself can say as much.*

Witnesses at the trial, however, testified that Cook made no secret of her close relationship with Sheppard. The owner of the Dolphin Alehouse described the origins of stolen silver and other goods found on Cook. "She confess'd that she had them from Jack Sheppard, and added, with a vulgar double Entendre, that she was Jack Sheppard's Washerwoman, and had many a time wash'd his three Pieces betwixt her."

The two Kates were acquitted, but prosecuted a second time on a separate indictment. Keys was acquitted a second time. Cook was sentenced to four months and fined.

Elizabeth Lyon had been locked up when her lover was put to death. She turned up a year later as Edgworth Bess at the trial of another thief named James Little. From the constable's testimony, it's clear that she'd been intimate with Little. The lawman described discovering the thief at Lyon's abode in Pattin's Alley, his breeches and stockings hanging on the bed. Little was wearing nothing but a coat. He was convicted and hanged. For Lyon, it was another man dead and gone.

Lyon herself was convicted of burglary in 1726. At her trial, she was described as still heartbroken over Sheppard. A witness in the case described Lyon sipping on a dram of gin, fingering a half-dozen teaspoons that she kissed longfully, and saying, "These were left me by my Dear, John Sheppard, and I have just fetch'd them out of Pawn."

Elizabeth Lyon was sentenced to transportation.

XIX

THE DOWNFALL OF JONATHAN WILD

*The Reason I have to expect ill Treatment from the Populace, gives
me much Uneasiness and strikes me with great Terror. . . . Lord have
Mercy upon me. Lord Receive me.*
—FROM A LETTER (ALLEGEDLY) BY JONATHAN WILD

By 1725, Jonathan Wild was falling out of favor. Still, the length of his run
had been extraordinary. He was able to accomplish what he did because
he was precise. But when he started getting sloppy and overconfident, he
began to lose control. Arrogance prompted him to raise prices on returning stolen items to their rightful owners. His minions feared their master,
but his pride made it ever more enticing for them to take a shot at him.
Biographer H. D. elucidated:

> *It is certain, that the greatest Part of his dark Proceedings wou'd still
> have continu'd a Secret to the World had it not been, that in his gay
> Hours, when his Heart was open, he took Pleasure in recounting his
> past Rogueries, and with a great deal of Humour, bragg'd of his biting
> the World; often hinting, not without Vanity, at the poor Understand-
> ing of the greatest Part of Mankind, and his own superior Cunning.*

As his adversaries' fame rose, even in their deaths, Wild's own reputation correspondingly declined. Blake's blow had given many rogues
similar murderous ideas, as the author of the 1745 collection *A Select
and Impartial Account of the Lives, Behaviour, and Dying Words, of the Most
Remarkable Convicts* wrote, "There were Numbers of them who had taken

AN INVITATION TO WILD'S HANGING

it into their Heads to deprive him of Life." As such, the thief-taker's battle against such forces took their toll: "His Escapes in the apprehending [of] such Persons were sometimes very narrow."

One of Wild's major missteps occurred when he allowed one of his top thieves, Roger Johnson, to skate after a major jewel heist. In doing so, he failed a great many people of quality in restoring their stolen goods. For the rich, the question was obvious: If Wild couldn't get their valuables back to them, what good was it to have him around? If only one class turned against him, Wild probably could have survived, but now both rich and poor wanted him gone. Three months after surviving his bout with Blueskin's knife, Wild had to fight for his life again, all his careful work now under attack.

Three years earlier, in 1722, Wild had purchased a large new sloop for £500 to ferry stolen goods to the shores of Belgium. To head his ship, Wild had selected Captain Roger Johnson, who besides not being a captain also had precious little sailing experience. Many men adopted the title of captain during the era for doing nothing more than dressing and acting the part.

Johnson was, however, an extremely successful bandit, and he and Wild got along well. He was an erstwhile pimp to Mother Jolly at the King's Arms Tavern in Drury Lane until he took to the road. He did so not as a highwayman but as a clergyman, working the scam known as Preaching the Parson. He used a godly aura to earn trust and then asked to change some coins, switching counterfeit ones for the real deal and making off down the road. Other accounts speak of him as being well versed in the "passing lay," a hustle in which a card sharp slow-plays his opponent, whereas the opponent believes he held the advantage.

After hooking up with Wild, the men enjoyed tremendous success in their smuggling endeavors. It was a lucrative affair, and for Wild, who had grown accustomed to the finer life, it nicely offset his monthly expenses. At the Installment of Knights of the Garter at Windsor in 1724,

Johnson bravely accumulated £3,000 worth of stolen jewelry. He even pickpocketed the Prince of Wales. Making such a score against the rich didn't come without consequences, however, and when Wild was tasked with handing Johnson over for arrest, he instead hid and protected him. According to Frank McLynn, Wild did so selfishly for fear that Johnson knew too much and would give away proprietary secrets if captured. Notwithstanding a healthy fear of each other, Wild and Johnson were close, maybe even friends. Johnson's wife, Rosamond, even lived at the Wild residence for a spell in the winter of 1724–25.

So when Thomas "Country Tom" Edwards swore vengeance against Johnson, it was destined to become a prolonged affair, pulling Wild into the middle to aid his captain repeatedly. Edwards was the owner of The Goat tavern, which Marshal Hitchen used in his Q&A in "The Regulator." Wild had thrown Edwards into the pen at least twice, but the waggon-lay expert, as *Select Trials* describes him, was "indefatigable in his Calling." He once trailed a coach for "100 Miles" to secure a heist, and he carried this tenacity into his pursuit of Johnson. Country Tom wanted to rid the world of Roger Johnson for good.

In February 1725, Edwards stumbled on his prey six miles east of London, in Stratford. Edwards apprehended Johnson and, with the help of a constable, held him at the Three Crowns Alehouse. Before proceeding, the three men grabbed a drink, and the delay gave Johnson the opportunity he needed to dispatch word to the thief-taker. Wild and Quilt Arnold grabbed their weapons and took to their horses to free their ally from peril once again.

When the two men arrived in Stratford, they intentionally caused such a disturbance that Johnson was able to flee in the confusion. Wild had interceded once more to ensure that Johnson remained a free man, but this time the authorities intervened against the thief-taker. His obstruction of justice had been too flagrant. When London officials learned of Wild's misconduct, he didn't stick around to see what they had in store. He made himself scarce for nearly three weeks.

Wild was on the defensive, a position that didn't suit him. When reports surfaced that he was not only wanted but on the lam, he could hardly stand it. He responded as he always had when looking to enhance his image. He took to the press and went on the attack. He placed an intimidating ad offering a reward for the slanderers who had besmirched his name in print. Then he paraded around London to contradict reports that he had fled the city.

Only a man with considerable connections could have pulled off such a blatant sting against Edwards. After Wild's move, some of these connections looked to make the most of the moment and use Wild's decline against him. *A Select and Impartial Account* records that "The Magistrates in London and the Middlesex, thought themselves oblig'd by the Duty of their Offices to take Notice of him; this occasion'd a Warrant to be granted against him, by a Worshipful Alderman of the City."

On February 15, following a visit from Mrs. Catherine Statham about a piece of stolen lace, Wild was arrested by Thomas Jones, the high constable of Holborn, and two city constables near Wood Street. A separate raid grabbed Arnold.

Wild was held at the Rose Sponging House. A magistrate was summoned. Wild sat by the fire in the kitchen. Onlookers gathered. What better time for a speech?

I wonder, good People, what it is you wou'd see? I am a poor honest Man, who have done all I could to serve People when they have had the Misfortune to lose their Goods by the Villany of Thieves; I have contributed more than any one Man living to bringing the most daring and notorious Malefactors to Justice, yet now by the Malice of my enemies, you see I am in Custody, and am going before a Magistrate who I hope will do me Justice; why should you insult me therefore? I don't know that I ever injur'd any of you; let me intreat you therefore, as you see me lame in body, and afflicted in Mind, not to make me more uneasy than I can bear; if I have offended against the Law it will punish me, but it gives you no right to use me ill, unheard, and unconvicted.

On edge and a bit sensitive, Wild requested a coach come directly to the door of the Rose Sponging House because of his gout, which made it hard to walk. He was taken to the home of justice of the peace Sir John Fryer, former lord mayor of London, who examined the thief-taker at his home over the course of several hours. Due to an ailment of his own, Fryer didn't even rise from his bed to have Wild remanded to prison.

Wild was committed to Newgate on an initial charge for interfering in the arrest of Roger Johnson. But then three justices charged him with a separate felony involving stolen lottery tickets and a £50 bank note. It wasn't the last time that evidence against Wild changed course. Gerald Howson notes that "Nothing more is heard of these charges, and it looks as if they had been improvised to stop Wild from getting bail." The government was trying to find a crime that would stick.

A letter dated February 23, 1724, from Secretary of State Townshend to Recorder Thompson, shows that the government was lining up potential witnesses against Wild, with Thomas Butler in play as a pawn.

Sir,

The Justices of the Peace, who committed Jonathan Wyld to Newgate, having acquainted me that there is in that Prison one Butler who can be a good Evidence against this Jonathan Wyld, and stands committed only for a crime that is Bailable, his Majesty who would have the said Jonathan Wyld prosecuted with the utmost rigour, as a most notorious and dangerous Offender, would have you admit the said Butler to Bail, if his crime be bailable, as is represented.

Townshend

Even if they didn't have a definitive case against Wild, a second letter from Townshend the same day shows that the government was forging ahead with other details of Wild's prosecution. Townshend instructed Nicholas Paxton, the prosecuting solicitor, that it would benefit their cause to try Wild before the King's Bench Court instead of on his home turf at the common-law court at the Old Bailey, where in all probability the thief-taker would exert considerable influence on the proceedings.

Sir,

The Justices of the Peace who committed Jonathan Wyld to Newgate having represented how necessary it is that particular care should be taken in the prosecution of such a dangerous fellow, His Majesty thinks fit that you should attend and carry on the Prosecution against the said Jonathan Wyld, the Justices of the Peace concerned will put into your hands the Evidences they have against him, and you will lay them before Mr. Attorney and Mr. Sollicitor General for their opinion & Direction in the Management of this Prosecution. And you will know of them whether it would not be more proper to get such a notorious Offender tried at the King's Bench Bar, than at the Sessions in the Old Bailey, where as it is conceived he will be wholly amongst his Abettors and Dependents.

Townshend

Legal expert John Langbein refers to this tactic, in which "the monarch and the government . . . provided episodic reinforcement for criminal prosecution," as "Prosecution by the Executive."

By February 24, it was clear that the government had the goods on Wild. The case went far deeper than Butler. They had discovered Wild's secrets. Recorder Thompson read the Warrant of Detainer aloud in open court:

I. That for many Years past he had been a Confederate with great Numbers of Highwaymen, Pickpockets, House-breakers, Shop-lifters, and other Thieves.

II. That he had formed a kind of corporation of thieves, of which he was the head or director, and that notwithstanding his pretended services, in detecting and prosecuting offenders, he procured such only to be hanged as concealed their booty, or refused to share it with him.

III. That he had divided the town and country into so many districts, and appointed distinct gangs for each, who regularly accounted with him for their robberies. That he had also a particular set to steal at churches in time of divine service: and likewise other moving detachments to attend at court, on birth-days, balls &c. and at both houses of parliament, circuits, and country fairs.

IV. That the persons employed by him were for the most part felons convict, who had returned from transportation before the time for which they were transported was expired; and that he made choice of them to be his agents, because they could not be legal evidences against him, and because he had it in his power to take from them what part of the stolen goods he thought fit, and otherwise use them ill, or hang them as he pleased.

V. That he had from time to time supplied such convicted felons with money and cloaths, and lodged them in his own house, the better to conceal them; particularly some, against whom there are now informations for counterfeiting and diminishing broad pieces and guineas.

VI. That he had not only been a receiver of stolen goods, as well as of writings of all kinds, for near fifteen years past, but had frequently been a confederate, and robbed along with the above-mentioned convicted felons.

VII. That, in order to carry on these vile practices, to gain some credit with the ignorant multitude, he usually carried a short silver staff, as a badge of authority from the government, which he used to produce, when he himself was concerned in robbing.

VIII. That he had under his care and direction, several warehouses for receiving and concealing stolen goods; and also a ship for carrying off jewels, watches, and other valuable goods, to Holland, where he had a superannuated thief for his factor.

IX. That he kept in pay several artists to make alterations, and transform watches, seals, snuff boxes, rings, and other valuable things, that they might not be known, several of which he used to present to such persons as he thought might be of service to him.

X. That he seldom or never helped the owners to the notes and papers they had lost, unless he found them able exactly to specify and describe them, and then often insisted on more than half the value.

XI. And lastly, it appears that he has often sold human blood, by procuring false evidence to swear persons into facts they were not guilty of; sometimes to prevent them from being evidences against himself, and at other times for the sake of the great reward given by the government.

Jonathan Wild had no more secrets. While his methods of business had been somewhat out in the open, these eleven articles left nothing to the imagination. Where did the government learn the intricacies of Wild's tactics? The Warrant of Detainer is so all-encompassing that it obviously wasn't thrown together hastily. Facts like these don't just appear out of thin air. They must have been gathered over an extended period from a source who knew Wild's business inside and out.

Recorder Thompson was just such a person. He had held his post as recorder, or chief judge, since 1714, around the time Wild was getting his start under Marshal Hitchen. For more than a decade, Thompson and Wild had worked together to bring numerous criminals to supposed justice, and Thompson receives credit for writing the clauses directed at the thief-taker in the 1718 Transportation Act, the so-called "Jonathan Wild's Act." After Parliament passed that piece of legislation, Thompson warned Wild to focus on catching thieves and to abandon his side business in stolen property. Wild answered by having a thief steal the velvet seats out of Thompson's coach, then offering his assistance to the recorder to help retrieve his property, to see if Thompson would stand behind his words. Thompson didn't bite.

But why shut Wild down now? Had the thief-taker gone a step too far when he failed to return the jewels stolen by Captain Johnson? Perhaps it was because Middlesex County magistrates were readying charges of their own against Wild, and London didn't want to appear either negligent or complicit. Maybe the government had been waiting patiently for Wild's weakness to show.

In the press, speculation mounted. The *Daily Journal* reported on March 4, "We hear that a Pardon is passed for a Person who is capable of making great Discoveries against Jonathan Wild."

Whatever the cause, powerful men were working behind the scenes to end the thief-taker's run. One way or another, the government was determined to get him.

On February 27, the press joined the chorus of antipathy. Bernard Mandeville, under the guise of *Philanthropos*, authored four articles that appeared in the *British Journal* throughout March. (In April the articles appeared as a collection, *An Enquiry into the Causes of the Frequent Executions at Tyburn*, under his real name.) Mandeville put thief-taking methods under a microscope. He discussed *theftbote*, the practice of dealing directly with pilferers to arrange for the payment for, and return of, stolen goods. Mandeville noted that it had turned the kingdom into a land of "aiders and abettors." Mandeville suggested that London's crime problem was unique and triggered by its practices in the prosecution and treatment of offenders once apprehended.

Like Defoe, Mandeville recognized the city's troubling reliance on the thief-taker. "As soon as any Thing is missing, suspected to be stolen, the first Course we steer is directly to the Office of Mr. *Jonathan Wild*." He also questioned the wisdom of robbery victims paying for the return of what he considered useless (but in fact damning) items. "If nothing could be made of Letters, Papers, and Things of that Nature, such as have no known Worth, and are not readily turned into Money, the numbers of Whores and Rogues, young and old, that are employ'd in the Diving Trade, would decrease considerably; many of them, from a Principle of Prudence, refusing to meddle with any Thing else." But Mandeville didn't mince words when it came to Wild's fate: "A profess'd Thief-Catcher, above all, ought to be severely punish'd, if it can be proved that he has suffer'd a known Rogue to go on in his Villany, tho' but one Day, after it was in his Power to apprehend and convict him, more especially if it appears that he was a Sharer in the Profit." Other London writers lined up in like fashion.

The only scrap of sympathy Wild could find came in late April and early May, when the *British Journal* followed Mandeville's essays with a letter about a thief from the turn of the eighteenth century who recognized that Wild wasn't the first to make his trade as a thief-catcher. Those who came before Wild had held the reins of authority just as tight.

"Thief-Catchers are our absolute Masters," the old thief said, "and they have Intelligence from Tapsters, Ostlers, and Porters, &c. at Inns." Should a thief refuse an assignment or directive, the thief-takers of old would "immediately have us committed for some former Crime; or . . . Bring Evidence to swear away our Lives wrongfully." In summation, this street veteran avowed that "There would be but few Thieves, and but few Robberies committed, were it not for Thief-Catchers." But he also noted of Wild:

> It is certain that the Correspondence he kept up with Highway-Men, Housebreakers, Rogues of all Sorts, was for some Years, beyond Example; and that none of his Predecessors or Contemporaries, enjoy'd the Superintendency over Thieves with such an absolute Sway, or so long successfully as himself. No person was ever more universally known in his Occupation.

The first round of "Authentick" books and catchpenny biographies on Wild's life appeared in advertisements as early as March 24. Poets and balladeers grabbed hold of the subject matter and followed suit shortly after. Some newspaper editors joined the conversation by pointing fingers at one another with accusations of complicity in publishing Wild's ads in their papers. *The Weekly Journal or the British Gazetteer*: "Pray how many Pounds have you had of Jonathan Wild, now in Limbs, for advertising. . . . And no Questions ask'd . . . for being a second-hand Pimp to Debauchery. . . . Your Advertisements were no small Encouragements to Villany and Debauchery."

Prison didn't stop Wild from conducting business. According to the *London Journal* of March 20, "Mr. Jonathan Wild's Confinement in Newgate, we hear, has not prevented his serving the Publick, as he terms it; for which it is not doubted but he will meet a Reward, Several Person have lately applied to him for Things that have been stole[n]; and we are told, he gives his Advice Gratis."

Wild also called for Mrs. Statham, who had paid him a visit prior to his arrest. He wanted to finish the case regarding her missing lace. He chatted with the old woman and arranged for the return of her property. Under Wild's instruction, she paid a porter ten guineas. This payment, albeit indirect, meant that money had been accepted for the return of stolen goods without pursuing the thief per the Transportation Act of 1718. Records of later proceedings show that he "did not then, nor any time since, discover or apprehend, or cause to be apprehended and brought to Justice, the Persons that committed the said Felony."

Wild had committed a felony under the law that people associated with him—the Jonathan Wild Act—and while in prison, no less. He had always been so careful, but the move was boneheaded, and also unnecessary. What was the benefit for Wild? He couldn't possibly have needed the ten-guinea reward that badly, and, in prison, he knew that all eyes were trained on him. Perhaps his vanity was creeping in again, and he wanted to show that he was still in charge. Maybe his battle wounds were really starting to take effect. Ordinary Purney painted a vivid picture of the rather decrepit prisoner: "He had Wounds and Scars still remaining in his Head, Body and Legs. He appeared to be very much disordered and confused in his Thoughts, which he said was owing to those Wounds, and in particular to two fractures in his Skull, which disordered his Brain, tho' cover'd with silver Plates." The thief-taker had become a shell of his former self. *The Tyburn Chronicle* noted that when Wild needed them most, his "Cunning and Courage forsook him."

In Newgate, Wild's savings paid for a place on the Master's side and his own cell. He secured the legal services of Mr. Serjeant Baynes and Mr.

Kettleby. On April 10, Wild's team requested a postponement, which was granted. From their perspective, pushing back his day of judgment certainly couldn't hurt matters, but in this instance, it only provided authorities with more time to shore up the case against him. When Irish bandit Henry Kelley was arrested a few weeks later, he offered information on the thief-taker and Mrs. Statham. The government's case now looked even better.

Throughout the spring, Wild's trial date muddled through a succession of postponements, false starts, and misreports. At one point, *Parker's Penny Post* reported that Wild's syphilis ointment had caused him to salivate uncontrollably. If he was drooling all over the courtroom, he couldn't very well defend himself properly. This Writ of Salivation failed to secure his salvation.

The government had no dearth of options. They lined up one witness after another for the prosecution. In an effort to rile the snakes, they rounded up Wild's acquaintances as well: John Green, Rosamond Johnson (the captain's wife), and a pregnant Elizabeth Doyle, who, it was reported, was "capable of making far greater Discoveries of the dark Transactions of Jonathan Wild, than any other whatsoever." Then William Field ratted on Abraham Mendez, who was arrested on April 1. Mendez and Field took turns smearing each other throughout the spring of 1725.

In the meantime, Wild began making lists. In his mind, all he needed to do was remind everybody just how important he was, which he did in "A List of the persons discover'd, apprehended, and convicted of several Robberies on the Highway; and also for Burglaries and House-breakings; etc." The directory named sixty-seven criminals, including thirty-five highwaymen and twenty-two housebreakers, all hanged because of the thief-taker.

When Defoe came sniffing around Newgate, Wild seized the opportunity. He didn't want his list to remain a courtroom ruse. Like always, he pushed to go public. As Frank Wadleigh Chandler notes in *The Literature of Roguery*, "At Wild's imprisonment he [Defoe] hastened to procure an interview and communicated to the anxious public his exclusive information through notices in *Applebee's Journal.*" Wild got the press coverage he desired, and in return, Applebee and Defoe got Wild's exposé.

On May 8, 1725, *Applebee's* published an abbreviated inventory of the criminals whom Wild had brought to "justice," along with the promise of a more in-depth look at the document at a future date. A week later, on May 14, Wild handed out his list in pamphlet form to members of the jury outside the Old Bailey during a pretrial appearance. The list contains errors of inclusion, exclusion, and otherwise, which impelled some critics, such as *The Tyburn Chronicle*, to castigate Wild for his poor bookkeeping and failed memory.

In the end, Wild's list did him little good. It merely pointed back to him as sole director of the executions of sixty-seven people. He came off not as a great lawman but as a mass murderer. *Select Trials* confirms that members of the court were far from impressed. "If a strict Enquiry was to be made after the Motives of his apprehending those Criminals named in his List, we should find that they were private Interest, old Grudges, or fresh Quarrels, and not the least Regard to Justice and his Country, &c."

Nobody was buying the charade anymore.

The rejection stunned Wild. He couldn't believe that everyone was deliberately overlooking the service he'd provided—ridding the country of thieves. He had fallen for his own theatrics. Others now saw through the guise and understood him to be a self-centered backstabber, but Wild had bought into his role as a servant to England, whole cloth. He believed himself above the law. He had convinced himself of the dream, but the dream was crashing down.

Ordinary Purney wrote that a dejected Wild wondered if he wouldn't have been better off had Blueskin Blake finished the job.

XX

THE TRIAL OF JONATHAN WILD

From out of the populous city men groan,
And the soul of the wounded crieth out.
—JOB 24:12

On Saturday, May 15, the trial of Jonathan Wild commenced, Sir Baron Page, Recorder William Thompson, and Lord Mayor George Merttins among the eminent participants. Despite Townshend's letter, the case was heard not at the King's Bench Court, as suggested, but at the Sessions House at Old Bailey. Attorney General Yorke tried the case for the Crown.

Thomas Butler's pardon proved unnecessary. The government decided to focus on Wild's transaction with Mrs. Statham. He was indicted on two counts, the first for stealing £40 worth of lace. The trial testimony reveals how events at Mrs. Statham's house had unfolded. Henry Kelley testified first.

A former con and hopeless coiner, Kelley came from Ireland on Wild's own ship, helmed by Captain Johnson. Once in London, Kelley called on Rosamond, the captain's wife, at Wild's house. There he met Wild and enjoyed a few tumblers of gin. Another caller, Peg Murphy, arrived shortly thereafter with a pair of clogs as a gift for Mrs. Wild. After a couple of rounds of gin, Wild inquired what direction Kelley would be traveling on his way home.

"To my Lodging at the Seven Dials," Kelley answered.

"Why then, I'll tell you what," said Wild. "There's an old blind bitch, that keeps a shop within twenty Yards of Holbourn-bridge, and sells fine

A BROADSIDE DEPICTING THE DAY OF WILD'S EXECUTION

Flanders Lace; and her Daughter is as blind as herself: Now, if you'll take the Trouble of calling upon her, you may speak [cant for "steal"] with a Box of Lace. I'll go along with you, and show you the Door."

The plan was agreed upon.

At Statham's, Wild stood watch while Kelley and Murphy stole eleven pieces of lace. Kelley's testimony of Wild's location during the heist cleared him of a capital offense. The defense team argued that since Wild had never entered the home, he couldn't be charged with a felony. Wild was acquitted on the first count against him.

The second indictment fell under the Jonathan Wild Act—receiving stolen property without bringing the culprit to justice. Kelley's description of the post-heist conference demonstrated the tough position in which thieves found themselves when venturing to get paid.

"We all went back to his House, where we opened the Box, and found eleven Pieces in it," said Kelly. "He [Wild] asked us if we'd have ready Money, or stay till an Advertisement came out? Stock was pretty low with us at that Time, and so we chose ready Money, and he gave us three Guineas, and four Broad Pieces."

"I can't afford to give any more, for she's a hard mouth'd old Bitch," said Wild, "and I shall never get above ten Guineas out of her."

Statham testified that Wild didn't accept a reward for her stolen lace, but had instructed her to pay a porter the ten guineas. She did as instructed, and in a short time, all but one piece of her lace was returned. She returned to Newgate to show Wild her gratitude.

"Now, Mr. Wild, what must I give you for your Trouble?"

According to Statham, Wild answered, "Not a Farthing, Madam, not a single Farthing; I don't do these Things for worldly Interest, but for the Benefit of poor People who have met with Misfortunes . . . and as you are a Widow, and a good Christian, I desire nothing of ye but your Prayers, and for them I shall be thankful. I have a great many Enemies, and God knows what may be the Consequence of this Imprisonment."

This description of the heathen Wild calling for God's blessing—after all the evil he'd done—drove the courtroom to laughter. But Wild saw a sliver of vindication. Statham had said it herself: He hadn't accepted the money directly. But that didn't matter. A reward was given, he had arranged the transaction, and no felon was apprehended. That's how both the judge and jury saw it as well.

The trial proceeded in convoluted arguments. Wild's lawyers contended that Wild couldn't be prosecuted for receiving the lace if nobody had been found guilty of stealing it in the first place. Wild attempted to ask Mrs. Murphy just that: "I beg your Lordship will ask her, who stole the Lace?"

Recorder Thompson had seen this tactic before—Wild's sleight of hand and calculated misdirection. Thompson hushed the defendant. Wild never should have attempted to fight the charges on legality. Once again, when he needed it most, his shrewdness abandoned him. He later acknowledged that if he had properly acknowledged his situation as "dangerous," he would have played his hand differently and called in favors from Wolverhampton, of all places. But it hardly would have mattered. Wild's time had come. The *London Journal* described his position: "Had he not been convicted on this Indictment, there were others on which he would have been tried; which were needless, in regard this was Capital."

The jury received its instructions, deliberated for half an hour, and found Wild guilty on the second charge.

He was brought to the bar.

"What have you to say, why Judgment of Death should not pass upon you?" he was asked.

Crestfallen, Wild admitted his guilt with regards to the stolen lace. He spoke timidly.

My Lord, I hope I may even in the sad Condition which I stand, pretend to some little Merit in respect to the Service I have done my Country, in delivering it from some of the greatest Pests with which it was ever troubl'd; my Lord, I have brought many bold and daring Malefactor to just Punishment, even at the Hazard of my own Life, my Body being cover'd with Scars I receiv'd in these Undertakings; I presume, my Lord, to say, I have some Merit, because at the Time the Things were done, they were esteem'd meritorious by the Government; and therefore I can hope, my Lord, some Compassion may be shewn on the Score of these Services.

Officials bound his thumbs with whipcord. Thompson told him to make good use of his time left on Earth by repenting, and added that he had warned the thief-taker.

Wild's displeasure knew no bounds, which "Jonathan Wild's Complaint," a broadside hawked on the street, encapsulated. In his time of need, not one soul came to his defense.

Sad Wild thus vents the anguish of his heart.
Thus of his inauspicious fate complains,
As he with gloomy brow surveys his chains.
Ingrateful country! Zealous for thy good,
How often have I hazarded my blood?
Nor have I arms alone, but arts employ'd,
Swords, Pistols, and damnation have defy'd . . .
But you, my faithful servants everywhere,
Whom I have train'd up with a father's care,
Sure you some grateful sentiments will have
And drop a tear upon your master's grave . . .
You by me were made
Successful artists in the thieving trade;
I taught ye to lead comfortable lives
To keep a train of whores, and starve your wives;
Go on and prosper, bravely play your parts,
nor leave unpractis'd any of your arts!
Be rogues renown'd, and trample on the laws
And like true bloods, revenge your patron's cause.

In the days following his trial, it was announced that "the lace woman at Holborn Bridge," Catherine Statham, was entitled, in consideration of her testimony and evidence against Wild, to the £40 reward for his conviction.

After his trial, Wild went on a four-day hunger strike. On May 19, the Dead Warrant was issued. He was granted no reprieve.

In a final bid to save his life, Wild petitioned the King and played a low card. He had been the dedicated husband of six wives, and his current one needed him. From "The Humble Petition of Jonathan Wild": "I have a sickly wife loaded and oppressed with grief, who must inevitably come to the grave with me, if I suffer, or lead a most miserable life, she being already non-compos mentis [not of sound mind]."

He wasn't wrong. Wild's wife, Mary, wasn't stable. She twice tried to kill herself after hearing of her husband's death sentence, which made him her second consecutive husband that Tyburn was taking. After Mary Wild was cut down, she aided her husband by delivering his petition to the King's men on the morning of May 20.

In the document, Wild recognized his previous unlawful actions. "I have indeed been a most wicked and notorious offender," he wrote, but from there he went on to applaud himself for having never been guilty of murder or treason, which afforded him great comfort in the midst of his "calamity and affliction." Nearly a hundred people went to the gallows on his account, but Wild's hands didn't knot the noose, so he absolved himself of culpability. In a final flourish, he offered to compile a new list demonstrating that still more criminals were at large whom he could bring in, if only given the chance, if only reprieved.

The *Daily Journal* published a copy of his plea on May 22. Elsewhere, newspapers were readying the city for the big event, advertising good seats on sale to view Wild's forthcoming hanging parade. Space at the Bull Head next to St. Sepulchre's Church was going for as much as five shillings per person.

Within Newgate, Wild talked often and sometimes incoherently of his past accomplishments. He brought up the likes of Mrs. Knap's murderers: Dun, Rag, Thurland, and White. He touted his capture of Jack Sheppard, James Shaw, and Blueskin Blake. Frederick J. Lyons notes that his rants "would wander aimlessly from one topic to another, as though he were talking to the empty air. Then suddenly, he appeared to be aware of the presence of his listener, and apologized for his obtuseness," and he'd point to his head in apology.

His execution date was set for Monday, May 24, and he was moved to the Condemned Hold. All hope was lost. Wild's body grew weak from lack of nourishment. He had started picking at food again, but his eating habits remained sparse. He was lethargic. He refused spiritual counsel or the opportunity to visit the chapel, afraid that onlookers would mock him visiting God's house, or that the gawkers would interrupt him. He blamed his body.

On Wild's night of the Black Dog, he grew inquisitive. He asked to receive the sacrament. He queried Ordinary Purney on a host of spiritual matters: What happens to the soul in the initial moments after leaving the body, what was "the local situation of the other World"? He took special interest in the "meaning of the words, Cursed is every one that hangeth on a Tree." Purney urged him to repent. Instead, Wild asked about suicide. How did the Greeks and Romans fare so well in lore after self-murder? Purney reminded him of the cowardice inherent in the act, its unholiness in Christianity.

Wild concurred and retired for the evening.

At two a.m., he mustered the courage to kill himself. He didn't want to submit himself to the spectacle that awaited him at Tyburn. This way he still had control. He downed a vial of laudanum, a mixture of opium and alcohol. His head dropped, and he fell to the floor.

Before much time had passed, a couple of prisoners noticed him laid out in the Condemned Hold. They grabbed hold of him and tried to enliven him, walking him in the cell until he came around. He was pale and sweaty, but no veteran of drugs. If he'd taken less, it would have stayed in his stomach and killed him, but he'd taken too much. He vomited, and the elixir of death spattered onto the floor below.

Wild couldn't even kill himself properly.

"The Reward of Cruelty" by William Hogarth

XXI

HANGING THE THIEF-CATCHER

By the Jury he's Cast, and his Sentence is pass'd
That he must to Tyburn be led,
And there in a String a full Hour must swing,
'Till he was Dead, Dead, and Dead, Dead . . .
—N. P., WEIGHLEY, ALIAS WILD: A POEM

Foul weather battered England in the spring and summer of 1725. Dark clouds loomed, and rain fell almost daily amid high winds and cracking thunder.

On May 24, the day of Wild's execution, his long-lost son from his first marriage arrived. The young man was nineteen years old and had come to London to see his old man. Wild and son didn't reunite, however. Authorities learned of the young man, described as an unruly sort, and suspecting that he might cause a commotion, London's civic leaders locked him up for the day.

In his prime, Wild was brave, charismatic, and fit. He had displayed ingenuity and great intelligence in his craft. By the time of his march to Tyburn, Wild was none of these things. According to Ordinary Purney, he had "render'd himself delirious by Poyson." He was still incapacitated. He could scarcely speak even if he'd wanted to. They loaded him in the cart, wearing his calamanco nightshirt. Three condemned men accompanied him.

The cart bounced along the road and he with it, still numb. The daylight spirited him a bit, and slowly he came around—to a great hostile crowd. No young ladies were tossing flowers. London had grown tired of his act. People hurled stones and clods of earth. A rock thrown from a window split his forehead, blood pouring down his face. His cart mates were wounded as well. Purney ditched the malefactors to spare himself.

The working class of London often sympathized with their own, but not today. The mob shouted triumphantly with fury and chanted the name of Blueskin Blake.

Witnesses to Wild's march included poet John Byrom, a member of the Royal Society, who ran with some of London's most powerful and intellectual. In his *Private Journal and Literary Remains*, Byrom mentions Wild on six occasions that include his fall, arrest, trial, and execution, which gives us an idea of the importance of the event, as well as a sketch of it. "Jo Clowes called on me about eleven to go see Wild, who went by to be hanged to-day; I stood at Abingdon's coffeehouse door. Jonathan sat in the cart between two others, in a nightgown and periwig, but no hat on, a book in his hand, and he cried much and the mob hooted him as he passed along." In a verse letter to an acquaintance, Byrom described the populace singing in the streets at the sight of the great thief-taker in such despair.

> *Good law! how the houses were crowded with mobs,*
> *That look'd like leviathan's picture in Hobb's,*
> *From the very ground-floor to the top of the leads,*
> *While Jonathan past thro' a Holborn of heads.*
>
> *From Newgate to Tyburn he made his Procession,*
> *Supported by two of the nimble profession:*
> *Between the unheeded poor Wretches he sat,*
> *In his Night-gown and Wig, without e'er a hat;*
> *With a Book in his Hand he went weeping and praying,*
> *The Mob all along, as he pass'd 'em, huzzaing.*

In *Applebee's Journal*, Defoe notes the same lack of sympathy: "In all the innumerable Crowd, there was not one Pitying Eye to be seen, nor one Compassionate Word to be heard," just more exultant "Hollooing and Huzzas."

By the time Wild reached Gray's Inn Gate, he had returned to his senses. He knocked back a glass of his beloved wine at Griffin Tavern. In St. Giles, the procession halted for a drink at the White Lion.

Wild took it all in, so many faces, all shouting.

"What a strange Rig they run upon me!" he said to no one in particular.

An invitation ticket to the affair had been issued beforehand. It reads:

To all the Thieves, Whores, Pick-pockets, Family Fellowes, etc., in Great Brittain & Ireland. Gentlemen & Ladies You are hereby desir'd to accompany ye worthy friend ye Pious Mr. J— W—d from his seat at Whittington's Colledge [Newgate] to ye Tripple Tree, where his last Exit and his Corps carry'd from thence to be decently Interr'd amongst his Ancestors. Pray bring this Ticket with you.

Wild arrived at the hanging tree, his head split open and body bruised. He had taken a beating. The blood reached down to his nightshirt.

The hangman readied the condemned: Robert Harpham, Robert Sandford, William Sperry, and Jonathan Wild. The thief-taker sat contemplatively in the cart. When the other malefactors stood, Wild remained seated, halter around his neck. When Sperry and Sandford were tied up, Wild finally stood. The blood from his wounds contrasted with the paleness of his skin. He and Harpham said a prayer. The rowdy crowd continued throwing stones, some of which even injured the hangman.

The hangman goaded the horse, dropping Wild and Harpham. Wild grabbed onto Harpham to slacken the rope, and then, around three p.m., he was gone.

No one rushed to save his body from the surgeons. In fact, that's exactly what the crowd wanted. The corpse was loaded into a coach, and the sheriff assured the mob that the dissectors would have at it.

The remains of Jonathan Wild were buried in the middle of the night at St. Pancras churchyard. Officials endeavored to keep commotion to a minimum as he was laid to rest beside his favorite wife, Elizabeth Mann. Days later an empty coffin was found near Kentish Town accompanied by a thin iron sheet, the coffin plate, which read MR. JONATHAN WILDE, DIED MAY 24, 1725, IN YE 42ND YEAR OF HIS AGE.

Somebody had dug him up.

On June 5, the *Daily Journal* reported details of a body on the shore in Whitehall. Except the bones were missing. What remained was a pile of "Skin, Flesh, and Entrails," obviously the leftovers from a surgical dissection. The *Daily Journal* supposed that the carrion was Jonathan Wild because "the Skin of the Breast was hairy."

The trail for the missing skeleton quickly went cold.

A century later, Wild's skeleton turned up in the hands of a surgeon. It had been passed from one surgeon to another since his death. In 1847, Dr. Frederick Fowler sent the skull to a James Deville in the Strand, a prominent phrenologist, without revealing its identity, but asking if anything could be learned of the person's character. Deville's certified report reads, in part: "This is the skull of an individual possessing some useful faculties for mechanical operations, going about and comprehending things readily; but he is a singular character, with a large portion of brain in the region of the propensities. And under disappointment of his own importance, pecuniary difficulties, or intoxication, he would be very likely to commit crime." Fowler then gave the skeleton—"in a perfect state, with the exception of the thumb of the left hand, and part of the forefinger of the right hand, which are missing"—to the Royal College of Surgeons.

Despite the opprobrium surrounding his death, Wild's absence wasn't universally applauded. A little more than a month had passed when the reality of the situation became evident. The city had no one else in place to deal with crime. The *Daily Journal* of July 5 commented, "'Tis remarkable that since the Dissolution of Jonathan Wild, not one Felon has been convicted capitally, which by some is attributed to a Reform amongst the Rogues, and by others to the Want of a proper Person to detect them; but be these Masters as they may, most or all agree, that the giving of Mr. Wild his *Quietus* was just and absolutely necessary."

According to the *London Journal*, Wild bequeathed his son £300.

After the younger Wild was released from prison, he boarded a ship to become a servant in the plantations of America. Historian Sir Walter Besant wondered whether "Perhaps, somewhere in Virginia, there are still living descendants of Jonathan Wild," but Besant thought better of it. "The historian, however, must admit that the young man was more likely to follow his father's steps and be hanged."

Jonathan Wild was dead only two days before the *Daily Journal* reported that Quilt Arnold had taken up with the "relict of Jonathan Wild," meaning the man's widow. Arnold intended to marry the boss's wife.

A year later, Arnold either joined Mary's previous suitors in the grave or went missing. The last mention of the thief-taker's lieutenant comes after he went tracking the murderer Edward Burnworth, alias Frazier, who had a £300 bounty on his head. *Select Trials* documents the meeting between Burnworth and Arnold in an Old Bailey alehouse in which Arnold found himself on the wrong side of a loaded pistol.

"Damn ye," Burnworth said to Arnold, "what Business have you with me? Do you think to set up the Trade of Thief-taking upon your own Account, now your old Master is hang'd? Ye Dog! It would be but tipping ye Justice to blow your Brains out." Instead of killing him, Burnworth forced on Arnold a glass of brandy mixed with gunpowder. "Now, down on your Knees, you Son of a Bitch. Drink this, and with it may be your eternal Damnation, if ever you offer to molest me, or any of my Acquaintances."

Arnold was never heard from again.

Abraham Mendez and William Field spent the summer of 1725 arresting and re-arresting each other. Mendez attempted to keep the Lost Property Office afloat for a stretch at a house on Bury Street. Then he worked as a thief-taker and at various jails as a turnkey, including a stint at Newgate. He remained active through the 1740s and '50s. His reputation as a loyal, honest, trustworthy worker never changed. A biography of him appeared in 1750, *The Life and Merry Adventures of Abraham Mendez, a Jew, Footman to Jonathan Wild, and a Runner at Newgate 40 Years*.

Field was indicted over and over again throughout the 1720s, always beating the rap, until finally he got his comeuppance. He was transported to Annapolis in 1730.

Marshal Charles Hitchen once wrote that it would be just as much advantage to the city to have one thief-taker brought to justice as a hundred thieves. In the end, London got both. But even with Wild gone, Hitchen continued to suffer. He still hadn't lived down the stories about the molly house. The Society for the Reformation of Manners kept a close eye on Hitchen, and ultimately his own predilections led to his death in 1727.

By now he was getting on in years, at least fifty. Still, he enjoyed the nightlife now and again. Hitchen began the evening of March 29 with a couple of pints at the Royal Oak in the Strand with Richard Williamson. The night ended at the Talbot Inn in Charing Cross, where Hitchen had a reputation for bringing soldiers from time to time. There Hitchen had the chamberlain make up a bed and bring wine for him and Williamson.

The next morning, Hitchen was accused of sodomy. He was taken into custody and committed to Newgate. At his trial on April 12, Hitchen was acquitted of the felony charge of committing the act, but found guilty of the misdemeanor of assault and attempted sodomy.

He was sentenced to six months in prison, a £20 fine, and an hour in the pillory on Katherine Street in the Strand. In the eighteenth century, men accused, convicted, or otherwise connected with sodomy especially riled the masses. But Hitchen held no illusions about what would greet him at the pillory. He paid officials and made arrangements, hoping to survive the stint.

He arrived on Katherine Street in a suit of armor and had arranged for a buffer of carts around the pillory to serve as protection. None of it mattered. The mob tore him to shreds. The *Daily Post* wrote that he "was very severely handled by the populace." *Parker's Penny Post* reported that "he appear'd as a tatter'd Scarecrow to fright Owls by Night."

Hitchen survived only half an hour before the undersheriff whisked him off to the relative safety of prison, where he spent the next six months. When he emerged in October, the Court of Aldermen dismissed him from his post as marshal. He had survived the pillory and endured prison. Granted his freedom, he had nothing left. He died a broken and penniless man a short time after his release.

After interviewing Wild, Defoe prepared another pamphlet. He wasn't going to miss out. As agreed and advertised, *Applebee's* published the names of the additional malefactors on Wild's "List" on May 15, 1725. In exchange, Defoe landed Wild's authorized story, which handily allowed *Applebee's* to disavow the authenticity of all other publications.

On June 8, the Blackfriars publisher released "The True, Genuine, and Perfect Account of the Life and Actions of Jonathan Wild; Taken from good Authority, and from his own Writings." It went through three printings in a matter of days.

Defoe's pamphlet spells out Wild's entire operation in forty pages and showcases interviews with clients (or, rather, victims) of the thief-taker, criminal associates, and turnkeys from Newgate. Defoe added dialogue to his account, making the story even more vivid. One passage includes a conversation with a female client—the scene beginning over a pot of tea—that contains more than two pages of nearly uninterrupted dialogue.

Defoe shows Wild little compassion, especially the thief-taker's habit of employing the young. But Defoe handles Wild's adolescence much as he did Robinson Crusoe's: a young man bent on adventure, unwilling to be confined to the tedium of a never-changing workday. The young buckle-maker wanted some excitement. No harm there, but by the end of the tale, Defoe has little sympathy for the criminal mastermind.

> *Thus ended the Tragedy and was a Life of horrid and inimitable Wickedness finish'd at the Gallows, the very same Place where, according to some, above 120 miserable Creatures had been hang'd, whose Blood in great measure may be said to lye at his Door, either in their being first brought into the thieving Trade, or led on it by his Encouragement and Assistance; and many of them at last betray'd and brought to Justice by his Means; upon which worst sort of Murther he valued himself, and would have it pass'd for Merit, even with the Government itself.*

XXII

"To Deliver Myself from This Death of a Life"

No man hath tasted differing fortunes more,
And thirteen times have I been rich and poor.
—Daniel Defoe, *The Review*

By the latter half of the 1720s, Daniel Defoe's work at London newspapers was coming to an end. He had become an old man in a young man's game. He concluded his contributions at *Applebee's* and the *Daily Post* as well. The *Political State of Great Britain* was Defoe's last work in the field, which he edited for less than a year in 1729 and 1730, following the death of its previous editor, Abel Boyer.

Defoe continued to write and publish pamphlets. His interests remained as varied as ever, from civic improvements to sociological issues. A few of his later works included *The Complete English Tradesman*, *A System of Magick*, and *The Political History of the Devil*. He published a pamphlet called "Mere Nature Delineated," describing the discovery of a boy living in the wild in a German forest. When Peter the Wild Boy, as he became known, was brought to England, the news captivated the public. As always, Defoe was on it, his finger firmly on the pulse of public interest.

But not all was well. In the fall of 1725, Defoe endured painful health problems. He underwent a lithotomy to remove stones from his bladder. It was an archaic procedure at best. First, the patient's wrists were tied to his ankles. The surgeon inserted a finger into the rectum, then

PORTRAIT OF DANIEL DEFOE FROM THE BRITISH NATIONAL
MARITIME MUSEUM
(painter unknown)

either—pick your poison—a long silver catheter into the urethra or an incision to the perineum. All, of course, sans anesthesia. Survival wasn't certain. Defoe shared his experience with his readers in one of his final *Applebee's* pieces. "Here's a Man cut for the Stone, and perishes in the Operation, torn and mangled by the merciless Surgeons, cut open alive, and bound Hand and Foot to force him to bear it; the very Apparatus is enough to chill the Blood, and sink a Man's Soul within him."

For some of Defoe's sociological treatises in the 1720s, he used the pseudonym Andrew Moreton, Esq. Not long fooled, readers soon identified Moreton as Defoe. *Read's Journal* publicly acknowledged the point in October 1728. Moreton didn't mince words. In *Augusta Triumphans: Or the Way to Make London the Most Flourishing City in the Universe*, he concluded with an essay titled "An Effectual Method to Prevent Street Robberies," in which he laughed off the pathetic state of the capital city's watchmen, calling them "decrepid, superannuated Wretches, with one Foot in the Grave, and the t'other ready to follow; so feeble, that a Puff of Breath can blow 'em down: Poor Mortals! Much fitter for an Alms-house than a Watch-house. A city watch'd and guarded by such Animals, is wretchedly watch'd indeed." Years had passed, but little had been done to lessen the problem. He wrote a second pamphlet on the issue that year, "Second Thoughts are Best and Street Robberies Consider'd."

Augusta Triumphans found Defoe in a retrospective mood. In the past, he had often given the impression of a rascal, a friend deadpanning you, hoping to get a rise. In his writing, he could be blustery, extremist, or pushing absurdity, as he had in the "Shortest Way" pamphlet. But in *Augusta Triumphans*, his mind wandered, touching on an array of subjects, including the establishment of a London-based university, a music academy, a hospital for foundlings, and the hazards of excessive gin drinking. He also reflected on the nature of criticism:

> *A Man who has the Publick Good in View, ought not in the least to be alarm'd at the tribute of Ridicule which Scoffers constantly pay to projecting Heads: It is the Business of a Writer, who means well, to go directly forward, without regard to Criticism, but to offer his Thoughts*

as they occur; and if in twenty Schemes, he hits but on one to the Pur-
pose, he ought to be excused failing in the Nineteen for the Twentieth
Sake.

If ever a man knew criticism, it was Defoe. As Paul Scanlon notes, nearly all of the surviving references to him by his contemporaries come in "the form of personal attack," and no one did more to disparage Defoe's reputation than Alexander Pope, who immortalized Defoe in *The Dunciad.*

Ear-less on high, stood pillory'd D—
And T— flagrant from the lash, below:

Pope later amended the couplet:

Ear-less on high, stood un-abash'd Defoe,
And Tutchin flagrant from the scourge, below:

In retrospect, Pope's words appear comparatively benign. But Defoe's inclusion in *The Dunciad* had far-reaching and long-lasting effect, plaguing him for the rest of his years.

In *Augusta Triumphans*, he acknowledges that he is reaching his last days. "I have but a short Time to live, nor would I waste my remaining Thread of Life in Vain, but having often lamented sundry Publick Abuses, and many Schemes having occur'd to my Fancy, which to me carried an Air of Benefit; I was resolv'd to commit them to Paper before my Departure, and leave, at least, a Testimony of my good Will to my Fellow Creature." The final pamphlet he authored, "An Effectual Scheme for the Immediate Preventing of Street Robberies," appeared in 1731.

In the fall of that year, Defoe was seventy years old and once again on the run from creditors. He had overextended himself in the purchase of a property in Colchester. A Mrs. Brooke was hounding him for payment on a bill long unpaid, or paid but without proof or receipt in hand.

He had unpaid rents owed all over town. Even the chamberlain of Stoke Newington was on his case for money. He also needed money for a dowry for the wedding of his daughter Sophia to Henry Baker. He wasn't destitute, but he was deeply in debt. The author of *Robinson Crusoe* couldn't afford to relax in his golden years.

The debt to Mrs. Brooke wound up in court. When obliged to pay her £400, Defoe made himself scarce to avoid debtors' prison. He fled to the city, to Cripplegate, back where it all began. He boarded in Rope-maker's Alley from the fall of 1730 to April 1731. A gate known as Far-thing Latch connected Ropemaker's Alley to Grub Street, and the owner of the gate charged a farthing for safe passage between the two neighbor-hoods. Defoe hid out, exhausted.

Defoe's final letter, dated August 12, 1730, addresses his son-in-law, Henry Baker. "I am at this time under a weight of very heavy illness, which I think will be a fever." But Defoe was also brokenhearted, weak, and isolated from those he loved. He lamented that he might never see his seven-month-old grandson David.

> *It is too much for me. Excuse my infirmity. I can say no more: my heart is too full. I only ask one thing of you as a dying request. Stand by them when I am gone. . . . I am so near my journey's end, and am hastening to the place where the weary are at rest, and where the wicked cease to trouble; be it that the passage is rough, and the day stormy, by what way soever He pleases to bring me to the end of it, I desire to finish life with this temper of soul in all cases: Te Deum Laudamus. [We praise thee, O God.]*

Daniel Defoe died, alone, on Saturday, April 24, 1731.

The official cause of death was given as "Lethargy," which we might understand as exhaustion.

He was buried within the Dissenters' burial ground in Bunhill Fields, his name entered into the burial registry as "Dubow." A Cripplegate his-torian remarked, "Such is fame! The Parish Clerk knew him not."

On May 1, the *Universal Spectator and Weekly Journal* ran the fol-lowing second-page notice: "A few Days ago died Daniel Defoe, Sen. A Person well known for his numerous writings."

The *Daily Journal* reported his death with a bit more biography, saying that he possessed "great natural Genius; and understood very well the Trade and Interest of this Kingdom." The paper ran additional death notices, reports of various ship's arrivals and departures, news of a man apprehended for theft, and an advertisement offering a reward for the return of a lost bank note, "No questions asked."

No biographers came knocking to write his life story. Except for a few pieces, his library was auctioned off shortly after his death. Daniel Defoe was forgotten.

EPILOGUE

LEGENDS

Defoe had invented a new way to examine the world, and today's journalists are his descendants.
—JOHN J. MILLER, *WALL STREET JOURNAL*

Today, in the Hunterian Museum at the Royal College of Surgeons, across from Lincoln's Inn Fields in London, the first thing to greet visitors is the skeleton of the old thief-taker general of Great Britain and Ireland. Jonathan Wild's skeleton remains with the surgeons who anatomized him.

In 1728, three years after Wild's death, John Gay released *The Beggar's Opera*, an immensely popular ballad opera that ran for sixty-two consecutive shows, the most successful production of its century. The satire of Prime Minister Robert Walpole's corrupt administration remains popular to this day. The thief-taker Peachum is based on Jonathan Wild. In the opening scene, Peachum fingers through his account books: "A Lawyer is an honest Employment, so is mine. Like me too he acts in a double Capacity, both against Rogues and for 'em; for 'tis but fitting that we should protect and encourage Cheats, since we live by them."

Henry Fielding's *Life and Death of Jonathan Wild, the Great* appeared in 1743, further cementing Jonathan Wild's image. Six years later, brothers Henry and John Fielding established the Bow Street Runners, London's first police force. Of eighty parish constables in Westminster, Henry Fielding banded together the only six he could trust among them. Thief-taking and reward money continued well into the nineteenth century, along with all the other crimes that Wild had organized. London's Metropolitan Police Service was established in 1829.

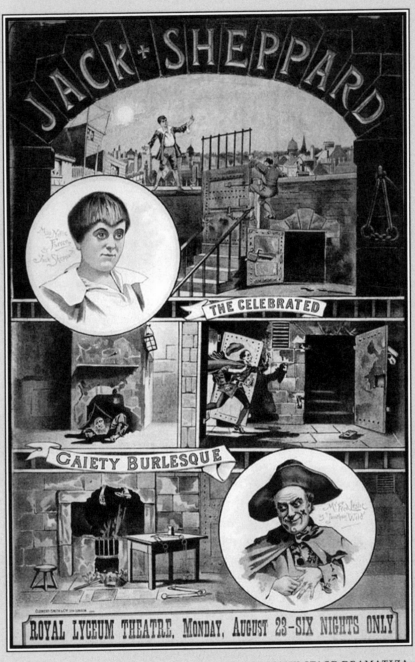

An 1885 poster advertising one of the many stage dramatizations of Jack Sheppard's life and death

By the time Edward Viles's romance *Blueskin* was released in 1868, of which, author S. M. Ellis noted, Wild is presented as "the most devilish creature ever conceived. He murders some one in nearly every chapter"—Wild was firmly established as the villain. Jack Sheppard, on the other hand, became revered. London denizens long appreciated those who fought back against Newgate. Captain Macheath in *The Beggar's Opera* was based on the infamous jailbreaker. But it was in the mid-nineteenth century, when William Harrison Ainsworth wrote *Jack Sheppard: A Romance*, that Sheppard mania returned. Ainsworth's tale battled *Oliver Twist* by Charles Dickens for market share, both first running simultaneously in the pages of *Bentley's Miscellany* from 1839 to 1840. Ainsworth and Dickens had conceived their stories together while perusing the pages of *The Newgate Calendar*. Dickens's Bill Sikes derives from Hell & Fury Sykes.

On the heels of *Jack Sheppard*'s popularity came a bevy of plays. Sheppard's resurgence not only captivated readers, but his name was also causing a stir on the streets again. Many blamed the fictional accounts for instigating fresh crimes and thuggery. It was soon illegal to use his name in further theatrical productions. A prison inspector, looking to ascertain the deleterious effects of Sheppardism, interviewed prison-school children. J. L. was fourteen years old and in the clink for pickpocketing £25. His response to the inspector:

The first time I was ever at the theatre was to see Jack Sheppard. There were two or three boys near to the house who were going, and they asked me. I took sixpence from the money I used to lay up weekly for clothes. The next time I went, which was the week after, I borrowed the money from a boy; I returned it to him the Saturday after. I then went many times. I took the money from my mother out of her pocket as she was sitting down, and I beside her. There was more than sixpence in her pocket. I got a great love for the theatre, and stole from people often to get there. I thought this Jack Sheppard was a clever fellow for making his escape and robbing his master. If I could get out of gaol, I think I should be as clever as him; but after all his exploits, he got done at last.

In America, outlaws Frank and Jesse James admired Sheppard and closed their letters to the *Kansas City Star*, "Signed, Jack Sheppard." In 1920s Berlin, Bertolt Brecht and Kurt Weill collaborated on *The Threepenny Opera*, a retelling of *The Beggar's Opera*. One of the *Threepenny* songs—"Mack the Knife" in English—became a musical standard and gave crooner Bobby Darin a number-one hit in 1959.

But none of it would have happened if not for Daniel Defoe and his pamphlets on the two criminal geniuses, Wild and Sheppard. He may have brought them to life with his detail-rich biographies, but precious little praise came his way for his troubles. For half a century, few remembered Daniel Defoe. Then, in 1785, George Chalmers wrote the first biography on the writer, and slowly, the accolades mounted. By 1870, the "ear-less," pilloried author had become a national hero. When his bones were disinterred for a monument, a riot nearly ensued. He rests near John Bunyan and William Blake in Bunhill Fields and stands among them as a literary titan.

His writing propelled journalism into the future and gave us: the celebrity criminal, the gossip column, investigative reporting, tabloid journalism, and the true crime genre. Our obsession with highwaymen, outlaws of the West, train robbers, and organized crime bosses all begins with Defoe. His work has influenced countless writers since, including Truman Capote, Norman Mailer, Gay Talese, Hunter S. Thompson, Tom Wolfe, and more. Defoe hardly received the praise due him when living, but in death, he has received the greatest acclaim possible, in that so many people still read, study, argue over, and emulate his work.

APPENDIX

CANTING DICTIONARY

Abram: Naked.

Abram cove: Poor fellow.

Autem mort: Married woman.

Belly cheat: An apron.

Betty: An instrument to break a door.

Bite the roger: Steal the portmanteau.

Bleating cheats: Sheep.

Booze: Drink.

Bousing cheat: Bottle.

Brush: Fly or run.

Budge: One that slips into a house in the dark and steals what he can lay hands on.

Bugbar: Dog.

Bung: Purse.

Cackling cheat: Chicken.

Cackling farts: Eggs.

Cank: Dumb.

Canniken: Plague.

Chapt: Dry, or thirsty.

Clincher: Crafty fellow.

Cly the jerk: To be whipped.

Cobble colt: Turkey.

Coker: Lie.

Cone: Man.

Couch: To lie down.

Couch a hog's head: To go to sleep.

Cramp-rings: Bolt or shackles.

Crashing cheats: Teeth.

Cull, or Cully: Fop, or one that may be easily fooled.

Damber: Rascal.

Dark man: Night or evening.

Dimber: Pretty.

Drawers: Hose, stockings.

Drousie: Peeping.

Dub: Enter or go into a house.

Earnest: A part or share.

Famble cheats: Rings or gloves.

Fambles: Hands.

Fan-grasp the cove: Agree with a man.

Fencing cully, or cull: A receiver of stolen goods.

Fib: To beat.

Flick the peter: Cut the cloak bag.

Flicker: Glass.

Flogging cove: Beadle of Bridewell.

Fogus: Tobacco.

Gage: Pot or pipe.

Gallant: Rum.

Gentry-mort: A gentlewoman.

Gigg: Nose.

Gigger: A door.

Gilt: Picklock, or crowbar.

Glazier: One that creeps in windows and lets in another to rob a house.

Glim flashy: Angry.

Glym-stick: Candlestick.

Glymmer: Fire.

Grannum: Corn.

Grinders: Teeth.

Gropers: Blind men.

Grunting cheat: Suckling pig.

Grunting peck: Pork.

Gybe: Any writing or a passport.

Heave a booth: To rob a house.

Heaver: Breast.

Hog: Shilling.

Hornman beak: Constable.

Jockum gage: Chamber pot.

Ken: House

Libben: A private dwelling-house.

Libege: Bed.

Lifter: Crutch.

Lips: Guns.

Loure: Money.

Lurries: All manners of clothing.

Make: Halfpenny.

Marinate: Transported.

Maund: Beg.

Maunders: Beggars.

Mish: Shirt.

Mower: Cow.

Mower beater: Drover.

Mumpers: Genteel beggars.

Muns: Face.

Mynt: Gold.

Nab: Head.

Nab cheat: Hat.

Napper: Cheat or thief.

Napper of naps: Sheep stealer.

Nazy: Drunken.

Nazy cove: Drunkard.

Nub: Neck.

Ogles: Eyes.

Old Mr. Gory: Piece of old gold.

Oracker: An arse.

Pannam: Bread.

Panter: Heart.

Peck, or peckidge: Any sort of meat.

Peeper: Looking glass.

Peery: Fearful.

Pikes: To run away.

Plant: To lay in place, or hide.

Pouting kane: Bar or tavern.

Prance: Horse.

Prancers: Horse stealers.

Prating cheat: Tongue.

Prigs: All sorts of thieves.

Quacking cheat: Duck.

Queer: Base or roguish.

Queer ken: Prison.

Raise a cloud: To take tobacco.

Rattling-mumpers: Coach beggars.

Ridge cully: Goldsmith.

Ruff peck: Bacon.

Ruffin: Devil.

Ruffler: A notorious rogue.

Rum buzzing welts: Cluster of grapes.

Rum mort: A curious wench.

Rum pad: Highwayman.

Rum padders: Horse.

Rumboy'd: Sought after with a warrant.

Rumville: London.

Salomon, or Solomon: Mass.

Scallen ken: Broker's shop.

Scour: To wear.

Skippers: Barn.

Smacking cove: Coachman.

Smelling cheat: Flower or nosegay.

Smiter: An arm.

Snudge: One that lies underneath a bed or in some other covert place to watch an opportunity to rob the house.

Spangles: Ends of gold or silver.

Squeeker: Bar-boy.

Stall wimper: Bastard.

Stampers: Feet.

Stamps: Shoes.

Starter: Question.

Stow your wilds and plant 'em: Be careful of what you say.

Swang: Shop.

Tip: Give.

Topping cheat: Gallows.

Topping cove: Highway.

Tour: To look.

Track up the dancers: Go up the stairs.

Trim: To hang.

Tumbler: Cart.

Wap: Copulate.

Watcher: Silver.

Whit: Newgate.

Win: Penny.

Abridged and edited from "Jonathan Wild's Canting Dictionary," which appeared in *The History of the Lives and Actions of Jonathan Wild, Thief-Taker; Joseph Blake, alias Bleuskin, Footpad; and John Sheppard, Housebreaker,* author unknown.

ACKNOWLEDGMENTS

I must recognize Gerald Howson's book, *Thief-Taker General*. He stridently took time to leave a road map for future generations looking into Jonathan Wild. It's a dogged piece of work, allowing for others, like myself, to not have to start from scratch. Speaking of books, *Select Trials* are also fascinating books, and the great number of occasions Jonathan Wild's name appears really puts in perspective how much he was at the center of the London legal proceedings at the time. I'd like to pass my appreciation on to a few of the kind people who helped me when I ran across them: Judy Robinson at the British Library in London and Nathan Dorn and Gary Johnson at the Library of Congress in Washington. Being able to grasp (with gloves, per the rules) *Applebee's Weekly Journal* from 1721, stained with coffee or tobacco, I couldn't help but take a moment to feel the link to the past and ponder some of the hands who likewise held the paper while sitting in a coffeehouse, outlaws' hands like Wild, or Defoe himself.

I'd like to thank James Jayo at Lyons Press for first saying yes, and then using a sharp editing eye, as well as Lauren Brancato. And thanks to my agent, Elise Capron of Dijkstra Literary Agency, for all of her time and efforts, but also for her kindness and support.

Also, my gratitude to Chris Reilly for a fridge full of IPA, no matter if he looked on in dismay as I guzzled instead of sipped; Public Radio App for introducing me to WUMB Boston, for nice and steady background music; and my technical advisor, Mr. Ben Soltesz.

Betti Skirboll and Jim and Kris Meighan, thanks for a great deal, but also it's of great value and encouragement to see enjoyment in books.

Finally, Jamie (a very reluctant and disgruntled editor), Hank, Emerson, and Scarlett, thanks for always being happy to see me, and everything else.

NOTES

Introduction: A Brawling Back-Alley Bunch

x. charges another with corpus swelling: Pat Rogers, "Defoe or the Devil," *London Review of Books*, 11:5 (1989), pp. 16–17.

x. "simpletons or rascals": Maximillian E. Novak, "The Defoe Canon: Attribution and De-Attribution," *Huntington Library Quarterly*, 59:1 (1996), p. 92.

x. "look craven": P. N. Furbank and W. R. Owens, "Who Wrote What? The Question of Attribution 3," *Eighteenth-Century Fiction*, Vol. 9, No. 2 (Jan. 1997).

xi. "an accepted fact by every Defoe scholar": Maximillian E. Novak, "Daniel Defoe and *Applebee's Original Weekly Journal*: An Attempt at Re-Attribution," *Eighteenth-Century Studies*, Vol. 45, No. 4 (2012), pp. 585-608.

xii. "Now at the termination": Arthur Griffiths, *The Chronicles of Newgate*, p. v.

xii. "As I am quick to conceive": Daniel Defoe, *Augusta Triumphans*, p. 8.

Prologue: The Triple Tree

xiii. To close the scene: London Metropolitan Archives [LMA], "Lastly to the Fatal Place of Execution" [Anon.], Reference Code: SC/GL/PR/P1/TYB/M0008982CL.

xiii. "All Good people pray": Walter Thornbury and Edward Walford, *Old and New London: A Narrative of Its History, Its People and Its Places*, p. 484.

xiii. "The shape of love's Tyburn that hangs up simplicity": William Shakespeare, *The Works of Shakespeare: Love's Labour's Lost*, p. 88.

xv. *I understand the root of it is dry*: *Description of Tyburn*. John Taylor, The Water-Poet (http://www.unc.edu/~charliem/taylor.htm).

xv. in 1196 with William Fitz Osbert: Alfred Marks, *Tyburn Tree: Its History and Annals*, p. 54.

xv. Dr. John Story became the first person: Arthur Lawrence Hayward, *Lives of the Most Remarkable Criminals, Who Have Been Condemned and Executed*, p. x.

xv. "the executioner had cut him": Ibid.; John Bayley, *The History and Antiquities of the Tower of London: With Memoirs*, Vol. 1, p. 152.

xvi. "The Sight has had an extraordinary": Samuel Richardson, *Letters Written to and for Particular Friends: On the Most Important Occasions,* Letter CLX. From a Country Gentleman in Town, to his Brother in the Country, describing a publick Execution in London, p. 239, retrieved from Eighteenth-Century Collections Online [ECCO]. Text Creation Partnership (http://quod.lib.umich.edu/e/ecco/004845953.0001.000/1:3?rgn=div1;view =toc).

xvi. "Many cart loads of our fellow": Henry Fielding, "An Enquiry into the Causes of the Late Increase of Robbers," *The Works of Henry Fielding: Complete in One Volume, with Memoir of the Author,* p. 793.

xvii. "And being hanged a little while": Thomas B. Howell and Thomas J. Howell, "The Confession of Thomas Norton," *Cobbett's Complete Collection of State Trials and Proceedings for High Treason,* p. 988.

Chapter One: The Dissenter

3. "a middle-sized spare man": *London Gazette* (January 11–14, 1703).

4. "hang'd . . . purg'd from the Face": *The Shortest Way with the Dissenters: Taken from Dr. Sach-ll's Sermon, and Others, Or Proposals for the Establishment of the Church,* pp. 13–19 [SW].

4. "no more outrageous": . Maximillian E. Novak, *Daniel Defoe: Master of Fictions: His Life and Ideas,* p. 173 [MN].

4. "Defoe was a gambler": Ibid., p. 177.

5. "mind impatient of confinement . . . beseech your Lordship": Daniel Defoe, ed. by George Harris Healey, *Letters of Daniel Defoe,* pp. 1–2 [*Letters*].

5. "prisons, pillories, and such like": Ibid., p. 2.

5. "passive courage": Ibid., p. 6.

6. "Two hundred thousand Englishmen": Daniel Defoe, *Selected Writings of Daniel Defoe,* p. 83.

6. "Our name is Legion": Ibid., p. 85.

6. "mixtures of Blood": Daniel Defoe, *A True Collection of the Writings of the Author of The True-Born Englishman,* Preface, p. x. [*True Collection*].

6. "the dramatic gesture": Paula R. Backscheider, "No Defense: Defoe in 1703," *PMLA,* Vol. 103, No. 3 (May 1988), p. 275.

7. maneuver invaded "the Conscience": appears in MN, p. 178, from the 1706 pamphlet "The Source of Our Present Fears Discover'd," A4.

7. "Swear that if he ever met him": Daniel Defoe, "A Dialogue between a Dissenter and the Observator," *A Collection of the Writings of the Author of The True-Born Englishman*, p. 225.

7. barreling out a window: MN, p. 179.

7. "a disordered mind": Quoted in Paula R. Backscheider, *Daniel Defoe: His Life*, p. 104 [PB].

7. "On Thursday Daniel de Foe": *Post Man and the Historical Account*, May 22–25, 1703.

8. "messengers" seized him, according to the *London Post*: *The London Post*, May 21–24, 1703. Appears in *The Nation*, Vol. 87, No. 2255 (September 17, 1908), p. 259.

8. George Croome, and the man: LMA CLA/047/LJ/01/0471. Sessions of the Peace, January 13, 1703, and Gaol Delivery, January 15, 1703.

8. nickname "Dismal": Claude Rawson, ed., *Politics and Literature in the Age of Swift: English and Irish Perspectives*, p. 124.

8. *Sir in Some Letters*: *Letters*, p. 8.

8. Court records show that: LMA CLA/047/LJ/01/0475. Sessions of the Peace, July 5, 1703, and Gaol Delivery, July 7, 1703.

8. The "True & Perfect Kallendar": LMA MJ/SR/2015. Sessions Roll: Gaol Delivery, July 1703.

9. "Of the Lord Mayor . . . pay off against Defoe": John Robert Moore, *Defoe in the Pillory and Other Studies*, p. 21.

9. "That no Man is qualified": "Reformation of Manner: A Satyr," *True Collection*, p. 64.

9. *L——l, the Pandor of thy Judgment-Seat*: Ibid., p. 70.

10. as rain drizzled down: PB, p. 117.

11. *The time being near expired*: *Fog's Weekly Journal* (June 12, 1731).

11. "No man in England": John Robert Moore, *Daniel Defoe: Citizen of the Modern World*, p. 104 [DD].

12. Defoe paid at least twenty guineas: PB, p. 107.

12. "The author had some great": E. M. Forster, *Aspects of the Novel*, p. 57.

12. "Pray, ask that gentleman": Daniel Defoe and Howard Maynadier, "Appeal to Honour and Justice," *The Works of Daniel Defoe*, Vol. 8, p. 232.

13. "with my hand, my Pen": *Letters*, p. 3.

13. "He is a very capable man": appears in DD, p. 145.

Chapter Two: The Streets of London

15. *The houses of Old London*: Thornbury and Walford, *Old and New London*, Vol. 1, p. 2.

15. Because of government planning laws: Patrick Pringle, *Hue and Cry: The Story of Henry and John Fielding and Their Bow Street Runners*, pp. 18–19 [PP].

15. The Thames overflowed [London description]: Kirstin Olson, *Daily Life in the Eighteenth Century*, p. 58; Frank McLynn, *Crime and Punishment in Eighteenth-Century England*, pp. 1–2 [FM]; and Mary Dorothy George, *London Life in the Eighteenth Century*, pp. 84–86, [MDG].

16. Population: 660,000 in 1712 from Gerald Howson, *Thief-Taker General: The Rise and Fall of Jonathan Wild*, p. 22 [GH], and 630,000 in 1715 from Tim Hitchcock, Robert Shoemaker, et al., "London History—London, 1715–1760," Old Bailey Proceedings Online (www.oldbaileyonline.org, version 7.0, September 5, 2013) [OBP].

16. greater rate of deaths than births: PP, p. 19.

16. "good for a few and bad for most": PP, p. 17.

16. *While worshippers were thronging the churches*: Ibid.

16. "The city was seen as sucking": Fergus Linnane, *London's Underworld: Three Centuries of Vice and Crime*, p. 24 [FL].

16. William Johnson—a butcher: William Jackson, *The New & Complete Newgate Calendar*, pp. 145–6 [NNC].

17. during this period in London at around 115,000: Patrick Colquhoun made this claim in *A Treatise on the Police of the Metropolis* (3rd ed.), p. xi.

17. The Bloody Code: FM, p. xi; National Archives, "Education: Crime and Punishment" (http://www.nationalarchives.gov.uk/education/candp/punishment/g06/g06cs1.htm).

18. "stand and deliver.": Anon., *The History of the Lives and Actions of Jonathan Wild, Thief-Taker; Joseph Blake, alias Bleuskin, Footpad; and John Sheppard, Housebreaker* (3rd ed.), p. 73 [*Bleuskin*].

18. "the school in which most highwaymen": Henry Fielding, *The Works of Henry Fielding*, Vol. 12, p. 31.

18. he fired a flintlock: FM, p. 58.

18. English highwaymen . . . possessions to their victims: FM, pp. 61–2.

18. "Madam, your charms": Charles George Harper, *Half-Hours with the Highwaymen*, Vol. 2, p. 108.

19. "God damn you, you double-refined": Christopher Hibbert, *Highwaymen*, p. 35.

19. "The whole appears as a vast wood or forest": Fielding, *The Works of Henry Fielding*, Vol. 5, p. 432.

19. "knocked on the head for his poverty": Charles Mackay, *Memoirs of Extraordinary Popular Delusions and the Madness of Crowds*, Vol. 1, p. 252.

20. for as little as sixpence: Christopher Hibbert, *The Road to Tyburn: The Story of Jack Sheppard and the Eighteenth-Century London Underworld*, p. 62 [CH].

20. "nocturnal fraternity": John Timbs, *Club Life of London*, Vol. 1, p. 39.

20. or toss a prostitute into a barrel: CH, p. 72.

20. historians argue . . . flattened noses: Sir Walter Besant, *London in the Eighteenth Century*, Vol. 6, p. 475.

20. Bucks had no problem breaking into a home: FL, p. xx.

21. "There is no humour in my countrymen": *The Spectator* (August 8, 1712); Joseph Addison and Sir Richard Steele, *The Spectator; with Notes, and a General Index*, Vol. 2, p. 185.

21. more than five hundred: Jack Lindsay, *The Monster City: Defoe's London, 1688–1730*, p. 56 [MC].

21. "These Houses, which are very numerous": *M. Misson's Memoirs and Observations in Travels over England*, Translated by Mr. Ozell, pp. 39–40.

22. The "Liquor of Azam": *Post Man and the Historical Account* (July 29–31,1703).

22. "Tinctura Amara Stomatica": *Post Man and the Historical Account* (October 29–31, 1719).

22. "A Medicine of Inestimable Worth": *Daily Journal* (May 24, 1725).

22. *An Enquiry into the Question, where the Swallow*": *Weekly Journal or Saturday's Post* (November 14, 1724).

Chapter Three: Jonathan Wild Comes to the City

23. "above his trade": Daniel Defoe, *The True and Genuine Account of the Life and Actions of the Late Jonathan Wild*, p. 3 [TG].

23. The eldest of five siblings: Ibid., p. 2.

25. his father died shortly: "Jonathan Wild," *Oxford Dictionary of National Biography*. This source puts Wild's father's death at around 1699, when Wild was sixteen years old.

25. left for a life in the city: *Select Trials for Murders . . . at the Sessions-House in the Old Bailey*, Vol. 2, p. 228 [ST].

25. In London, he hired on: TG, p. 3.

25. Wild took employment as a "setter": GH, p. 12.

25. he told the owner: *The Life of Jonathan Wild from his Birth to his Death . . . By H. D., late Clerk to Justice R*—— (2nd ed.), pp. 4–6 [HD].

26. "Very well," said the horse's owner: Ibid., pp. 5–6.

26. with nine pence to his name: Ibid., p. 7.

27. Wild had been doing the trick for years: Ibid., p. 3.

27. Off they went to Warwick: Ibid., p. 8. In the second edition, Warwick is changed to Gloucester, but Warwick makes more sense, as it's on the way to London from Wolverhampton.

28. Wild says he spent four years: Jonathan Wild, "An Answer to a Late Insolent Libel," Preface [Libel].

28. "in some measure let into the secrets": Ibid.

28. founded in 1555: Thornbury and Walford, *Old and New London*, p. 368.

28. "punishment, correction, or reformation": PP, p. 30.

29. "Everyone who went into prison": Ibid., pp. 30–31.

29. The Compter, like other prisons: GH, pp. 15–17.

29. "Sir, we arrest you in the King's": Thornbury and Walford, *Old and New London*, p. 368.

29. *Here about seventy people*: GH, pp. 16–17.

30. 300 inmates, out of a total of 1,500: Ibid., p. 17.

30. "Making the Black Dog Walk": Peter Ackroyd, *London*, p. 401.

30. "Women and children of both sexes": PP, p. 31.

30. By 1711, he had gained: Frederick J. Lyons, *Jonathan Wild: Prince of Robbers*, p. 11 [LY].

30. "Liberty of the Gate": TG, p. 4.

30. cant is private and unchanging: John C. Hotten, *A Dictionary of Modern Slang, Cant*, pp. x, 6–7. A Canting dictionary can be found in Charles Hitchen's "The Regulator," as well as one titled "Jonathan Wild's Canting Dictionary" in Anon., *The History of the Lives and Actions of Jonathan Wild*.

31. "a common street-walker": *The Tyburn Chronicle*, Vol. 2, pp. 142–3.

31. "a kind of Oracle": HD, p. 14.

32. Two notable men: GH, p. 19.

32. "A Schedule of what monies . . . cant remember being Small": LMA, CLA/047/LJ/17/018/B.

Chapter Four: The *Review*

33. "I grasp at any kind of opportunity": Michel de Montaigne, Emil Julius Trechmann (translator), *The Essays*, Vol. 1, p. 254.

33. "Cities in general fascinated Defoe": John Richetti, *The Cambridge Companion to Daniel Defoe*, p. 158.

33. "when murthering men in the dark": Appears in Walter Wilson and Daniel Defoe, *Memoirs of the Life and Time of Daniel De Foe*, Vol. 1, p. 69.

35. "A pamphlet in the seventeenth century": J. B. Williams, *A History of English Journalism*, p. 7.

35. "I wanted your newes paper": Ibid, p. 8.

35. *The Observator: In Question*: W. P. Trent, "Defoe—The Newspaper and the Novel," *The Cambridge History of English Literature*, Vol. 9, Sir Adolphus William Ward and Alfred Rayney Waller, eds., pp. 3–4.

35. in excess of 400,000 words: PB, p. 141.

36. The storm hit [Great Storm info]: *Daily Mail* (January 6, 2012).

36. "the greatest and the longest storm": Daniel Defoe, *The Storm*, p. 282.

36. "the first substantial work of modern journalism": John Miller, "Writing Up a Storm," *The Wall Street Journal* (August 13, 2011).

36. "one of the earliest extended journalistic": Nicholson Baker, "The Greatest Liar," *Columbia Journalism Review* (July 28, 2009).

36. *A Weekly Review of the Affairs of*: First issue. Available at: https://play .google.com/store/books/details?id=cHkPAAAAQAAJ.

37. After a month, its circulation: PB, p. 153.

37. "setting the Affairs of Europe": *Review* (February 19, 1704).

37. "mean Stile" and called his verse "rough": *True-Born Englishman*, Preface.

37. "After our Serious Matters": *Review* (February 19, 1704).

38. "any such Apparitions, Ghosts": *Review* (March 29, 1705).

38. "a drunken Justice fallen": *Review* (May 23, 1704).

38. "Solemn and Tedious Affair": *Review Collection*, Preface (January 1705).

38. "Advice from the Scandal Club": MN, p. 31.

38. "All men are not Historians": *Review*, A Supplementary Journal to the Advice from the Scandal Club (September 1704).

38. "Defoe's *Review* was actually intended": Christopher Flynn, "Defoe's *Review*: Textual Editing and New Media" (http://english.illinoisstate .edu/digitaldefoe/archive/spring09/multimedia/review/ defoe_final .html).

40. "a Man in the Dark": *Letters*, p. 16.

40. Dr. Arbuthnot's austere quarters: Thomas Wright, *The Life of Daniel Defoe*, p. 184 [TW].

40. "abuse of human": John Timbs, *Club Life of London*, p. 23.

40. also a Tory club: TW, p. 184.

40. "so self-conceited": Ibid.

40. "As to our Brethren" . . . "we will forgive": *Review* (February 19, 1704).

41. "Author of the Review": William Lee, *Daniel Defoe: His Life, and Recently Discovered Writings*, Vol. 1, pp. 263–4 [Lee].

41. "two stupid illiterate Scribblers": *The Examiner*, No. 16 (November 16, 1710); *The Works of Jonathan Swift*, p. 301.

41. "I am perfectly illiterate": *Review* (December 16, 1710). Appears in Walter Wilson and Daniel Defoe, *Memoirs of the Life and Time of Daniel De Foe*, Vol. 3, Wilson, p. 189.

41. "Will nothing make a man a schollar": Daniel Defoe, Karl Daniel Bülbring (ed.), *The Compleat English Gentleman*, Issue 2, p. 199.

41. "If we think of his contemporaries": DD, pp. 274–5.

42. "The poor *Review* is quite exhausted": John Gay, "The Present State of Wit. In a Letter to a Friend in the Country," *The Works of Jonathan Swift: Containing Interesting and Valuable* . . ., Vol. 2, Jonathan Swift, Thomas Roscoe, p. 400.

42. "Still convinced that novelty": PB, p. 477. XX. "One of these authors": Jonathan Swift and John Hawkesworth, *The Works of Dr. Jonathan Swift: Accurately Revised in Twelve* . . ., Vol. 3, p. 215.

Chapter Five: The Marshal and the Buckle-Maker

43. *These are some of the remarkable*: Libel, p. 26.

45. *To Mr. A— Merchant*: Ibid., p. 29.

46. intimidation, confession, and possession: Ibid., p. 16.

46. formed a committee to investigate: GH, p. 50.

46. "2,000 persons who lived by": LMA, COL/OF/02/081. Marshals. Comes Aldermen's Complaint, Articles/Complaints against Hitchen, Hitchen's Answer and Suggestions for Detecting Thieves.

46. Another complaint against Hitchen: Ibid.; GH, p. 51.

46. "Answer of Charles Hitchen": LMA, COL/OF/02/081. Marshals.

46. "nine pages of foolscap": GH, p. 52.

47. "a rendezvous and nursery": Peter Cunningham, *Handbook of London: Past and Present*, Vol. 1, p. 285.

47. "trussed chicken": CH, p. 56.

48. "During the time of discipline": Anon, *The Midnight Spy*, p. 122.

48. "One of the Cant Words": TG, p. 5.

48. mill kens, files, bridle culls: LY, p. 61.

49. one in 1691: TG, pp. 7–8; GH, pp. 36–7.

49. "when the poor Adventurer": TG, pp. 8.

50. defined in canting dictionaries: Charles Hitchen, "The Regulator," pp. 19–20 [Regulator].

51. *I am very sensible*: Libel, p. 13.

51. "several Brandy-Shops": Ibid.

52. "What do you think I bought": Ibid., p. 14.

52. surely "Swing for it": Ibid., p. 15.

53. respectable bailiff's wife: Ibid., pp. 24–5.

53. "poker, fire-fork . . . mangled": Ibid., p. 29.

53. "We'll catch the Whores Birds!": ST, p. 250.

53. Beech Lane: GH, p. 61.

53. "a great rage": Libel, p. 26.

53. "he-whores" . . . "No, ye fool": Ibid., p. 30.

54. "The Marshal was very merry": Ibid., p. 31.

Chapter Six: Thief-Catcher General of Great Britain and Ireland

55. *He was now master*: TG, p. 20.

57. "She had some time so provoked" . . . "in a grateful consideration": *The Tyburn Chronicle*, Vol. 2, p. 147.

57. Wild's house on Cock Alley: PP, p. 34.

58. *You know, my Bloods*: ST, pp. 229–30.

59. *I happen'd to hear*: Ibid., p. 230.

59. "Let us see how the Bear": *J—N W—ld's Skittish & Baboonish New Proclamation*, British Library, MSS SUR/RP/5361 BOX 125 946 BC, System # 003960399.

60. "to come to my felonious": Ibid.

60. As Frank McLynn explains: FM, p. 21.

60. *Sir, I only come to serve*: ST, p. 231.

61. Technically, a thief-taker: John S. Dempsey and Linda S. Forst, *An Introduction to Policing*, p. 6.

62. *Lost on Friday Evening*: *Daily Courant* (May 26, 1714).

62. "Whereas there some time": *Post Man and the Historical Account* (May 22–24, 1716).

63. Wild had earned at least £200: GH, p. 72.

63. "Blue-Boar in the Old Bailey": *Daily Courant* (December 24, 1714).

63. owned by a Mrs. Seagoe: ST, p. 233.

63. "a Velvet Pulpit cloth": *Post Man and the Historical Account* (September 23–25, 1718).

63. three fundamental rules . . . "threatening Speeches": TG, p. 14.

64. The first person sent to the gallows: ST, p. 218; GH, p. 71. Thanks to Gerald Howson for noting this chronology, and his uncovering of the article from the *Post Boy*, dated September 27, 1714, which corresponds to Wild's list.

64. "A List of the persons discover'd": ST, p. 216.

64. Parrot, Parker, and Chance: GH, p. 73.

64. *The Prisoner [Parrot] came*: ST, p. 267.

65. he didn't remain free for long: Ibid., p. 218.

65. Portuguese Jew: Karen A Macfarlane, "Jewish Policemen of the 18th Century," *Journal of Modern Jewish Studies*, Vol. 10, Issue 2 (2011), pp. 223–44.

65. Quilt Arnold information: ST, Vol. 1, pp. 358–9; Mary Clayton, "Quilt Arnold," *London Lives, 1690–1800* (www.londonlives.org, version 1.1, June 17, 2012) [LL].

65. clerk of the western/northern roads: GH, p. 146.

65. "Secretary, and Groom of the Chambers": *Daily Journal* (February 17, 1725).

65. "blood money": Blood Money, National Archives, E 407/30.

65. On Saturday, March 31, 1716: ST, p. 261.

66. *Whereas on Friday the 30th*: *London Gazette* (March 31, 1716–April 3, 1716).

66. The *Weekly Packet* further reported: *Weekly Packet* (March 31, 1716–April 7, 1716).

66. Isaac Rag, Timothy Dun, Will White: ST, pp. 261–7.

67. "In an instant, some fellows": ST, pp. 263–7.

67. "rob any they should meet": *Weekly Journal or British Gazetteer* (May 26, 1716).

67. Isaac Rag gave: OBP, January 1715 (s17150114-1); OBP, October 12, 1715, Isaac Rag.

68. William White, thirty-four: White, Thurland, Chapman bios, ST, p. 264.

68. shop at Colchester in Essex: OBP, Ordinary of Newgate's Account, June 1716 (OA17160608).

68. Dun had surrendered himself: *Weekly Packet* (May 12–19, 1716).

68. A hard case, he had been: *Weekly Journal or British Gazetteer* (July 28, 1716).

68. "he must follow the old Business": ST, p. 265.

69. "Treasury Warrants": Treasury Warrants: July 21–25, 1717, *Calendar of Treasury Books*, Vol. 31: 1717 (1960), pp. 458–65 (http://www.british -history.ac.uk/report.aspx?compid=85435&strquery=jonathanwild).

70. Isaac Rag, for all his help: Middlesex Sessions Papers—Justices' Working Documents, July 1717, LL, LMSMPS501630052.

70. We know they denied his petition: *Original Weekly Journal* (December 14–21, 1717).

70. "If the same Person": *Post Man and the Historical Account* (May 22–24, 1716).

71. Defoe later noted: TG, pp. 21–22.

72. 68 Ship Court: *London Topographical Record*, Vol. 2, p. 95.

72. the Cooper's Arms: *Notes and Queries*, Vol. 78, p. 332.

72. birthplace of painter William Hogarth: Timbs, *Curiosities of London*, p. 558.

72. From the King's Head: *The Political State of Great Britain*, Vol. 29 (May 31, 1725), pp. 505–06.

72. One technique he used: FL, pp. 2–3.

72–73. the Spruce Prig . . . Mr. Lun: HD, pp. 38–39.

73. even took on Parliament: GH, p. 149.

73. "My Life on't": HD, p. 37.

73. *Many a poor Boy*: TG, pp. 32–33.

73. "So, Mr. Son of a Bitch" [Butler episode]: ST, pp. 278–80; HD, p. 57.

74. *News from Newgate*: "The Proceedings—Associated Records," OBP.

74. "This became common practice": "The Proceedings—The Value of the Proceedings as a Historical Source," OBP.

75. *Although initially aimed*: Ibid.

75. "privately stealing" . . . "Jonathan Wild": OBP, September 6, 1716 (17160906).

76. By 1718, he had brought down: GH, p. 76.

76. *He is about 37*: Advertisement, OBP, January 13, 1716 (a17160113-1).

76. "Head Theif-Catcher": *Weekly Journal or British Gazetteer* (January 19, 1717).

76. "Thief-Taker General of Great Britain": *Weekly Journal or Saturday's Post* (February 28, 1719).

76. "inimitable Boldness . . . brutal Courage": TG, pp. vi–vii.

76. *Nay, Advertisements*: TG, p. 20.

77. "a pushing, enterprizing Nature": TG, pp. 17–18.

Chapter Seven: Jack Sheppard, Apprentice

79. *Sheppard was the very embodiment*: FL, p. 9.
79. At the workhouse school: CH, p. 42.
80. In Spitalfields: Peter Linebaugh, *The London Hanged*, p. 9 [LH].
80. Sir William Fazakerley: Horace Bleackley and Stewart Marsh Ellis, *Jack Sheppard*, p. 2 [BL].
80. "a complete pocket Hercules": Ibid., p. 3.
80. "bore no little resemblance": Ibid.
81. "having a perfect Boy's Countenance": *Parker's London News or the Impartial Intelligencer* (November 11, 1724).
81. "Impediment, or Hesitation": *Daily Post* (September 4, 1724).

Chapter Eight: The Regulator

82. *Set Forth in Several*: Libel, title page.
82. bullying, bribery, and corruption: GH, p. 101.
82. sixty criminals to justice: Libel, Preface.
82–83. "Act for the Further" . . . "Unless a person doth apprehend": *The Statutes at Large*, Vol. 13, pp. 473–4.
83. "This Act was so directly aimed": TG, p. 31.
83. "A Fellow, who by his Conduct": *Weekly Journal or Saturday's Post* (January 3, 1719).
84. "King of Gipsies": Regulator, p. 5.
84. "an ignorant and impudent insult to the reader": NNC, p. 229.
84. "far too stupid to be effective": LY, p. 221.
84. "a clumsy performance": Besant, *London in the Eighteenth Century*, Vol. 6, p. 498.
84. "illiterate": William Robert Irwin, *The Making of Jonathan Wild*, p. 12.
84. "excruciating" . . . "unintended humour": GH, p. 104.
84. Hitchen composed a numbered list: Regulator, p. 16.
85. "The Thief, the Gaol": Ibid., p. 4.
85. "By His Skittish and Baboonish Majesty": British Library, *Skittish & Baboonish New Proclamation*, MSS SUR/RP/5361 BOX 125 946 BC, System # 003960399.
85. *Be it known to All*: Ibid.
85. pamphlet was "most stupid": *The Tyburn Chronicle*, Vol. 2, p. 147–48.
86. "only 'exposés' of this underworld": GH, p. 104.
86. "The names of the Flash Words now in Vogue": Regulator, p. 19.

86. *What are all that heap of Boys:* Ibid., p. 10.

86. "I see they live well": Ibid., p. 12.

86. "a Leg of Mutton": Ibid., p. 13.

87. "His Majesty's Seven-Year Passengers": LH, p. 9.

87. six hundred a year: Bernard Bailyn, *Voyagers to the West*, p. 294.

87. "the most cruel insult": Benjamin Franklin and William Temple Franklin, *Memoirs of the Life and Writings of Benjamin Franklin*, Vol. 4, p. 100.

87. "tender parental" . . . "may possibly change their natures": Benjamin Franklin and Albert Henry Smyth (ed.), *The Writings of Benjamin Franklin*, Vol. 3, p. 46.

88. £40 . . . £10 a head: GH, pp. 91–5.

88. gone nearly insane: LY, p. 128.

88. Riddlesden's Bond of Transportation: LMA, MJ/SP/T/02/002.

88. he reached Annapolis: GH, p. 137.

88. "Tallow Chandler and Soapmaker": *American Weekly Mercury*, No. 176, p. 45 (April 25–May 2, 1723); *American Weekly Mercury*, Vol. 4 (1722–23).

88. settling back into Newgate: *Daily Journal* (September 22, 1721) as appeared in *American Weekly Mercury*, Vol. 4, p. 45.

89. Meff . . . hanged at Tyburn: NNC, Vol. 1, pp. 263–6; ST, Vol. 1, pp. 70–73.

89. Meff is one of nineteen men: ST, p. 219.

89. "If I had been safe landed": NNC, p. 264.

89. ran headlong into Jonathan Wild: *The Weekly Journal or Saturday's Post* (August 19, 1721).

89. "Some evil genius attended me": NNC, p. 264.

89. *I have had enough of this restless*: Ibid. p. 266.

89. "One would think": Ibid.

90. "Nocturnal Adventures": Libel, p. 12.

90. Mother Clap's abode on Field Lane: GH, p. 63.

90. "I'll be reveng'd" . . . "fine Green Hats": Libel, pp. 31–32.

90. "Any gentleman that wants": Ibid., p. 41.

91. *Account of the Tryal:* British Library, *An Account of the Tryal, Examination, and Conviction of Several Notorious Persons Call'd Sodomites*, System Number 002216347, Shelfmark 1851.c.10 (35).

91. "No one but an exceedingly vain man": LY, p. 130.

92. *On a sudden we found street robberies*: Defoe and Maynadier, ed., "Lives of Six Notorious Street Robbers," *The Works of Daniel Defoe*, Vol. 16, p. 371.

93. "that they may be blinded": Regulator, p. 6.

93. Wild had run through a string of relationships: Wild, *Oxford Dictionary of National Biography*; TG, p. 18.

94. "and always a Seraglio of Mistresses": HD, p. 70.

94. "Mr. Wild, the famous": *Applebee's Original Weekly Journal* (September 26, 1719).

94. "We hear Jonathan Wild": *Weekly Journal or Saturday's Post* (October 3, 1719).

94. offering a one-guinea reward: *Post Man and the Historical Account* (October 29–31, 1719).

94. He also threw his hat: *Weekly Journal or Saturday's Post* (October 10, 1719).

94. "a Man of the most exemplary": *A Collection of Miscellany Letters: Selected Out of Mist's Weekly Journal*, Letter XLIX, p. 147.

Chapter Nine: Crusoe and Flanders

95. *I was alone, circumscrib'd*: Daniel Defoe, *The Life and Strange Surprizing Adventures of Robinson Crusoe*, pp. 184–5 [RC].

95. four-acre lot: PB, p. 380.

95. Description of Defoe's house: PB, p. 476; Edward Forbes Robinson, *Defoe in Stoke Newington*, no page numbers.

95. Hackney Brook: Ibid.

95. "a gloomy and irregular pile of red brick": Ibid.

97. England's crime literature: Lincoln B. Faller, *Turned to Account: The Forms and Functions of Criminal Biography*, p. 2.

97. As Lincoln Faller points out: Roger D. Lund, ed., *Critical Essays on Daniel Defoe*, pp. 42–3 [CE].

97. "transfer of portable property": Ibid., p. 37.

98. "The Editor believes . . . a just History of Fact": RC, Preface.

98. "probably a very inadequate sum": Lee, Vol. 1, p. 293.

98. Taylor registered the work: George Atherton Aitken, *Romances and Narratives*, Vol. 1, Introduction, p. ii.

98. "The first part of *Robinson*: Joseph Spence and Edmond Malone, *Observations, Anecdotes, and Characters of Books and Men*, p. 298.

98. nothing but a fad: MN, p. 6.

99. "historic Kind of Writing": Henry Fielding, *Tom Jones*, Vol. 2, p. 285.

99. "new Province of Writing": Henry Fielding, *The Miscellaneous Works of Henry Fielding*, Vol. 1, p. 91.

101. "the Court pronounced Judgment": *Post Boy* (February 14–16, 1721).

101. "with the exceptions of his initials": Lee, Vol. 1, p. 264.

101. Letters from Defoe to . . . de la Faye: *Letters*, p. 451.

Chapter Ten: The Black Lion

103. "transition from industry to idleness": LH, p. 14.

103. *went on together for about six Years*: Daniel Defoe, *A Narrative of All the Robberies, Escapes, &c. of John Sheppard*, pp. 4–5 [*Narrative*].

104. *I may justly lay the Blame*: Ibid., pp. 5–6.

105. "Unhappy Wretch!": Ibid., p. 6.

106. "He made a mere jest": Anon., *The History of the Remarkable Life of John Sheppard*, pp. 3–4 [History].

106. a "violent-tempered Amazon": BL, p. 3.

106. "had a very great Contempt": Arthur Lawrence Hayward, ed., *Lives of the Most Remarkable Criminals*, p. 275.

106. "Don't tell me such melancholy": Ibid., pp. 275–6.

106. "This Action acquired a reputation": ST, p. 134.

107. Wild's brother Andrew: Thomas Seccombe, *Lives of Twelve Bad Men*, p. 245.

107. "orgy of spirit-drinking": MD, p. 27.

107. *But English drunkards*: *True Collection*, p. 23.

108. "People reeled about the streets": FL, p. 25.

108. "gin-flamed insanity": MD, p. 42.

108. Judith Defour: OBP, 1734, Trial of Judith Defour (t17340227-32); OBP, Ordinary of Newgate's Account, March 1734 (OA17340308).

108. "a cause as well as a result of their craving for gin": MD, p. 40.

109. "'Tis a growing Vice": Charles Davenant, *An Essay upon Ways and Means of Supplying the War*, p. 134.

109. "a collection of sinners": Daniel Defoe, *The Complete English Tradesman*, Vol. 2, p. 80.

109. London's leaders met at Hicks Hall: LL, Middlesex Sessions: SM/OC, April 28, 1721 (LMSMOC400000249–51).

109. "proper method to suppress": Ibid.

110. *Beer, happy Produce of our Isle*: William Hogarth, John Ireland, and John Nichols, *Hogarth's Works: With Life and Anecdotal Descriptions of His Pictures*, Vol. 2, p. 66.

111. *Gin, cursed fiend!*: Ibid., p. 68.

111. "had given himself up": Hayward, *Lives of the Most Remarkable Criminals*, p. 274.

111. Sheppard and Wood: LH, p. 16.

111. "then fell to robbing almost everyone": *Narrative*, p. 9.

111. making off with nine silver spoons: ST, p. 134.

111. Thomas twice had been indicted: Ibid.

112. "burnt in the hand": OBP, August 1723, trial of Thomas Sheppard (t17230828-24) and (t17230828-43).

Chapter Eleven: Celebrity Gangbuster

113. *I made it my Business to search*: ST, Vol. 1, pp. 296–7.

113. "I remember I had occasion": TG, p. 25.

115. the Mint offered sanctuary: FM, p. 3; Timbs, *Curiosities of London*, pp. 508–9.

115. "By 1712 the authorities": Ibid.

115. "last of the 'bastard sanctuaries'": Ibid.

115. When a representative from the coroner's: John Timbs, *Historic Sketches, Remarkable Duels, Notorious Highwaymen, Rogueries, Crimes*, p. 350.

116. Wild staffed his corporation precisely: Ibid., p. 28.

117. "I am serv'd by a parcel": Ibid., p. 32.

117–18. "Jonathan," he said . . . "fierce butcher": Ibid., pp. 35–36.

118. The government closed the Mint: *The Weekly Journal or Saturday's Post* (July 20, 1723), reprinted in Timbs, *Curiosities of London*, p. 509.

118. "Blood being flush'd": OBP, Ordinary of Newgate's Account, February 1721 (OA17210208).

118. William Colthurst, shortly: Blood Money, National Archives, E 407/30.

118. As a butler in the comfortable home: ST, Vol. 1, p. 175.

119. such as the "Slip" and the "Palm": GH, p. 179.

119. "No Life is so gloomy": ST, Vol. 1, p. 186.

119. at the Queen's Head Tavern: GH, p. 173.

119. The Hawkins gang had taken: ST, Vol. 1, pp. 162–98.

120. "The prisoner at first": Ibid., p. 113; OBP, December 1721, trial of Butler Fox (t17211206-41).

120. "I expect to die": Ibid., p. 174.

120. "Lord Jesus, come quickly!": Ibid., p. 180.

120. "hang'd in Irons on a Gibbet": Ibid., p. 197.

121. The assault was savage: Ibid., p. 127; GH, p. 175; OBP, January 1722, trial of James Shaw, alias Smith, alias Thomson Richard Norton, alias Watkins (t17220112-14).

121. "squeazing the chats": GH, p. 178.

121. capture had grown to £140: OBP, January 1722, trial of James Shaw, alias Smith, alias Thomson Richard Norton, alias Watkins (t17220112-14); ST, Vol. 1, pp. 126–8.

121. "The Prisoner, Shaw": Ibid.

122. Field's duplicitous word supported: LL, September 1720 (t17200907-33) and October 1720 (t17201012-23).

122. *There is no doubt but he is an ill Man*: ST, Vol. I, p. 166.

123. "Major Kerrick, the chief": *Daily Journal* (July 4, 1722).

123. "delighted" in sexual pleasures: *Ordinary's Account* (July 18, 1722), ECCO.

123. "God damn ye": ST, Vol. 1., p. 204.

124. His defense was pronounced "frivolous": OBP, July 1722, trial of John Molony, James Carrick (t17220704-51).

124. "laughed and smiled upon all": *Ordinary's Account* (July 18, 1722), ECCO.

124. Wild took home at least £900: GH, p. 196; FL, pp. 2–7.

124. "They write from Bath and Bristol": *Daily Journal*, November 2, 1721, as appeared in GH, p. 125.

124. As Gerald Howson points out: GH, pp. 125–6.

125. Wild began his days: *Bleuskin*, Preface, p. 1; GH, p. 120.

125. "pint of sherry": GH, p. 120.

125. "Hang or Save": *Bleuskin*, Preface, p. 1.

125. valet de chamber: *Weekly Journal or Saturday's Post* (February 28, 1719).

125. haughty dinners: Alexander Smith, *Memoirs of the Life and Times of the Famous Jonathan Wild*, p. 14.

125. "awkward familiarity": *Common Sense: Or, the Englishman's Journal. Being a Collection of Letters*, Vol. 2 (December 23, 1738), p. 276.

125. Duke's Head on Red Cross: Rev. George Weight, "Statistics of the Parish of St. George the Martyr, Southwark," *Journal of the Royal Statistical Society*, Vol. 3 (January 20, 1840), p. 55.

126. warehouse in Newington Butts: GH, p. 142.

126. "trap-doors, sliding panels": Cunningham, *Handbook of London*, Vol. 1, p. 118.

126. escaped convict named Jones: Thornbury and Walford, *Old and New London*, Vol. 2, p. 426.

126. unearthed a skull and bones: Ibid., p. 426; *Court Gazette* (August 17, 1844).

126. "two strangely constructed houses": *Lloyd's Weekly* London newspaper (August 11, 1844).

126. chimney sweep named Williams: *Catholic Telegraph* (September 14, 1844), Vol. 13, p. 293.

127. blood money certificates: Blood Money, National Archives, E 407/30.

127. Duncan Campbell: GH, p. 117.

127. "His business in all Things": HD, p. 63.

127. £100 more: *Daily Journal* (September 26, 1721); John H. Langbein, *The Origins of Adversary Criminal Trial*, pp. 149–50; *Weighley, alias Wild*, p. 38; GH, p. 125.

127. "Here he played his Card": *Weighley, alias Wild*, title page, p. 38.

Chapter Twelve: Cleverest of All

129. *Sheppard was now upon his wicked*: History, p. 6.

129. Jack Sheppard met his older brother: CH, p. 99.

129. For their first score: ST, p. 135.

129. as "generous" in this matter: Ibid.

129. In February 1724: Ibid.

129. found refuge at the Queen's Head: CH, p. 99.

130. skittles: Joseph Strutt, *The Sports and Pastimes of the People of England from the Earliest Period*, p. 221; Hackwood, *Old English Sports*, p. 223; John Nichols, *The Gentleman's Magazine*, Vol. 65, p. 304.

130. "brutal and foul tempered": CH, p. 100.

130. Card games, such as basset: MC, p. 50.

130–31. "Betting was universal" . . . "speed of his footman": Ibid.

131. "This Vice is the more dangerous": Fielding, *An Enquiry into the Causes of the Late Increase of Robbers*, p. 92.

131. Onlookers sometimes joined the fray: MC, p. 54.

131. "famous Stoke Newington ass woman": *Daily Journal* (October 7, 1728).

131. "the Atlas of the Sword": Timbs, *Curiosities of London*, p. 503.

131. boxing's first champion: BoxRec.com http://boxrec.com/media/index.php/James_Figg And http://www.ibhof.com/pages/about/inductees/pioneer/figg.html.

132. "At the Boarded House": *Daily Courant* (April 21, 1718); BoxRec had Figg entering the fight game in 1719, not 1718.

132. "Chubs that we might make a Penny": *Narrative*, p. 12.

132. A proven athlete, Sykes: *Weekly Journal or Saturday's Post* (May 16, 1719).

133. Sykes had plans: ST, p. 135; BL, p. 6.

133. Sheppard had a razor: *Narrative*, p. 13.

134. "All staring up": Ibid.

134. Some say that Sheppard: BL, p. 6; Anon., *Authentic Memoirs of the Life and Surprising Adventures of John Sheppard*, p. 9 [*Authentic Memoirs*].

134. "I was well enough diverted": *Narrative*, p. 13.

135. "cracksmen": BL, p. 7.

135. "But where are they Escap'd to?": *History*, p. 9.

136. taken just ten minutes: Ibid., p. 10.

136. Even the keepers: Ibid.

136. "The underworld of London": BL, p. 9.

137. Afterward, Grace, who needed his share: ST, p. 136.

137. Lamb . . . sentence of transportation: OBP, July 1724 (s17240708-1).

137. "like a dog to his vomit": *History*, p. 10.

137. "been a thief almost from the cradle": NNC, p. 391.

137. As a boy, Blueskin went to school: *Bleuskin*, p. 72; ST, p. 165.

138. "You double Pox'd Salivated": *Bleuskin*, p. 72.

138. He amassed a pretty penny: Ibid., p. 102.

138. with a saber gash: GH, p. 195.

138. Yet, in prison: *Bleuskin*, p. 78.

138. "Having heard that two": ST, pp. 162–3.

138. "I was call'd up about": Ibid., p. 131.

Chapter Thirteen: Wild versus Sheppard

141. *He [Wild] was the uncrowned*: BL, p. 11.

141. "I was indeed twice at a Thief-Catcher's": *Narrative*, p. 16.

141. *I have often lamented*: Ibid., pp. 15–16.

142. Sheppard helped Pargiter out of the ditch: *History*, p. 14.

142. "Roman Antiquities": *British Journal* (September 5, 1724).

143. He armed himself: *Bleuskin*, p. 81.

143. "He was concern'd along": *Narrative*, p. 15.

143. "Cherchez la femme!": Alexandre Dumas, *Théatre complet de Alex. Dumas*, Vol. 2, p. 103.

143. She disclosed: *Narrative*, p. 14.

144. "Yesterday one Shepheard": *Daily Journal* (July 25, 1724).

144. "an older, hard-bitten figure": Richard Holmes, *Defoe on Wild and Sheppard*, p. ix [Holmes].

145. "discours'd with great freedom": *The Flying Post Or Weekly Medley* (January 11, 1729).

145. It's estimated that the serial impeacher: GH, p. 19.

145. His name and signature: Blood Money, National Archives, E 407/30.

145. "all of a piece": *Narrative*, p. 11.

146. "In a Day or two after": Ibid.

146. Sheppard admitted to it all: *History*, p. 16; OBP, August 1724, trial of Joseph Sheppard (t17240812-52).

146. "'Tis impossible to describe": J. Cooke, ed., *Moll Flanders* (1765 edition), p. 295 [*Moll*].

Chapter Fourteen: The Trial of Jack Sheppard

147. *Sheppard, the notorious housebreaker*: *Applebee's Original Weekly* (August 1, 1724), reprinted in Lee, pp. 383–4.

147. the distinguished lord mayor [all trial notes and testimony]: ST, pp. 131–2; OBP, August 1724, trial of Joseph Sheppard (t17240812-52); OBP, Ordinary of Newgate's Account, September 1724 (OA17240904).

150. "I told him all the particulars": ST, p. 138.

150. wished that "Field may repent": *Narrative*, p. 10.

151. "Yes, so my great Lord": BL, p. 19.

151. Lumley Davis, on the other hand: *Authentic Memoirs*, pp. 19–20.

152. *He got loose from his chains*: OBP, Ordinary of Newgate's Account, September 1724 (OA17240904).

152. "Yesterday, several Persons": *Post Boy* (September 5–8, 1724).

152. "I have sometimes procured": *Narrative*, pp. 11–12.

153. first week of September: *Weekly Journal or Saturday's Post* (September 5, 1724).

153. "disorder'd in his senses" . . . "dash'd out his Brains": *British Journal* (September 12, 1724).

153. John Ketch . . . executioner: CH, pp. 184–5.

153. John Price, who held the post: Andrew Knapp, William Baldwin, NNC, p. 61.

154. *To show you that I am in charity*: *London News* (September 7, 1724).

154. "In connexion with *Applebee's*": William Minto, *Daniel Defoe*, p. 127.

155. "Well done, my lad": ST, p. 159.

155. "trusty comrade": OBP, December 1724, trial of William Page (t17241204-47).

155. He had drinks with friends: *History*, pp. 21–2.

155. Black Jack Tavern, was renamed: Jacob Larwood and John Camden Hotten, *The History of Signboards: From the Earliest Times to the Present Day*, p. 386.

156. "There's a stag!": BL, p. 23.

156. "mean girl": Ibid.

156. "Pistols presented to his Head": *Evening Post* (September 10–12, 1724).

156. "I have brought my hogs": *History*, p. 26.

157. "his old mansion": Ibid.

157. *His Escape and his being*: Ibid., pp. 27–8.

157. "At least one prisoner literally": CH, p. 163.

Chapter Fifteen: Mr. Applebee's Man

159. *Newspapers became less political*: Minto, *Daniel Defoe*, p. 126.

159. "On Tuesday Night": *Applebee's* (September 5, 1724).

159. "Sheppard took to the Hedges": *Applebee's* (September 12, 1724).

159. "a Divine" "composed and cheerful": *Applebee's* (September 12, 1724, reprinted in Lee, Vol. 3, pp. 304–05.

160. Nathaniel Mist . . . fourteen arrests: "Nathaniel Mist," *Oxford Dictionary of National Biography*, Vol. 38, pp. 377–80.

160. "*Applebee's Weekly Journal* was intended": MN, p. 510.

160. "non-political essay": James Sutherland, *Defoe*, p. 255.

160. Starting at *Mist's* and continuing at *Applebee's*: MN, p. 511.

160. "lighter touch": Ibid., p. 579.

160. "essays on suicide": Ibid., pp. 510–11.

160. *When he could think of nothing better*: Sutherland, *Defoe*, p. 255.

161. waste his efforts defending: John J. Richetti, *The Life of Daniel Defoe: A Critical Biography*, pp. 342–4.

161. "A Brother Journal Man": *Applebee's* (February 18, 1721), reprinted in Lee, Vol. 2, pp. 340–42.

162. "1. Scene by scene construction": Edd Applegate, *Literary Journalism: A Biographical Dictionary of Writers and Editor*, p. xiv.

162. *a gentleman well known*: Reprinted in John Forster, *Oliver Cromwell, Daniel De Foe, Sir Richard Steele, Charles Churchill*, p. 150.

163. received advances from publishers: Holmes, p. xii.

163. Besides *Mist's* and *Applebee's*: Lee, Vol. 3, p. xviii.

163. *In this way of talk*: *Colonel Jack*, printed by D. A. Talboys for Thomas Tegg, p. 9.

163. "a dirty glass-bottle-house boy": Ibid., p. 6.

163. "it was a story just waiting for any journalist": Holmes, p. xi.

164. upwards of £25: Ibid., p. xv.

164. yearly compensation for the ordinary: OBP, Ordinary of Newgate's Account, June 1716 (OA17160608).

164. *I mention'd to him*: Ibid.

164. "Clergymen and enterprising pamphleteers": Andrea McKenzie, "The Real Macheath: Social Satire, Appropriation, and Eighteenth-Century Criminal Biography," Huntington Library Quarterly 69.4 (2006), p. 590.

164. "whose business it is to extort confessions": *Moll*, p. 104.

164. *The ordinary of Newgate came to me*: Ibid., p. 93.

165. If need be, Applebee greased: Holmes, p. xv.

165. By midcentury, more than a thousand: Ibid.

165. "gingerbread men": *History*, p. 49.

165. "inhuman" and "barbarous": OBP, Ordinary of Newgate's Account, September 1724 (OA17240904).

165. "When he came to talk": CH, p. 205.

Chapter Sixteen: Blueskin's Penknife

167. *In his limitless ambition*: CH, pp. 130–1.

167. On October 2, Wild: *Evening Post* (October 13–15, 1724).

167. "Going to his Chamber-door": ST, p. 164.

168. Since 1540, the Barber-Surgeons: The Worshipful Company of Barbers (www.barberscompany.org).

168. Blueskin did Wild's bidding: *Bleuskin*, pp. 77–8.

168. For his efforts . . . £420 reward: GH, p. 196.

168. gifted Blueskin with a musketoon: Ibid., p. 184.

169. gold watch snaked: *Bleuskin*, p. 76.

169. Edward Polit and William Blewit: *Bleuskin*, p. 72; OBP, Ordinary of Newgate's Account, November 1724 (OA17241111).

169. "worthless companion": *Narrative*, p. 15.

169. "had made dreadful Havock": *History*, pp. 33–34.

169. "The young Generation of Thieves": TG, p. 21.

169. fiddle-loving young woman: Bleuskin, p. 82.

169. "I believe you will not bring £40": ST, p. 164.

170. "I cannot do it," Wild said: *History*, p. 39.

170. "I'll send you a good Book": ST, p. 164.

170. He pulled out his penknife: *Daily Journal* (October 15, 1724); ST, pp. 164–68.

170. "Muslin Stock": *Evening Post* (October 13–15, 1724).

170. for the rest of October: GH, p. 229.

170. "into the Sessions House Yard": *London Journal* (October 17, 1724).

170. "He answer'd that none prompted": OBP, Ordinary of Newgate's Account, November 1724 (OA17241111).

171. "Blood, nor I neither": ST, p. 163.

171. "The Villain triumph'd afterwards": *London Journal* (October 17, 1724).

171. "Blueskin's Ballad.": Sir Walter Scott, *The Works of Jonathan Swift*, Vol. 13, pp. 328–31.

172. The year 1724: GH, pp. 210, 300.

172. addressed his "Humble Petition": File of letters from Mr. Fowler, Royal College of Surgeons, RCS-MUS/3/3/11; *The Times* (May 6, 1841).

172. "great trouble and charge": Arthur Griffiths, *The Chronicles of Newgate*, p. 258.

172. "The Consideration thereof is adjourned": LMA, microfilm X109/249.

172. Wild never received the Freedom: GH, p. 211.

172. "very handsome Sum" . . . "'tis hoped": *Applebee's* (June 6, 1724), reprinted in Lee, Vol. 3, pp. 271–2.

173. "Ask me no such Questions": *History*, pp. 30, 60.

173. "John Sheppard, the Malefactor": *Applebee's* (October 10, 1724); Lee, Vol. 3, p. 316.

174. "There is scarce a Smith in London": *Narrative*, p. 17.

174. Kneebone attempted to intercede: Ibid.

174. "Those audacious Criminals": TG, p. 15.

174. "I wanted still a more useful": *Narrative*, p. 18.

Chapter Seventeen: The Castle

175. *I found there was not a moment*: *Narrative*, p. 19.

175. "Released thus from all surveillance": Griffiths, *The Chronicles of Newgate*, p. 184.

175. He took to his task [entire escape]: *Narrative*, pp. 19–28; ST, pp. 141–2; *Weekly Journal or Saturday's Post* (October 17, 1724); BL, pp. 27–8; CH, pp. 169–78.

177. since a group of rebels . . . 1716: BL, p. 29; *Narrative*, p. 20.

177. "The Keepers say the Door": *Narrative*, p. 20.

178. "Lord, what noise": Ibid., p. 23.

179. "I was once more . . . a Freeman": Ibid.

179. a couple of bolts: *Authentic Memoirs*, pp. 45–8.

179. "the Devil himself": *Weekly Journal or Saturday's Post* (October 17, 1724).

180. "He is about 22 years of age": *Evening Post* (October 15, 1724).

180. "It could be seen as a duel": Holmes, p. x.

181. *Samson of Old: Authentic Memoirs*, p. 50.

181. King George I himself kept tabs on Sheppard's saga: BL, p. 37.

181. murdering Robert Mayer: *Daily Post* (November 10, 1721); *Historical Register, Containing an Impartial Relation of All Transactions Foreign and Domestick,* Vol. 6, 1721, p. 43.

181. Among the classifieds: *Evening Post* (October 17–20, 1724).

182. "It would have taken a shrewd onlooker": Holmes, p. xix.

182. "gone once more": *History*, Preface.

182. "Which was Sheppard?": Ibid., p. 31.

182. "mortal Aversion to Hemp": *Weekly Journal or British Gazetteer* (October 31, 1724).

182. "Jonathan recovers; curse on thy": *Daily Journal* (October 30, 1724).

182. *Mr. Applebee, This with my Kind Love*: ST, pp. 142–3.

183. "more likely to be genuine": CH, p. 188.

183. "for my Memorandums" . . . "I hope the Grace": *Parker's London News* (October 23, 1724).

183. brewhouse on Thames Street: *Weekly Journal or British Gazetteer* (October 31, 1724).

183. "The description the man gives": *London Journal* (October 31, 1724).

184. "For God's sake, who are you?": *Narrative*, p. 25.

185. "I cannot say it was in my Intention": Ibid., p. 27.

185. "Unless the young Refugee": *Authentic Memoirs*, p. 49.

185. "I step't towards the Hay-Market": *Narrative*, p. 27.

186. At a pawnshop at the sign: *Daily Journal* (November 2, 1724).

186. "loudly giving out Directions": *Narrative*, p. 28.

186. Sheppard walked out . . . valued at £60: Ibid.

186. black suit, ruffled shirt: *Daily Post* (November 2, 1724); *London Journal* (November 7, 1724).

186. "I made an extraordinary Appearance": *Narrative*, p. 28.

Chapter Eighteen: Forlorn at the Triple Tree

187. "Female of the Hundreds": *British Journal* (November 7, 1724).

187. "scoundrel": Lewis Saul Benjamin, *The Life of William Makepeace Thackeray*, p. 100.

189. shop of Nicks, a butcher: *Daily Journal* (November 2, 1724).

189. "At length my Senses": *Narrative*, p. 29.

189. "Murder!" he yelled: *Daily Journal* (November 2, 1724).

190. The news brought thousands: Ibid.

190. "Lost, the 1st of October": *Daily Post* (November 2, 1724).

190. "vow'd revenge": ST, p. 282.

190. "Cases within the Act passed": Townshend and Walpole, National Archives; SP, pp. 44, 81.

191. a letter pertaining to Wild: Townshend and Walpole, National Archives; SP, pp. 44, 81, f. 390.

191. At Newgate, Sheppard was secured: *British Journal* (November 7, 1724).

191. two guards on him at all times: *Evening Post* (October 31–November 3, 1724).

191. *Sir:—His Majesty being informed*: George Harris, *The Life of Lord Chancellor Hardwicke: with Selections from his Correspondence, Diaries, Speeches, and Judgments*, Vol. 1, p. 158.

192. On Tuesday, November 10: *Weekly Journal or British Gazetteer* (November 14, 1724).

192. "Youth and Ignorance": Ibid.

192. "who abetted" . . . "He averred that": Ibid.

193. "He was remanded back to Newgate": Ibid.

193. "We afterwards have an account": Harris, *The Life of Lord Chancellor Hardwicke*, p. 153.

193. *Since your Curiosity*: Reprinted in Lewis Saul Benjamin, *The Life and Writings of Philip, Duke of Wharton*, p. 149; BL, p. 42.

194. "It is your business": *Weekly Journal or Saturday's Post* (October 24, 1724).

194. Figg promised to have a drink: *History*, p. 48.

195. hopes for a royal pardon: *London Journal* (November 7, 1724).

195. "whereupon, some Amendments": *London Journal* (November 14, 1724).

195. If the condemned man . . . coffin and hearse: *Authentic Memoirs*, p. 69; BL, p. 53.

195. The infamous prison breaker . . . sharp knife: ST, p. 145.

195. haphazard suppositions: *Evening Post* (November 12–14, 1724).

195. tried to saw . . . burst through the wall: *Weekly Journal or Saturday's Post* (November 14, 1724).

196. In the cart, on his way to Tyburn: *British Journal* (November 14, 1724).

196. "disguised in Liquor": ST, pp. 168–9.

196. His failure to kill Wild: *Bleuskin*, p. 101.

196. "The Greater the Rogue": Ibid., p. 102.

196. "carry'd off by the Surgeons": *Evening Post* (November 12–14, 1724).

196. "Shortly after the scholar": Catharine Arnold, *Underworld London: Crime and Punishment in the Capital City*, pp 40–41.

196. "its appearances accompanied": Ibid.

196. "pious admonition": *Chambers's Journal of Popular Literature, Science and Arts*, Vol. 19, No. 947 (February 18, 1882), p. 111.

196. "You prisoners that are within": Thornbury and Walford, *Old and New London*, Vol. 2, pp. 483–4.

197. "unwilling that so notorious": Townshend and Walpole, National Archives; SP, pp. 44, 81, f. 372.

197. *the person with whom he seem'd the most pleas'd*: OBP, Ordinary of Newgate's Account, November 1724, (OA172412072412070004).

198. John "Half-Hanged" Smith: Marks, *Tyburn Tree*, pp. 221–2.

198. *when he was turned off*: The *Tyburn Chronicle*, Vol. 1, p. 69.

199. £500 on a good hanging day: Robert Hughes, *The Fatal Shore*, p. 34.

199. *To the Hundreds of Drury*: *Daily Journal* (November 16, 1724).

199. at 200,000 strong: Cunningham, *Handbook of London*, Vol. 2, p. 852; Leslie Stephen, ed., *Oxford Dictionary of National Biography*, Vol. 52, p. 61.

199. "preserve the Peace": *Parker's London News or the Impartial Intelligencer* (November 16, 1724).

200. By "Main Force": *Applebee's* (November 21, 1724), appears in Lee, Vol. 3, p. 335.

201. "His behaviour was modest": *Parker's London News* (November 17, 1724).

201. "I have now as great satisfaction": *Weekly Journal or British Gazetteer* (November 21, 1724).

202. "He behav'd very gravely": Ibid.

202. "Both as an author and as a political agent": Richetti, *Cambridge Companion to Daniel Defoe*, pp. 64–5.

203. "much Difficulty, and with uncommon": *Weekly Journal or British Gazetteer* (November 21, 1724).

203. *Hard Fate at Tyburn's*: Bleuskin, p. 4.

203. "kill'd him with kindness": *Authentic Memoirs*, p. 69.

204. the Riot Act: *Parker's London News* (November 20, 1724).

204. "Surely no malefactor": Charles E. Pearce, *Polly Peachum*, p. 21.

204. "When he arrived at the Tree": *Daily Journal* (November 17, 1724).

204. "To a large extent Sheppard's fame": Philip Rawlings, *Drunks, Whores and Idle Apprentices: Criminal Biographies of the Eighteenth Century*, p. 35.

205. At their trial on December 4: ST, p. 156; OBP, December 1724, trial of Edward Betty Katharine Betty, alias Cook, alias Macoon Katharine Keys (t17241204-15).

206. From the constable's testimony: OBP, October 1725, trial of James Little (t17251013-22).

206. "These were left me": OBP, March 1726, trial of Elizabeth Lyon, alias Sheppard, alias Edgworth Bess (t17260302-47).

Chapter Nineteen: The Downfall of Jonathan Wild

207. *The Reason I have to expect ill Treatment*: HD, pp. 78–79.

207. *It is certain*: Ibid., p. vi.

207. "There were Numbers of them": *A Select and Impartial Account of the Lives, Behaviour, and Dying Words, of the Most Remarkable Convicts*, Vol. 1, pp. 328–9.

209. new sloop for £500: GH, p. 227.

209. He was an erstwhile pimp: Ibid., p. 105.

209. "passing lay": ST, p. 281.

210. £3,000 worth of stolen jewelry . . . pickpocketed the Prince of Wales: GH, p. 214.

210. "indefatigable in his Calling": ST, p. 281.

210. Edwards apprehended Johnson: Ibid.

210. Wild's misconduct, he didn't stick around: Ibid., p. 282; Hayward, *Lives of the Most Remarkable Criminals*, p. 247.

211. He placed an intimidating ad: HD, p. 73.

211. "The Magistrates in London": *A Select and Impartial Account*, p. 329.

211. *I wonder, good People*: Ibid., pp. 329–30.

211. He was taken to the home . . . Fryer: *Daily Journal* (February 17, 1725).

212. "Nothing more is heard": GH, p. 235.

212. *Sir, The Justices of the Peace*: Townshend and Walpole, National Archives; SP, pp. 44, 81, f. 390.

213. The letter to Paxton: Townshend and Walpole, National Archives; SP, pp. 44, 81, f. 391.

213. "the monarch and the government" . . . "Prosecution by the Executive": Langbein, *The Origins of Adversary Criminal Trial*, p. 120.

213. Warrant of Detainer: *The Political State of Great Britain*, Vol. 29 (May 31, 1725), pp. 505–6; *The Tyburn Chronicle*, Vol. 2, pp. 124–5.

213. Thompson warned Wild: *Daily Journal* (May 17, 1725). It was reported at the trial that Wild "acknowledged his Guilt of the Fact and the frequent Admonitions given him by Mr. Recorder, to avoid such Practices"; *A Select and Impartial Account*, p. 332.

213. velvet seats out of Thompson's coach: HD, p. 25.

216. "We hear that a Pardon": *Daily Journal* (March 4, 1725).

216. Bernard Mandeville, under the guise: *British Journal* (February 27– March 27, 1725).

216. "aiders and abettors": *British Journal* (February 27, 1725).

216. "As soon as any Thing is missing": Ibid.

217. "Thief-Catchers are our absolute Masters": *British Journal* (May 1, 1725).

217. *It is certain that the Correspondence*: *British Journal* (April 24, 1725).

217. The first round of "Authentick": *Daily Journal* (March 24, 1725).

217. "Pray how many Pounds: *The Weekly Journal or the British Gazetteer* (May 15, 1725).

218. "Mr. Jonathan Wild's Confinement": *London Journal* (March 20, 1725).

218. "did not then, nor any time since": OBP, May 1725 (17250513).

218. "He had Wounds and Scars": OBP, Ordinary of Newgate's Account, May 1725 (OA17250524).

218. "Cunning and Courage forsook him": *The Tyburn Chronicle*, Vol. 2, p. 204.

219. Wild's syphilis ointment: *Parker's Penny Post* (April 30, 1725); GH, p. 257.

219. "capable of making far greater Discoveries": *Daily Journal* (May 5, 1725).

219. Wild's acquaintances . . . John Green: *London Journal* (May 8, 1725) named Green as a Wild "accomplice."

219. "A List of the Persons": ST, p. 216.

219. "At Wild's imprisonment": FWC, p. 160.

219. Wild got the press coverage: GH, p. 254; BL, p. 53.

220. "If a strict Enquiry": ST, pp. 220–1.

Chapter Twenty: The Trial of Jonathan Wild

221. former con and hopeless coiner, Kelley: OBP, July 1724, trial of Henry Kelley (t17240708-59).

221. "To my Lodging at the Seven Dials": Trial transcripts at ST, pp. 221–2; OBP, May 1725, trial of Jonathan Wilde (t17250513-55).

223. This description of the heathen Wild: *London Journal* (May 22, 1725).

224. He later acknowledged . . . "dangerous": OBP, Ordinary of Newgate's Account, May 1725 (OA17250524).

224. "Had he not been convicted": *London Journal* (May 22, 1725).

224. "What have you to say" . . . *My Lord, I hope*: *A Select and Impartial Account*, p. 332.

225. "Jonathan Wild's Complaint": Library of Congress, The Funeral Procession of the Celebrated Mr. Jonathan Wild, "The Complaint of Jonathan Wild" (February 15, 1725), LC control no. 98504181; ST, pp. 282–4.

225. "the lace woman at Holborn Bridge": *Daily Journal* (May 18, 1725).

226. Wild went on a four-day hunger strike: OBP, Ordinary of Newgate's Account, May 1725 (OA17250524).

226. "The Humble Petition of Jonathan Wild": British Library, Humble Petition of Jonathan Wild. Shelfmark 1851.c.10 (40) System # 003923026.

226. Wild's wife, Mary: *Parker's Penny Post* (May 26, 1725); TG, p. 19.

226. Space at the Bull Head: *Daily Post* (May 21, 1725).

226. his rants "would wander": LY, p. 213.

227. "the local situation" . . . "Cursed is every one": OBP, Ordinary of Newgate's Account, May 1725 (OA17250524).

227. He vomited: *The Political State of Great Britain*, Vol. 29 (May 31, 1725), p. 506.

Chapter Twenty-One: Hanging the Thief-Catcher

229. Foul weather battered England: *Daily Journal* (July 5, 1725); *Political State of Great Britain*, Vol. 29 (June 30, 1725), p. 584; Lee, Vol. 3, pp. 400–04.

229. The young man was nineteen: Besant, *London in the Eighteenth Century*, Vol. 6, p. 502.

229. "render'd himself delirious": OBP, Ordinary of Newgate's Account, May 1725 (OA17250524).

230. His cart mates were wounded: *Parker's Penny Post* (May 26, 1725); *London Journal* (May 29, 1725).

230. "Jo Clowes called on me": John Byrom and Richard Parkinson (ed.), *The Private Journal and Literary Remains of John Byrom*, Vol. 1, Part 1, p. 141.

231. "What a strange Rig they run upon me!": *Parker's Penny Post* (May 26, 1725).

231. *To all the Thieves, Whores*: LY, pp. 215–6; GH, p. 274.

231. He and Harpham said a prayer: *Weekly Journal or British Gazetteer* (May 29, 1725).

231. some of which even injured the hangman: *Parker's Penny Post* (May 26, 1725).

231. Wild grabbed onto Harpham: *Parker's Penny Post* (May 26, 1725).

232. MR. JONATHAN WILDE, DIED MAY 24: William Henry Flower, *Catalogue of the Specimens Illustrating the Osteology and Dentition . . .*, Royal College of Surgeons of England Museum, p. 49.

232. "Skin, Flesh, and Entrails": *Daily Journal* (June 5, 1725).

232. "This is the skull of an individual": *The Phrenological Journal and Science of Health*, Vol. 2, p. 429.

232. "in a perfect state, with the exception": Ibid., p. 428.

232–223. "'Tis remarkable that since the Dissolution": *Daily Journal* (July 5, 1725).

233. According to the *London Journal*: *London Journal* (May 29, 1725).

233. "Perhaps, somewhere in Virginia": Besant, *London in the Eighteenth Century*, Vol. 6, p. 502.

233. "relic of Jonathan Wild": *Daily Journal* (May 26, 1725).

233. "Damn ye," Burnworth said: ST, Vol. 2, p. 353.

234. various jails as a turnkey: Karen A. Macfarlane, "The Jewish Policemen of Eighteenth-Century London," *Journal of Modern Jewish Studies*, Vol. 10, Issue 2, p. 230.

234. Field was indicted: GH, p. 247.

234. Marshal Charles Hitchen once wrote: Regulator, p. 3.

234. Hitchen began the evening of March 29: ST, Vol. 3, pp. 74–75; OBP, April 1727, trial of Charles Hitchen (t17270412-41).

235. "was very severely handled": *Daily Post* (May 3, 1727).

235. "he appear'd as a tatter'd": *Parker's Penny Post* (May 3, 1727).

235. When he emerged in October: *Daily Post* (October 24, 1727).

235. *Applebee's* published the names: Lee, Vol. 1, p. 391.
236. *Thus ended the Tragedy*: TG, p. 40.

Chapter Twenty-Two: "To Deliver Myself from This Death of a Life"
237. "To DELIVER MYSELF": RC, p. 236.
237. It was an archaic procedure: Wendy Moore, *The Knife Man*, p. 46; William Coulson, *On Lithotrity and Lithotomy*; PB, pp. 493–5.
239. "Here's a Man cut": *Applebee's* (September 25, 1725), appears in Lee, Vol, 3, pp. 430–1.
239. *Read's Journal* publicly: *Read's Journal* (October 26, 1728), "alias D——l Def—e's Scheme."
239. "decrepid, superannuated Wretches": Defoe, *Augusta Triumphans*, p. 47.
239. *A Man who has the Publick Good*: Ibid., p. 3.
240. "the form of personal attack": Paul A. Scanlon, ed., *Moll Flanders*, p. 419.
240. *Ear-less on high, stood pillory'd D—*: *The Dunciad: An Heroic Poem*, p. 22.
240. *Earl-ess on high, stood un-abash'd Defoe*: *The Dunciad: With Notes Variorum, and the Prolegomena of Scriblerus*, p. 106.
240. "I have but a short Time": Defoe, *Augusta Triumphans*, p. 4.
241. "I am at this time under a weight": *Letters*, p. 475.
241. his name entered . . . "Dubow": TW, p. 385; Walter Wilson and Daniel Defoe, *Memoirs of the Life and Time of Daniel De Foe*, Vol. 3, p. 610.
241. "Such is fame!": Sir John James Baddeley, Lord Mayor of London, *Cripplegate, One of the Twenty-Six Wards of the City of London*, p. 302.
241. "A few Days ago died Daniel": *Universal Spectator and Weekly Journal* (May 1, 1731).
242. "great natural Genius": *Daily Journal* (April 28, 1731).

Epilogue: Legends
243. *Defoe had invented*: *Wall Street Journal* (August 13, 2011).
243. "A Lawyer is an honest": *The Beggar's Opera; In Three Acts*, p. 11.
245. "the most devilish creature": BL, p. 207.
245. Ainsworth and Dickens had conceived: GH, p. 209.
245. *The first time I was ever*: *The Sixth Report of the Inspector of Prisons for the Northern Districts of England* appears in Charles Mackay, *Memoirs of Extraordinary Popular Delusions and the Madness of Crowds*, Vol. 1, p. 253.
246. "Signed, Jack Sheppard": LH, p. 7.

SELECTED BIBLIOGRAPHY

Eighteenth-Century Newspapers

The following newspapers were searched between the years 1703 and 1731 for information on the principals of the story through the database 17th–18th Century Burney Collection Newspapers. Exact dates of articles are listed in the Notes.

British Journal, Daily Courant, Daily Journal, Daily Post, Evening Post, The Flying Post or Weekly Medley, Fog's Weekly Journal, London Gazette, London Journal, London News, The London Post, Mist's Weekly Journal, Original Weekly Journal (became *Applebee's Original Weekly Journal*; there are only a few years' worth of *Applebee's* available in the Burney Collection), *Parker's London News or the Impartial Intelligencer* (became *Parker's Penny Post* in 1725), *Post Boy, Post Man and the Historical Account, The Spectator, Weekly Journal or British Gazetteer, Weekly Journal or Saturday's Post, Weekly Packet, A Weekly Review of the Affairs of France.*

Eighteenth-Century Criminal Trials

The Old Bailey Proceedings Online (www.oldbaileyonline.org, version 7.0, September 5, 2013) [OBP].

Tim Hitchcock, Robert Shoemaker, Clive Emsley, Sharon Howard, and Jamie McLaughlin, et al., The Old Bailey Proceedings Online, 1674–1913.

Seventeenth- and Eighteenth-Century Literature

Anon. *The History of the Lives and Actions of Jonathan Wild, Thief-Taker; Joseph Blake, Alias Bleuskin, Footpad; and John Sheppard, Housebreaker.* Third ed. London: Edward Midwinter, 1726. Eighteenth-Century Collection Online [ECCO].

———. *The History of the Remarkable Life of John Sheppard, Containing a Particular Account of His Many Robberies and Escapes.* London: Applebee, 1724. ECCO.

———. *The Midnight Spy; Or, a View of the Transactions of London and Westminster; from . . . Ten in the Evening till Five in the Morning; Exhibiting a Great Variety of Scenes in High and Low Life, Etc.* London: J. Cooke, 1766.

Defoe, Daniel. *Augusta Triumphans: Or, The Way to Make London the Most Flourishing City in the Universe.* London: Printed for J. Roberts and sold by E. Nutt, A. Dodd, N. Blanford, and J. Stagg, 1728. ECCO.

———. *A Collection of the Writings of the Author of The True-Born Englishman.* London: n.p., 1703.

———. *The Fortunes and Misfortunes of the Famous Moll Flanders, The Second Edition, Corrected.* London: Printed for W. Chetwood, 1722.

———. George Healey, ed. *Letters of Daniel Defoe.* Oxford: Clarendon, 1955.

———. *The Life and Strange Surprizing Adventures of Robinson Crusoe, of York, Mariner: Who Lived Eight and Twenty Years All Alone in an Un-inhabited Island on the Coast of America.* London: W. Taylor, 1719.

———. *Life of Colonel Jack: And, a True Relation of the Apparition of One Mrs. Veal.* Oxford: Printed by D. A. Talboys, for Thomas Tegg, 1840.

———. *A Narrative of All the Robberies, Escapes, &c. of John Sheppard, Giving an Exact Description of the Manner of His Wonderful Escape from the Castle in Newgate ... Written by Himself.* London: Printed and sold by John Applebee, 1724.

———. *The Shortest-way with the Dissenters, Or, Proposals for the Establishment of the Church.* London: S.n., 1702.

———. *The Storm; Or, A Collection of the Most Remarkable Casualties and Disasters Which Happen'd in the Late Dreadful Tempest, Both by Sea and Land.* London: Printed for George Sawbridge, and sold by J. Nutt, 1704.

———. *The True and Genuine Account of the Life and Actions of the Late Jonathan Wild: Not Made up of Fiction and Fable, but Taken from His Own Mouth, and Collected from Papers of His Own Writing.* London: Printed and sold by John Applebee, in Black-Fryers, 1725.

———. *A True Collection of the Writings of the Author of The True-Born Englishman. Corrected by Himself.* London, 1703. ECCO.

Hitchen, Charles. "The Regulator, Or, A Discovery of the Thieves, Thief-Takers, and Locks, Alias Receivers of Stolen Goods in and about the City of London: With the Thief-Taker's Proclamation, Also an Account of All the Flash Words Now in Vogue amongst the Thieves, with an Explanation of Each Word: With an Exact List of the Convicts' Names That Was Condemn'd in the Year 1717, That Now Lies in Newgate to

Plead to His Majesty's Transportation Pardon." By a prisoner in New-gate. London: Printed for T. Warner, at the Black Boy in Pater-Noster-Row, 1718.

Hutton, Luke. *The Discovery of a London Monster Called the Black Dog of Newgate: Profitable for all Readers to Take Heed by*. Imprinted by G. Eld, for Robert Wilson. 1612. Early English Books Online.

Jackson, William. *The New & Complete Newgate Calendar; Or, Villany Displayed in All Its Branches: Containing Accounts of the Most Notorious Malefactors from the Year 1700 to the Present Time*. London: Alexr. Hogg, 1795. ECCO.

The Life of Jonathan Wild from his Birth to his Death . . . By H. D., Late Clerk to Justice R——. London: T. Warner, 1725. ECCO.

Pope, Alexander. *The Dunciad. An Heroic Poem*. London: A. Dodd, 1728.

A Select and Impartial Account of the Lives, Behaviour, and Dying Words of the Most Remarkable Convicts, from the Year 1700, down to the Present Time. London: Printed by J. Applebee, for J. Hodges, 1745.

Select Trials at the Sessions-House in the Old Bailey for Murder, Robberies, Rapes, Sodomy, Coining, Frauds, Bigamy, and Other Offences to Which Are Added Genuine Accounts of the Lives, Behaviour, Confessions, and Dying Speeches of the Most Eminent Convicts, from the Year 1720 to This Time. Vols. 1–3. London: Printed by J. Applebee for J. Hodges, 1742.

Select Trials for Murders, Robberies, Rapes, Sodomy, Coining, Frauds, and other Offences: at the Sessions-House in the Old Bailey. To which are added, genuine accounts of the lives, Behaviour, Confessions and Dying-Speeches of the Most Eminent Convicts. From the Year 1720 to 1724, inclusive. Vols. 1–2. London. Printed for J. Wilford. 1735.

Smith, Alexander. *Memoirs of the Life and Times of the Famous Jonathan Wild*. New York: Garland, 1973 (republished).

The Tyburn Chronicle: Or, The Villainy Display'd in All Its Branches: Containing An Authentic Account Of The Lives, Adventures, Tryals, Executions, and Last Dying Speeches of the Most Notorious Malefactors of All Denominations, Who Have Sufferer'd for Bigamy, Forgeries . . . In England, Scotland, and Ireland: From the Year 1700, to the Present Time. Vols. 1–2. London: Cooke, 1768. ECCO.

Weighley, Alias Wild: A Poem, in Imitation of Hudibras. To Which Is Annex'd, a More Genuine and Particular Account in Prose, than Any Yet Publish'd, of the Most Remarkable Events, and Transactions, of His Life, from the Time of His Birth to His Execution. Also Jonathan's Last Farewell and Epitaph . . . By

N. P., *many Years his intimate Acquaintance*. London: Printed for J. Robert, 1725. ECCO.

Wild, Jonathan. "An Answer to a Late Insolent Libel, Entituled, A Discovery of the Conduct of Receivers and Thief-takers, in and about the City of London." London: T. Warner, 1718.

Post-Eighteenth-Century Literature

Arnold, Catharine. *Underworld London: Crime and Punishment in the Capital City*. London: Simon & Schuster, 2012.

Backscheider, Paula R. *Daniel Defoe: His Life*. Baltimore: Johns Hopkins UP, 1989.

———. *Moll Flanders: The Making of a Criminal Mind*. Boston: Twayne, 1990.

Besant, Sir Walter. *London in the Eighteenth Century*. London: A. & C. Black, 1902.

Bleackley, Horace, and Stewart Marsh Ellis. *Jack Sheppard*. Edinburgh: W. Hodge & Co., 1933.

Chandler, Frank Wadleigh. *The Literature of Roguery*. Boston: Houghton Mifflin, 1907.

Cunningham, Peter. *Handbook of London: Past and Present*. London: John Murray, 1850.

Faller, Lincoln B. *Turned to Account: The Forms and Functions of Criminal Biography in Late Seventeenth- and Early Eighteenth-Century England*. Cambridge: Cambridge UP, 1987.

Fielding, Henry. *The Works of Henry Fielding, Esq., with a Life of the Author.* Vols. 5, 12. London: Richards, 1824. Miscellanies.

Franklin, Benjamin, and John Bigelow. *Autobiography of Benjamin Franklin*. Philadelphia: J. B. Lippincott, 1868.

Furbank, Philip Nicholas, and W. R. Owens. *Defoe De-Attributions: A Critique of J. R. Moore's Checklist*. London: Hambledon, 1994.

Defoe, Daniel, and George Atherton Aitken. *Romances and Narratives by Daniel Defoe*. London: Published by J.M. Dent, 1895.

———, and Karl D. Bülbring. *The Compleat English Gentleman*. London: D. Nutt, 1890. Issue 2.

———, and Howard Maynadier. *The Works of Daniel Defoe*. Vol. 1 and 16. London and New York: Chesterfield Society, 1903.

George, Mary Dorothy. *London Life in the Eighteenth Century*. New York: Harper & Row, 1964.

Griffiths, Arthur. *The Chronicles of Newgate*. London: Chapman & Hall, 1884.

Hackwood, Frederick William. *Old English Sports*. London: T.F. Unwin, 1907.

Harper, Charles G. *Half-hours with the Highwaymen: Picturesque Biographies and Traditions of the "Knights of the Road."* Vol. 2. London: Chapman & Hall, 1908.

Harris, George. *The Life of Lord Chancellor Hardwicke with Selections from His Correspondence, Diaries, Speeches, and Judgments*. Vol. 1. London: E. Moxon, 1847.

Hay, Douglas. *Albion's Fatal Tree: Crime and Society in Eighteenth-Century England*. New York: Pantheon, 1975.

Hayward, Arthur Lawrence, ed. *Lives of the Most Remarkable Criminals, Who Have Been Condemned and Executed for Murder, the Highway, Housebreaking, Street Robberies, Coining or Other Offences*. London: G. Routledge, 1927.

Hibbert, Christopher. *Highwaymen*. New York: Delacorte, 1968.

———. *The Road to Tyburn: The Story of Jack Sheppard and the Eighteenth-Century London Underworld*. Cleveland: World Publishing, 1957.

———. *The Roots of Evil: A Social History of Crime and Punishment*. New York: Little Brown, 1963.

Hogarth, William, John Nichols, and John Ireland. *Hogarth's Works: With Life and Anecdotal Descriptions of His Pictures*. Vol. 2. Edinburgh: Oliphant, Anderson & Ferrier, 1883. Second.

Holmes, Richard. *Defoe on Sheppard and Wild: The History of the Remarkable Life of John Sheppard; a Narrative of All the Robberies, Escapes &c. of John Sheppard; the True and Genuine Account of the Life and Actions of the Late Jonathan Wild*. London: Harper Perennial, 2002.

Howson, Gerald. *Thief-Taker General: The Rise and Fall of Jonathan Wild*. New York: St. Martin's, 1970.

Irwin, William Robert. *The Making of Jonathan Wild: A Study in the Literary Method of Henry Fielding*. Hamden, CT: Archon, 1966.

Langbein, John H. *The Origins of Adversary Criminal Trial*. Oxford: Oxford UP, 2003.

Lee, William. *Daniel Defoe: His Life, and Recently Discovered Writings: Extending from 1716 to 1729*. Vols. 1–3. London: Hotten, 1869.

Lindsay, Jack. *The Monster City: Defoe's London, 1688–1730*. New York: St. Martin's, 1978.

Linebaugh, Peter. *The London Hanged: Crime and Civil Society in the Eighteenth Century*. Cambridge: Cambridge UP, 1992.

Linnane, Fergus. *London's Underworld: Three Centuries of Vice and Crime*. London: Robson, 2003.

Lund, Roger D., ed. *Critical Essays on Daniel Defoe*. New York: G. K. Hall, 1997.

Lyons, Frederick J. *Jonathan Wild: Prince of Robbers*. London: M. Joseph, 1936.

Marks, Alfred. *Tyburn Tree: Its History and Annals*. London: Brown, Langham, 1908.

McLynn, Frank. *Crime and Punishment in Eighteenth-Century England*. New York: Oxford UP, 1991.

Minto, William. *Daniel Defoe*. London: Macmillan, 1879.

Moore, John Robert. *Daniel Defoe: Citizen of the Modern World*. Chicago and London: University of Chicago, 1958.

———. *Defoe in the Pillory and Other Studies*. Bloomington: Indiana University, 1939.

Novak, Maximillian E. *Daniel Defoe: Master of Fictions: His Life and Ideas*. Oxford: Oxford UP, 2001.

———. *Defoe and the Nature of Man*. London: Oxford UP, 1963.

O'Donnell, Bernard. *The Old Bailey and Its Trials*. New York: Macmillan, 1951.

Pringle, Patrick. *Hue and Cry: The Story of Henry and John Fielding and Their Bow Street Runners*. New York: Morrow, 1955.

Richetti, John J. *The Life of Daniel Defoe: A Critical Biography*. Oxford: Wiley-Blackwell, 2005.

———, ed. *The Cambridge Companion to Daniel Defoe*. Cambridge: Cambridge UP, 2008.

Seccombe, Thomas. *Lives of Twelve Bad Men: Original Studies of Eminent Scoundrels by Various Hands*. New York: G. P. Putnam's Sons, 1894.

Secord, Arthur Wellesley. *Studies in the Narrative Method of Defoe*. New York: Russell & Russell, 1963.

Seidel, Michael. *Robinson Crusoe: Island Myths and the Novel*. Boston: Twayne, 1991.

Sutherland, James Runcieman. *Defoe*. Philadelphia, NY: Lippincott, 1938.

Thornbury, Walter, and Edward Walford. *Old and New London: A Narrative of Its History, Its People, and Its Places*. London: Cassell, Petter & Galpin, 1887.

Timbs, John. *Club Life of London: With Anecdotes of the Clubs, Coffee Houses, and Taverns of the Metropolis, during the 17th, 18th, and 19th Centuries*. London: Richard Bentley, 1866.

———. *Curiosities of London*. London: David Bogue, 1855.

Trent, William P. *Daniel Defoe: How to Know Him*. Indianapolis: Bobbs-Merrill, 1916.

Wilson, Walter, and Daniel Defoe. *Memoirs of the Life and Time of Daniel De Foe: Containing a Review of His Writings and His Opinions upon a Variety of Important Matters, Civil and Ecclesiastical. In Three Volumes*. Vol. 1. London: Hurst., n.d.

Wright, Thomas. *The Life of Daniel Defoe*. New York: Anson D. F. Randolph, 1894.

Archive Material

British Library:

J—N W—ld's Skittish & Baboonish New Proclamation: MSSSUR/RP/5361 BOX 125 946 BC. General Reference Collection 1881.a.5.(28). System # 003960399.

An Account of the Tryal, Examination, and Conviction of Several Notorious Persons Call'd Sodomites. 1707: General Reference Collection 1851.c.10. (35). System # 002216347.

The Humble Petition of Jonathan Wild: General Reference Collection 1851.c.10.(39). System # 003923026.

London Metropolitan Archives [LMA]:

"Lastly to the Fatal Place of Execution" [Anon.], Reference Code: SC/GL/PR/P1/TYB/M0008982CL.

Sessions of the Peace, January 13, and Gaol Delivery, January 15, 1703: CLA/047/LJ/01/0471.

Sessions of the Peace, July 5, and Gaol Delivery, July 7, 1703: CLA/047/LJ/01/0475.

Sessions Roll: Sessions of the Peace and Oyer and Terminer, July 1703: MJ/SR/2014.

Sessions Roll: Gaol Delivery, July 1703: MJ/SR/2015.

Sessions of the Peace, February 22, and Gaol Delivery, February 24, 1703: CLA/047/LJ/01/0472.

Sessions of the Peace, July 5, and Gaol Delivery, July 7, 1703: CLA/047/LJ/01/0475.

Debtors Schedules: CLA/047/LJ/17/018/B.

Marshals: COL/OF/02/081.

Transportation of William Riddlesden: MJ/SP/T/02/002.

Bond of Mariners and Others to Justices of the Peace to Transport Felons: CLA/047/LJ/18/017.

Tyburn Ticket for Jonathan Wild: P69/BRI/B/044/MS14845.

Original Letter from Townsend to the Lord Mayor: CLA/035/02/021.

Proclamation by the Mayor for Reformation of Abuses in the Gaol of Newgate: CLA/035/02/045.

Royal College of Surgeons:

File of letters from Mr. Fowler, re. presenting the skeleton of Jonathan Wilde to the College. RCS-MUS/3/3/11.

National Archives, Kew, England:

Townshend and Walpole. Secretaries of State: State Papers: SP 44/81.

Blood Money. Exchequer of Receipt, Miscellaneous Rolls, Books and Papers: E 407/30.

Twenty-First-Century Periodicals—Online Sources

Backscheider, Paula R. "Firing off the Canon." *Novel: A Forum on Fiction* 24.1 (1990): 115–18. JSTOR.

———. "No Defense: Defoe in 1703." *PMLA* 103.3 (1988): 274–84. JSTOR.

Baker, Nicholson. "The Greatest Liar." *Columbia Journalism Review* (July 28, 2009).

Clayton, Mary. "Quilt Arnold," *London Lives*, 1690–1800 (www.londonlives.org, version 1.1, 17 June 2012) [LL].

"Defoe's Review: Textual Editing and New Media." *Digital Defoe* (http://english.illinoisstate.edu/digitaldefoe/archive/spring09/multimedia/flynn.pdf Web).

McKenzie, Andrea. "The Real Macheath: Social Satire, Appropriation, and Eighteenth-Century Criminal Biography," *Huntington Library Quarterly* 69.4 (2006): 581–605. JSTOR.

Miller, John J. "Writing up a Storm," *Wall Street Journal* (August 13, 2011).

National Archives. "Education: Crime and Punishment" (http://www .nationalarchives.gov.uk/education/candp/punishment/g06/g06cs1 .htm).

Novak, Maximillian E. "Daniel Defoe and *Applebee's Original Weekly Journal*: An Attempt at Re-Attribution," *Eighteenth-Century Studies* 45.4 (2012): 585–608. Project Muse.

———. "The Defoe Canon: Attribution and De-Attribution," *Huntington Library Quarterly* 59.1 (1996): 83–104.

Treasury Warrants: July 21–25, 1717. *Calendar of Treasury Books*, Vol. 31: 1717 (1960), pp. 458–65 (http://www.british-history.ac.uk/report.aspx? compid=85435&strquery=jonathanwild).

INDEX

Note: Page numbers in *italics* indicate pictures and engravings.